CREATING
DIGITAL MUSIC
AND SOUND

RotoVision

A ROTOVISION BOOK
Published and distributed by RotoVision SA
Route Suisse 9
CH-1295 Mies
Switzerland

RotoVision SA
Sales and Editorial Office
Sheridan House, 114 Western Road
Hove BN3 1DD, UK

Tel: +44 (0)1273 72 72 68
Fax: +44 (0)1273 72 72 69
www.rotovision.com

Copyright © RotoVision SA 2006

10 9 8 7 6 5 4 3 2 1

ISBN: 2-940361-27-4

Art Director: Tony Seddon
Design: Studio Ink
Copy editor: Gary Eastwood

Reprographics in Singapore by ProVision Pte.
Tel: +65 6334 7720
Fax: +65 6334 7721

Printed in China by Midas Printing
International Limited

CREATING
DIGITAL MUSIC
AND SOUND

THE ESSENTIAL HANDBOOK FOR THE HOME MUSIC STUDIO

CHRIS MIDDLETON

CONTENTS

There have never been more opportunities to get creative with digital audio and music, thanks to mass-market digital technology. You can get to grips with the basics of making professional recordings just by using some of the standard tools that come with your Mac or Windows PC–and if you're a Linux user, there are hundreds of free or shareware audio tools.

Music is also the most personal of media–and recording it is the most subjective of processes. This book is for you if you want to understand the basics and also be inspired by what other creative people are doing so you can pursue your own subjective vision.

Digital technology means that when you become a musician, a composer, a music producer, an audio engineer, or a sound designer you're joining a worldwide community of people who are passionate and talkative about what they do. But the real boon is having a professional recording studio and video-editing suite in your computer–and if you own a laptop that's a studio you can take with you wherever you go.

With the tools you may already have at your disposal, you can not only compose and arrange music, record sound, and edit, mix, and remix the results, but also add music and sound to

video, movies, animations, and Web sites; you can build soundtoys and sculpt generative music landscapes; and you can become an Internet radio broadcaster, blogger, or podcaster. You can even make music to a professional level on some cellphones. This book will explore all of this and more.

Music and sound have become part of a media stream that connects people in an infinite variety of ways, and that means a world of opportunities to share your work with others, to publish or sell it online, and to meet and collaborate with like-minded people.

Of course, the music industry itself is moving toward a model of selling tracks directly to listeners online or via the cellphone network, and that means that music, videos, animations, games, and graphics will start merging into a stream of rich content that we can access on our cellphones and media players–but also make for ourselves at home.

If you have access to a computer, then the only creative barriers are those of your ambition. So, what are you waiting for?

A book of this modest length and ambitious scope cannot hope to be a comprehensive guide to all of the software and hardware tools, recording techniques, and professional processes involved

in making and recording music and sound for musicians, videomakers, filmmakers, Web designers, and animators—each of these areas merits a lengthy book of its own, and each tool has its own instruction manuals, textbooks, magazines, and discussion boards.

What this book aims to do is something rather different. First, it is a creative introduction to a selection of tools and technologies that typify the much wider choices that are available to you.

More importantly, it is the first book to look at how music and sound is used across a variety of media. After all, even the most standard desktop technologies allow creative people everywhere to make music and add sound to Web sites,

to videos, movies, and animations, and to share it in hundreds of different ways, from client to client, from server to client, and from peer to peer.

What are the common factors? What are the unique challenges? This book aims to explore both questions and present you with a range of answers, from technical dos and don'ts to inspirational ideas and creative hints and tips. It will also give you lots of related information on issues that may prove vital in your work: such as how to protect your rights, for example.

But the most important parts of the book are the creative strategies—together with interviews with people who work in very different roles within these interrelated media: musicians; composers; film

editors; sound designers; software makers; and even a graphic designer who has pushed back the boundaries of design by using music and sound. What do they do? What tools do they use? What inspires them? And how do they turn inspiration into finished works?

I hope you enjoy the journey.

Chris Middleton

Chris Middleton

FROM VOICE TO FLAWLESS PERFORMANCE
Microphones, mic techniques, acoustics, and voice editing skills will all be covered in this book, together with equipment buying guides.

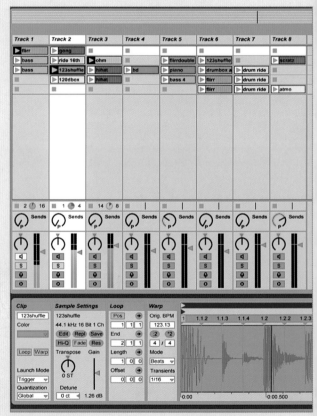

MUSIC AND SOUND TOOLS
The basic principles of music-making tools, like Ableton Live (pictured) will be explored, as pointers to more in-depth books on each software package. Ableton Live allows you to play with loops and beats in a live, DJ-style performance, beat-stretching and beat-matching loops and soundclips in real time.

FROM DESKTOP TO ABBEY ROAD
We'll approach sound-recording and music-making from both sides, exploring how the professionals do it, and how you can learn from their skills to produce great recordings on widely available desktop equipment.

SOUNDWAVES

ANALOG RECORDING

DIGITAL RECORDING

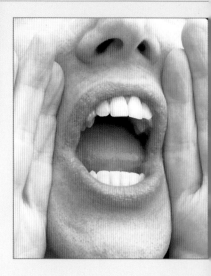

WHAT IS SOUND?

Sound is waves of pressure caused by vibrating objects—such as vocal cords and guitar strings. Clearly, waves of any sort can only exist where there are molecules to be moved around, so sound requires a medium in which to make waves. Normally, this is the air, though sound also travels through any "elastic" substance within which molecules can be pushed and pulled around. These waves of excited air molecules are gathered in our ears, and our brains perceive them as sound.

Sound, then, is both a physical phenomenon, and our perception of it. If we understand just enough of the physics, we can record sound well; but if we also appreciate sound's

psychoacoustic properties, then we can use sound and music to influence people's perceptions.

If you were able to take a side-on view of a simple soundwave, such as a sinewave, you'd see that it consisted of a series of cyclical, repeating peaks and troughs—known as positive and negative peaks. The positive peaks represent fronts of increased atmospheric pressure where air molecules are compressed more tightly together. Each of these is followed by a zone of lower than normal atmospheric pressure, called a rarefaction (represented in our imaginary side-on view by the negative peak). In any graphical representation, a waveform rises and falls beneath an imaginary centerline.

The distance between these positive and negative peaks is known as the signal's **amplitude**–or volume. Higher pressure sounds have higher peaks and deeper troughs, and we perceive them as louder.

We can see, then, that volume is actually a measure of sound pressure level (SPL). We measure SPL using the decibel (dB). It's vital to understand that the decibel

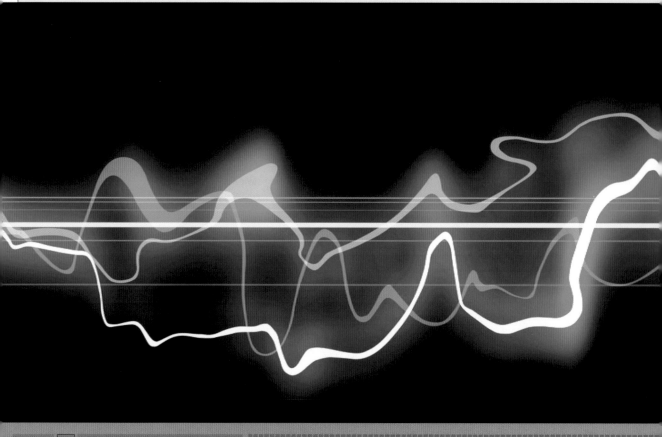

is a measurement of relative intensity, where the volume of a signal is compared to a reference level. In the physical world, we describe loud sounds in terms of high decibel counts (for example, 160dB for a fighter plane), but this is relative to the reference level at which we can hear no sound at all (0dB).

Within digital and analog recording systems, however, 0dB is not silence but the opposite—the measure of maximum loudness before distortion. In digital systems, signals that peak above 0dB cause "clipping," an unattractive, crackling distortion. If it seems odd to have 0dB meaning silence on the one hand, and maximum volume before distortion on the other, remember that in recording terms, this is the level of the signal before it is amplified. Signals need to be output at a maximum reference level of 0dB from the recording system before they are amplified (from zero, in effect) and played through your speakers.

SPEED OF SOUND THROUGH AIR

The speed of sound through the air is 1,130ft (344m) per second—just over one foot per millisecond. You can use this knowledge in your work. See Effects and The Virtual Guitarist to find out how.

SPEED OF SOUND THROUGH STEEL

Through steel, such as the rails of a subway system, sound travels at 16,600ft (5,060m) per second. This consideration can affect how you construct your working space for sound.

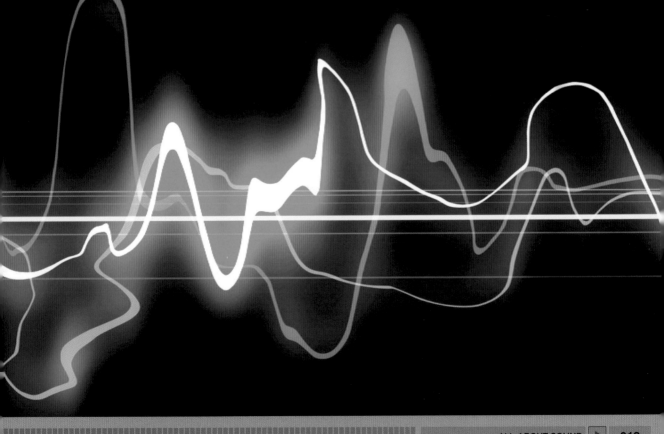

The **wavelength** is the distance through the air (or other medium) that a soundwave travels to complete one of its repeating cycles—one peak and one negative peak. The term is usually only applied to simple waveforms—constant tones whose wavelengths are easily measurable.

The speed at which one of these cycles is repeated every second is known as the soundwave's **frequency**, and it is expressed using the unit hertz (Hz)—the same unit we use to measure the speed of any cyclical event, such as the number of calculations performed every second by a microprocessor. If a soundwave completes 20 cycles a second, it is measured at 20Hz, and we perceive this sound as having a very low pitch. If it completes 20,000 cycles a second, it is measured at 20,000Hz (20kHz), and we

perceive it as having an extremely high pitch. Frequency and pitch, then, are intimately related. 20Hz-20kHz is the approximate audible spectrum of human hearing (we have 20:20 hearing). If you are standing in the middle of a road you will hear the sound of a speeding car long before the vehicle hits you, because sound travels faster than cars do. However, a fighter plane travelling faster than 1,130ft (344m) a second (Mach 1) will have passed over your head before you hear the sound its engines were making on its approach. This is because the plane is travelling faster than its own sound.

So, sound travels on average at 1,130ft (344m) per second through the atmosphere, but through seawater it travels more than four times quicker, at 4,900ft/sec (1,500m/sec). Through steel,

sound travels nearly 15 times faster (16,600ft/sec, 5,050m/sec) than it does through the air—which is why you hear the sound of a subway train through the rails first. In other words, the denser the medium, the faster sound travels through it. Sound travels through the air faster on hot days because the air is denser. All of this is relevant because it affects the way we might choose to design the spaces we use to record sound.

So far, so good, but what makes a car sound like a car, and a fighter plane sound like a fighter plane? After all, if a sound's frequency and amplitude were the only components of sound, then all musical instruments playing middle C (261.63Hz) would sound the same.

When a simple waveform, such as a sinewave, moves through one complete

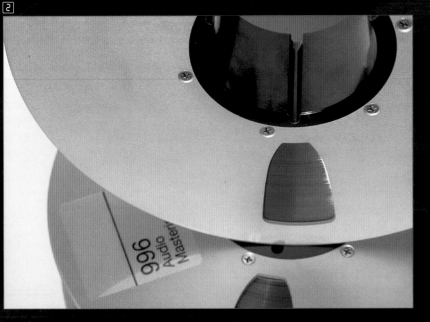

1. IN THE GROOVE
Vinyl recordings remain a boom industry thanks to DJs and the dance music market. Here the grooves of the disk are analogs of a soundwave, cut laterally into the surface of a master disk by a needle.

2. MASTER TAPES
Two-inch unmixed analog master tapes used to be standard in rock music recording. Even in the 21st century they remain standard in some studios, while others have moved to hard-disk recording and digital editing using software and hardware suites such as Digidesign's Pro Tools and software packages such as Steinberg's Cubase and Nuendo, Apple's Logic, and Cakewalk's Sonar.

3. PINPOINT PERFORMANCE
Reversing the recording process by running the needle through the laterally cut groove releases the stored energy. The vibrations are then turned back into electrical pulses, which are amplified and played through loudspeakers. Speakers turn the electrical pulses back into waves of air pressure that we hear as music.

cycle, it is said to have travelled through 360 degrees—or one complete **phase**. Of course, most sounds are not simple tones, but complex mixtures of different waveforms. In musical instruments, for example, their different materials and ways in which they are constructed and played create different characteristic sounds. However, let's assume for a moment that we have two simple, identical waveforms. If both are triggered at the exact same time and pass through one complete phase, their positive and negative peaks will correspond—they will be "in phase," and the volume of the combined signal will double. However, if one of the identical waves is delayed for a fraction of a second and triggered before a complete cycle of its identical companion has taken place, the signals will clash (they will be "out of phase"). Lastly, if the positive peak of one of the

two identical waves is triggered at the same point as the negative peak of the other, the two signals will cancel each other out (they will be in "antiphase").

DIGITAL SYSTEMS AND DYNAMIC RANGE

There is a direct correlation between the word length of a digital system, and its theoretical dynamic range. This is equivalent to six decibels (6dB) per bit (binary digit). A 16-bit system has a dynamic range of 96dB SPL (16 x 6dB), whereas a 24-bit (24-character word length) digital system has a dynamic range of 144dB (24 x 6dB). This, according to the Audio Engineers Society (www.aes.org) "approaches that of instantaneous hearing damage in as little as one exposure."

Most sounds consist of complex waveforms, the components of which move in and out of phase with each other, creating unique and characteristic blends of sounds and artifacts. More specifically, the fact that the "voice" of the same note played on a guitar, a saxophone, a violin, and a trumpet is so different from one instrument to the next is mainly due to the presence of frequencies other than the fundamental pitch (the actual note being played). These are known as "partials." When the frequency of a partial is a multiple of the original pitch (eg 440Hz x 2 = 880Hz), we call it an harmonic. The tones will sound related.

The last component of a soundwave after its amplitude, wavelength, speed, frequency, phase, and harmonics is its "**envelope**." This is the complete "package" of a sound, containing elements such as its **attack** (how quickly it hits peak amplitude)—a plucked violin string has a fast attack, whereas a bowed violin string has a slow one—and its **decay** (how long is takes to fade to silence).

So what have we learned? Well, the basics of soundwaves, but also the rudiments of sound synthesis. All of these sound parameters and more are what a synthesizer provides, along with oscillators that generate the sound, and controls for shaping waveforms.

But now we should get to the heart of the matter for any book about creating digital music and sound—namely, that sound is analog, and digital is merely the way we store, interpret, edit, and interact with the information we have gathered. Analog—as Real World Studios' sound engineer Marco Migliari once said to me—is everything that's going on outside the [digital] box. So let's look at both sides of the process.

ANALOG RECORDING

So-called analog processes are important to understand when working digitally because sound is not digital. As we've already explored, sound is waves of air pressure, and until recorded sound has been turned back into those pressure waves then it is merely information.

How we prefer to store that information, edit it, and translate it back into something we can hear is what the "analog versus digital" debate is all about.

So what does "analog" actually mean? An analog is anything that measures something and communicates it—physically—in a form we can understand. For example, the hands on an analog clock communicate the passing of time by spinning around. The word comes from the Greek analogos, meaning "in proportion."

Transducers are at the heart of any analog recording process. Far from being some archaic piece of equipment, a transducer is simply the term for anything that transforms one type of energy into a different type of energy.

Most analog recording processes transform soundwaves into electrical impulses. Next, they store those signals on magnetic tape, or they turn them into a different type of energy again: vibrations that are literally (in fact, laterally) cut into a piece

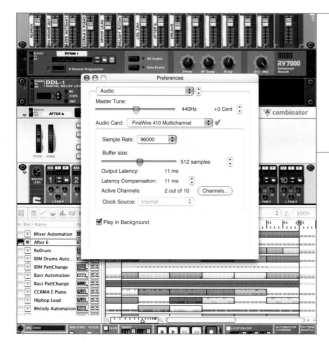

LATENCY
Because of the number of calculations your computer has to make to process digital audio, there will be a tiny delay—hopefully not noticeable to the human ear—between you hitting the key on a keyboard and the sound being triggered in your software sequencer. This is known as the latency of the system. On older, slower computers, latency can be a serious problem. Even very fast systems will begin to exhibit noticeable latency if you apply dozens of signal processors and effects across a number of tracks, as your processor is being asked to carry out a huge number of simultaneous calculations.

SOFTWARE SETTINGS
In any music- or audio-production package you can set the sampling rate and audio output device that the application will use. Shown: music application Reason, accessing an external soundcard.

of acetate by a needle. If you reverse the process by spinning the record so the needle runs along the groove, then the original sounds are reproduced and the stored energy is released. We call such processes "analog" because transducers are analogs: they measure sound and store it by effecting a change in a physical medium, such as by cutting a groove into a record.

Even if you plan to be the world's most digital musician you'll still use at least two or three analog processes and sets of transducers in your work: your microphone, which translates air pressure into electrical impulses; your speakers, which turn those impulses back into air-pressure waves; and your ears, which reverse the process again.

You can see how information might get lost in the journey through the analog domain—and where new information, such as noise (which I'll define as undesired information), might be introduced. Any analog devices we use to capture a sound, change its relationship with other

sounds, or play the sound back introduce extra steps that the soundwave has to take on its journey. Inevitably, this means that the sound will be changed subtly over the course of that journey—and that might mean it is degraded, modified, or enhanced. That's the creative challenge!

Sound is also affected in countless ways by the physical locations in which it is heard, recorded, and played back. It is important to realize that there is no "correct" environment for any of the above and when we record sound and music, we have little control over where and how someone will hear it. All we can do as producers and engineers is cover as many of the possible scenarios as possible—with audio, "luck" is always determined or tempered by a measure of good judgment.

All this might seem irrelevant to digital sound, but digital audio-editing packages go to great lengths to copy some of the methodology of analog processes and devices. To record unpredictable sound accurately from the real world you'll also

need to understand the predictable aspects of what microphones do, how sound behaves in different environments, and how to use your speakers (and your ears). Even if you work entirely digitally, the process will have been analog at some stage in the soundwave's journey.

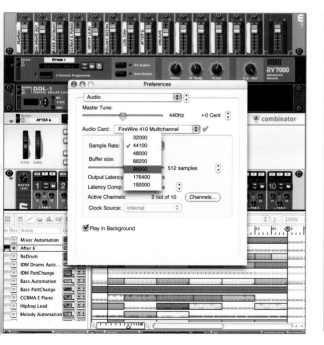

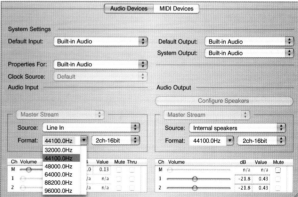

WATCH YOUR SAMPLE RATES!
If you record a sound—including an entire song or track—at one sample rate and then import it into an audio-editing package for further tweaks, make sure the settings of the new file match those of the soundfile you've imported. If you import a 48kHz audio file into a workspace that is set at twice the sample rate, 96kHz, the soundfile you've imported will play at half the normal speed. For more on this, Google the term "Nyquist Theorem."

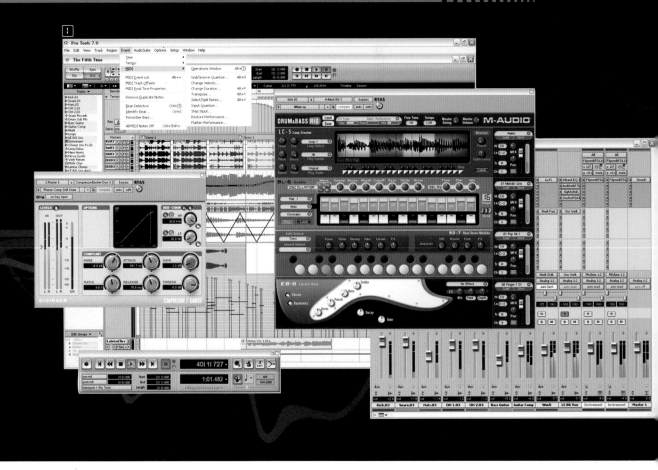

DIGITAL RECORDING

Computers don't understand music—despite the fact that notation is a simple form of code. The only language they do understand is binary, the counting system that uses sequences of 1s and 0s to represent calculations. In computing, each 1 means "on" (voltage through a switch) and each 0 means "off" (no voltage) to one of millions of switches somewhere in your processor.

The key to digital recording is **sampling**. Unlike analog recording, which we've already examined, digital systems analyze a waveform in minute detail thousands of times a second to build up a picture of the sound. This process is known as sampling. Sounds are subtle, nuanced things, and so the more detailed the analysis is, the more accurate the reproduction of the wave will be. Systems that sample a waveform the highest

number of times every second produce the most accurate recordings. The number of times a wave is sampled each and every second is called the **sample rate**, or **sampling frequency**.

■ A computer's sample rate is measured in hertz (Hz). So, if your computer's soundcard has an audio sample rate of 96kHz, for example, that means it can analyze a waveform up to 96,000 times every second. This is a common sampling rate in many 24-bit recording systems (see below).

■ The sampling rate you use must be at least double that of the highest frequency of the sound you are recording to sample it accurately.

■ Don't panic! You don't need to do the math yourself, as your system does the number-crunching for you, but as

the highest-frequency sound the human ear can detect is roughly 20kHz, and the lowest is roughly 20Hz, the minimum sampling rate for accurate digital recordings is anything over 40kHz—twice the highest frequency that most of us can hear.

■ All CD-recording systems, for example, have a sampling rate of 44.1kHz, set because it allows them to record most of the spectrum of human hearing accurately with a bit of room to spare. The technology to do this is known as PCM (pulse code modulation). Aggregating several streams of PCM sound information into a larger stream (a multiplex) means that more detailed and accurate information about the sound can be encoded and sent. This technique is called Time Division Multiplexing (TDM), which is the method used within Digidesign's Pro

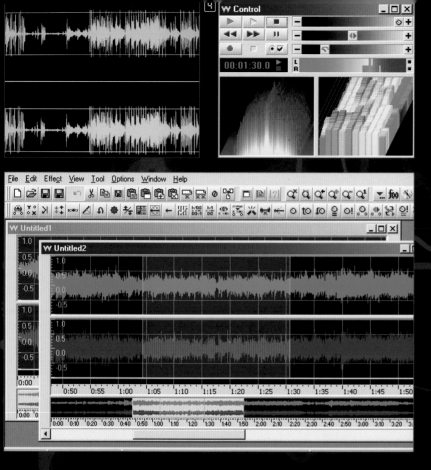

1. DIGIDESIGN PRO TOOLS
This suite of tools is one of the options you have at your disposal when choosing a music and sound application. Turn to page 42 for more information.

2. WAVE EDITING
Graphical readouts of a soundwave's amplitude and characteristic "envelope" can be edited on your PC, allowing you to "see" sound in order to work with it.

3. SLICING AND DICING
Digital information can be interpreted in many different ways. In this inexpensive PC sound-editing software, Goldwave, you can choose to examine the different frequency bands of a wave in 3-D.

4. EDITING THE WAVE
Most editing suites allow you to highlight sections of a soundwave and then apply a whole range of different parameters to it. (Software: Goldwave.)

Tools suite of professional software and hardware products for sound recording (page 42).

16- AND 24-BIT RECORDING
We know that digital systems only understand binary code. "Bit" is short for "binary digit," and as we know, a binary digit is either a 1 or a 0–"1" meaning "on" and "0" meaning "off." Computers are essentially calculating machines. They store the results of their calculations–such as their minute analysis of a soundwave–in strings of binary digits that tell a processor's millions of internal switches what to do. Software turns this type of information into something you can interact with via your monitor and your mouse.

Just as more samples per second equals more accurate recordings, so a longer string of binary digits means that more

information can be stored in it. The length of this invisible string of code is called the "bit depth." So a 24-bit system is simply one that stores information in strings of 1s and 0s that are 24 binary digits long (e.g. 111001100011011000111001) rather than 16, for example. The number of characters used to store the data is known as the "word length."

So why record at 24-bit if you're going to make a CD or create an MP3? Well, you can record at whichever bit depth you prefer, but the real answer (as with all digital media) is redundant detail. As in digital photography, it is better to capture as much information as you can to begin with and then see what you can lose than it is to record at lower resolution (bit depth) from the start. Either way, digital audio requires a lot of processing, and 24-bit files contain a massive amount of data. Think about

it: 96,000 samples a second over the course of a three-minute pop song equals 17,280,000 samples stored in strings of 24 bits. That's why you need a computer with a fast processor and lots of storage capacity (see page 21 for more information).

As your computer has to analyze a sound tens of thousands of times a second to sample just a tiny section of it, there can be a minuscule timelag between you talking into your microphone or hitting a key on your synth and your computer recording the information. This timelag is called the system's **latency**. It should only be a few milliseconds long (almost imperceptible to the human ear), but you need to keep that figure as low as possible to avoid noticeable timing problems. This will be discussed in various sections of the book.

MACS, PCS, AND LINUX

EXTERNAL MUSIC HARDWARE

SOUNDCARDS AND INTERFACES

WORKSTATIONS AND MULTITRACKERS

When computers, such as the clunky early Windows PCs, the first Apples to fall from the tree, and the much-loved (by some) Ataris, were first seriously introduced into recording studios in the mid-1980s, there was little that they could usefully do that you couldn't do faster, cheaper, and better with the application of a little human ingenuity. In those days even a modest professional studio might consist of a 16- or 24-track tape machine; a 24-track mixing desk; racks of signal processors and effects; maybe half a dozen analog or primitive digital synths; and perhaps a crude 8-bit sampler.

So it's a sobering thought that, bar the engineer's experience and skill, all the advantages of the first digital-assisted recording studios—and whole rooms full of bulky equipment—can now be boiled down to a few million lines of code on an average desktop computer. And if you have a laptop, more sobering still is the realization that an entire virtual studio can be held in a box that is half the size of a briefcase. Thousands of musicians today, be they professional artists such as Nitin Sawhney, who tours the world with a Pro Tools-based laptop recording new sounds and new collaborations, or DJs

and remixers, base their studio on a mobile solution, or have invested in both home-based and mobile setups. For many musicians, a well-specified laptop holds a copy of all the software on their main desktop computer, allowing the laptop to become a roving "ambassador" for their home or project facility.

APPLE MAC OR WINDOWS PC?
The perennial question of which computer platform to go for is perhaps best solved by asking yourself a few simple questions—such as what do you want to achieve today?

APPLE MAC
The self-contained Apple Macs are ideal for music production.

1. PC STUDIOS
Windows PC-based studios are the pragmatic solution, especially if you use your computer for non-music-related tasks. Laptops are an excellent option in terms of convenience and portability.

2. THE COMPUTER IN YOUR STUDIO
Whatever your choice of computer, it can be at the center of a range of music peripherals.

3. RAM
Always go for 1GB of RAM if you can upgrade your system. Ensure you're buying the right RAM chips for your type of computer.

MINIMUM AND RECOMMENDED SPECIFICATIONS: MAC/PC

Processors: 1GHz minimum; ideally 1.6GHz or higher.
Computers are designed to crunch numbers, digitize data, and provide a graphical means to interact with and edit information. So go for the highest specification Mac or PC you can. For music and sound, processors should be at least as fast as 1GHz, preferably a lot higher—say 1.6GHz or 1.8GHz. A lot of software manufacturers quote minimum and recommended specifications of less than this, but ignore this advice.

Hard Disk Space: 60GB minimum, preferably more.

The more the merrier. If you're recording audio, you'll very quickly be dealing with multi-megabyte file sizes on every individual track. That takes up a lot of space (not to mention processing power).

RAM: 1GB+
Again, many software makers quote minimum specifications of 256MB, and recommend 512MB of RAM. Ignore their advice and go for 1GB every time. RAM is inexpensive. (Doublecheck with an expert you're buying the right module.)

What kind of music do you want to make? Do you want a fully featured production suite for dealing with music, sound, video, and animation—or simply a means to sketch ideas, record demos, and jam with your friends?

This is another way of saying, what software do you want? Some packages run solely on one platform, such as CoolEdit (PC) and Logic Pro/Logic Express (Mac). However, many good-quality music and sound tools (Cubase, Reason, and dozens of others) work just as well on either platform. There are literally hundreds of music and sound tools out there.

The next question is: What do you want to achieve in the future? The computer you choose today needs to match the scale of your ambitions tomorrow—and

those ambitions will almost certainly get bigger, the deeper into digital music and sound you go.

If you already have a Windows PC, then be pragmatic and find out if your machine is fast enough and powerful enough to run music software alongside all of the other software you may have, such as Microsoft Office. See the box on the previous page for recommended system requirements.

If you have a desktop Windows computer, the next thing to establish is whether your integral soundcard is up to the task of recording and playing back master-quality audio, and if it has all the connections you're going to need—such as whether it can record surround sound, if you wish to make soundtracks for DVDs. Turn to the sections on soundcards

(page 28) and audio and data connectivity (page 35) for more information. You'll find surround-sound on pages 156-161, and also in the sections on mixing. You can choose to buy an external soundcard and interface, but one of the characteristics of desktop PCs is that they have integral cards—albeit in the back of your computer tower.

If you have, or desire, a Windows-based laptop, then you will need to purchase an external soundcard/interface, which you can connect via FireWire and/or USB. There are numerous modules on the market. Again, turn to pages 28-29.

The main advantage of Windows PCs is their ubiquity—which means low cost, easy maintenance, and wide availability of peripherals. Smaller software developers tend to write for Windows

PCs, as they can't afford to do otherwise—unless they're part of the open-source software movement (see box). Some hardware manufacturers, meanwhile, produce highly specified PCs with top-quality soundcards, drivers, interfaces, and software pre-installed for music and/or multimedia work. These can be pricey, but are certainly worth investigating—and could save you a great deal of time and effort attempting to set everything up to the same standard yourself.

However, if you are in the market for a dedicated music and sound computer—offering easy access to other digital media tools as well—then you'd be well advised to consider one of the latest Apple Macs. One of the Mac's advantages is that hardware and software all come from the same source, which makes for a stable and well-integrated system—

1. EASE OF USE
Digital music can lead to a tangle of cables and peripherals, so you may thank yourself for choosing a self-contained system, like a Mac or a laptop.

2. KEEP IT SAFE
Security is the disadvantage of a laptop—the CEO of an Internet security company once left his laptop, full of company secrets, behind at a security conference!

LINUX FOR MUSIC AND SOUND

Linux is an "open source" operating system you can run on your computer (within a partition, perhaps) if you feel drawn to the world of independent software development. Linux is a derivative of the Unix operating system, but its source code (the kernel of code at the heart of the system) is freely available for anyone to access, and is shared between a global community of developers that is committed to passing on its work with others. They are part of what's known as the "copyleft" movement, who are against the principle of copyright and the Microsoft and Apple world of proprietary systems.

With thousands of people freely writing and developing Linux software, new music tools—from fully featured suites to plugins and effects—are available on the Internet almost every day.

As a result, your best bet is to Google "Linux music" and see what's available, but you'll find some useful URLs and resources at the back of the book.

something that doesn't always apply to PCs. The elegant, minimal, and ergonomically designed Macs can be a huge boon to a home studio. Indeed, a self-contained machine like one of the beautiful iMac range is many professional musicians' computer of choice. Many top studios are Mac based as well. More third-party peripherals are becoming available, especially since the success of the iPod.

The other advantage is that Macs are, without exception, designed from the ground up to be hubs of creativity and entertainment. There is little that you can't create on a Mac if you can get hold of the software, the peripherals, and the support—which may mean relying on the Internet. For music and sound, however, you will certainly need to buy an external soundcard/interface, but most musicians prefer to have some form of external

interface, as it makes it easier to plug in mics, instruments, and cables, and access the hardware's controls if they need to.

File formats and compatibility are less of a problem these days; they only really become an issue if you are using plugins (see page 60). Check that your favored plugin works on your preferred computer platform.

As we increasingly source content and tools from the Internet and become members of global communities of interest, it's also worth bearing in mind that Macs are inherently more secure than PCs—if only because the majority of virus-writers have Microsoft's operating systems in their sights. That said, Apple's switch to Intel chips in 2006 may have a knock-on effect in terms of security, as it makes the system an easier target for malicious coders.

Another potential pitfall is that Macs produced after the changeover are different from those produced prior to it, such as the first two generations of iMac G5s. Future software iterations will have to be recompiled for the new processors, which might mean compatibility problems for anyone who invested in fully featured professional studio software before the changeover, but who has yet to upgrade their computer.

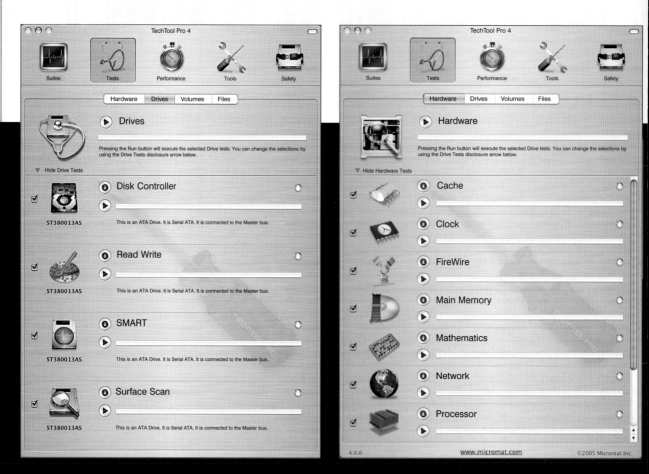

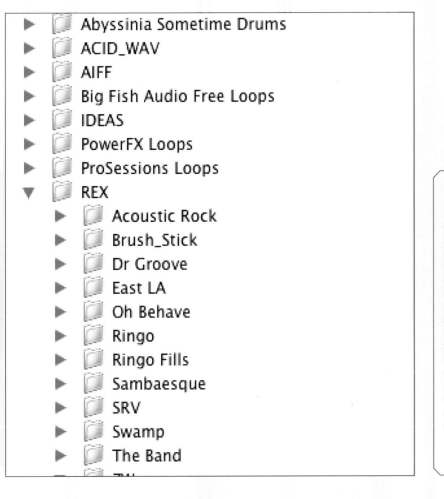

▶ Abyssinia Sometime Drums
▶ ACID_WAV
▶ AIFF
▶ Big Fish Audio Free Loops
▶ IDEAS
▶ PowerFX Loops
▶ ProSessions Loops
▼ REX
   ▶ Acoustic Rock
   ▶ Brush_Stick
   ▶ Dr Groove
   ▶ East LA
   ▶ Oh Behave
   ▶ Ringo
   ▶ Ringo Fills
   ▶ Sambaesque
   ▶ SRV
   ▶ Swamp
   ▶ The Band

FILE MANAGEMENT (LEFT)

File management is a vital issue with digital music and sound. You will rapidly build up a huge library of audio files, loops, samples, songs, mixes, and different file types—such as mixes saved for the Web. The sooner you put in place a simple means of storing, managing, tagging, and archiving your work, the better. If you don't do it from day one, you'll face a huge task trying to sort out hundreds or thousands of files later on—and you'll easily lose files that are essential components of songs. This is another reason to invest in an external hard disk for additional storage and backup.

MAINTAIN YOUR SYSTEM

Another reason for your computer running slowly, other than insufficient RAM, a slow processor, or a slow hard disk, is that your hard disk may have become cluttered and fragmented with thousands of bits of files and poorly sorted work. It's a good idea to run a diagnostic program that fixes common faults and errors, and "defrags" your disk. Backup your work before you run this, however. The software shown here, Tech Tools (Mac), is recommended by some resellers.

AVOID THE ARMS RACE!

With massive storage, fast processors, and huge RAM capacities all within reach of the most meager budget, it's easy to enter an arms race of "faster, better, more, more, more." This is especially true of music technology, and it is many musicians' weakness. You will soon have put together a home studio in your software alone that outflanks the capabilities of many professional studios of the recent past, and yet lurking in the back of your mind will be the suspicion that your music would sound better if only you could buy that new vocal plugin, perhaps a grand piano emulator, and then there's that new guitar rack simulator you've been coveting. The problem with this mindset is that we risk never mastering the basics of the dozens of tools we have, let alone discovering their full creative potential. Sometimes it's better to master every aspect of a small set of tools than to buy more tools and then rarely use them. You might even get some music recorded.

WORKSTATION KEYBOARDS

While it's tempting to abandon hardware synths, samplers, and other sound-generating keyboards/modules, one could make an invaluable addition to your studio both as your main controller keyboard via MIDI; as an expandable soundbank, as a musical sketchpad (if it has onboard sequencing capabilities, as this classic Korg Triton has), and as a live performance instrument. You may also find that having dedicated analog style controls on the keyboard's main interface is preferable to operating virtual controls via a mouse and computer keyboard.

Desktop computers and laptops are excellent number-crunchers and windows into a world of creative applications. However, a mouse and a QWERTY keyboard are far from ideal as musical tools or musical interfaces—they encourage us to be passive pointers and clickers rather than active musicians following our intuitions, emotions, and passions.

All acoustic and electric musical instruments—from guitars, drums, and keyboards, to the dozens of instruments in the strings and brass families—have one thing in common: they're designed to be extensions of the human body that allow us to communicate through a global language using our physicality as human beings. Digital technology in its purest form, on the other hand, has a habit of producing "boxes" packed full of amazing

sounds and effects, but which lack a human interface and ask us merely to sit down, slouch, plug them in, and select from a menu. They talk the digital language of 1s and 0s, ons and offs. Yet such processes can be inward looking and do not breed collaboration, which is part and parcel of making music.

Some recent digital music technology devices, such as Korg's Kaos Pad and the Alesis Airsynth, are the exception to the rule, in that they've added a form of intuitive human interface. The Kaos Pad allows you to play digital effects like a musical instrument by sliding your fingers back and forth across a touch-sensitive screen and tapping out rhythms, while the Airsynth brings to mind the Theremin of old by responding to your hand movements through the air. Both

were used live by Brian Eno recently in a rare, one-off London gig I attended with software pioneer Tim Cole.

Synthesizers, electric pianos, and samplers are terms that used to refer to pieces of dedicated musical hardware, which included not just a standard piano keyboard, but also built-in sounds and controls you could touch. Today, more and more of these instruments exist only as software/emulations, and the market for hardware synths and samplers is dwindling. Many hardware synths, though, are still available, and new models are being developed—at least, for now.

A traditional synth, sampler, or workstation keyboard remains an excellent addition to your home studio—and there's a lot to be said for mastering every aspect of a

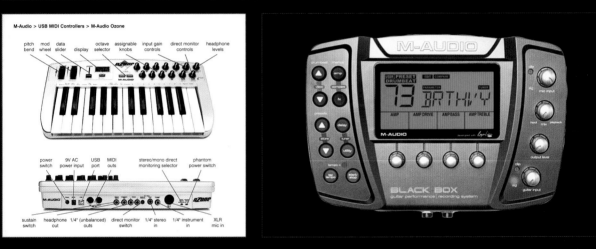

single instrument rather than buying into a constant software upgrade path. All synths are MIDI devices, whether through the old-style MIDI interface, or via USB or FireWire. (If you're not up to speed with MIDI, see pages 44-45.)

For many of you, the only musical interface you'll need is a simple MIDI controller keyboard. This is essentially a "dummy" (non-sound generating) keyboard that acts as a controller to your music software's (and your soundcard's) synthesizer. Controller keyboards come in numerous sizes, such as 37-, 49-, 61-, and 88-notes (keys). Controller keyboards send MIDI note and control information to your computer. Many feature a range of assignable control knobs and sliders. You can program these to control specific functions on a software synthesizer,

sampler, plugin, or virtual instrument– such as changing a sound's envelope, velocity, sustain, and so on. Controller keyboards are usually lightweight and portable, and connect to your computer via USB. Many come bundled with demo versions of music software.

However, guitarists, drummers, and wind/brass players take heart: you can also buy MIDI guitars, drum pads, and even breath-controlled MIDI synths.

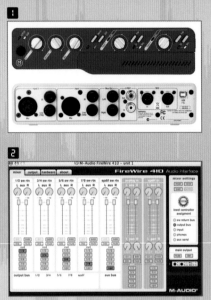

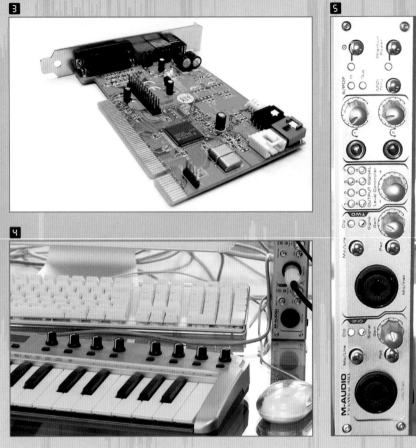

1. MBOX
Digidesign hardware interface for use with its Pro Tools LE system.

2. SOFTWARE
The onscreen interface that appears when you use an M-Audio FireWire 410 external card.

3. INTERNAL CARDS
Specialist internal card for PC-based systems.

4. DESKTOP STUDIO
Computer, soundcard, and MIDI keyboard—a complete studio setup.

5. CLOSE-UP VIEW
An M-Audio FireWire 410 external card.

All computers have some form of internal soundcard and onboard synthesizer for processing music and sound. However, for professional work, you should invest in a top-quality soundcard. Anything else will be a false economy.

Soundcards essentially come in two forms –cards that slot into your PC tower; and external, standalone devices (sometimes called "breakout boxes" or audio interfaces) that connect to your PC/Mac via FireWire or USB. Some internal cards come with an additional breakout box.

If you have either a Mac or a laptop, then you'll need to invest in an external device. This is by no means a disadvantage, as external cards are in many ways the best and most useful option, as they avoid you having to access the rear of your computer to make new connections or check for

faults. It's also useful being able to see the onboard peak indicator lights to check for clipped signals on input, rather than always having to rely on your software. Many cards come with some form of bundled software, which will usually present you with a simple onscreen, mixer-style interface for managing your inputs and outputs from the desktop.

One of your soundcard's primary functions is to convert analog signals into digital data that your computer can interpret– it's an analog to digital convertor—so the most important consideration (after compatibility) is to check the sampling rate. Go for a card that can sample sound at 24-bit at 96kHz.

Soundcards also serve as a single interface between your computer and the outside world for a whole variety of different audio

and data connections–information from which it sends to and from your computer via FireWire or USB.

If you mix and make music solely in software rather than via an external mixing desk or digital multitracker, then your soundcard will be the single point for managing external connections. It may be useful to keep all of your line-level inputs permanently wired up to avoid the hassle of constant unplugging and searching for leads.

Many soundcards also act as MIDI hubs, so you can plug an external hardware synth, sampler, controller keyboard, or MIDI signal processor (effects box) into your card, and this data will also be streamed to your sequencing package or music software via FireWire or USB.

LATENCY IN SOUNDCARDS

Latency (the minuscule delay between hitting a key or singing a note and this information registering on your computer) is an issue with some poorer-quality cards, and tends to be rooted in driver problems. ASIO 2 (Audio Stream In/Out) is a low-latency driver for the PC. Top-quality cards should have zero or near-zero latency. If you're still experiencing latency on your Mac or PC and you've eliminated the soundcard from the equation, then install more RAM, or buy a faster computer.

THE RISKS OF FIREWIRE

FireWire connections are supposed to be "hot swappable," which means that you can theoretically plug in or unplug your soundcard while it and your computer are switched on. Don't do it! There is a risk you may burn out your soundcard. By far the safest option is to leave your soundcard connected to your computer, but switch the soundcard off. Switch on your computer and wait for it to begin booting up before switching on the card.

6. A HUB FOR ALL CONNECTIONS
It makes sense to choose an external card that can act as a single point for all of your audio and data connections, data from all of which it will send in a single stream via FireWire (recommended) or USB.

Assuming you've invested in professional monitor speakers, then you'll drive these from your soundcard as well. Many cards offer multiple audio outputs so you can set up a surround sound monitor system direct from the card if you wish, or route signals to external signal processors.

■ Ensure that your card is Mac or PC compatible!

Most soundcards offer at least some of the following features. I would advise going for a card that's got the lot, as it will give you the broadest range of options for working with audio in a variety of different media.

■ At least two professional-quality balanced analog line inputs, for guitars and other instruments or modules that use 1/4in (0.6mm) jack plugs. See page 35.

■ One or two professional XLR mic connections. Having two will allow you to stereo-mic a room, for example. The XLR inputs are sometimes combined with the jack inputs into a single socket. See page 35.

■ A Mic/Line switch with each input; a Pad button for attenuating signals that have a tendency to be overloud, and a Gain control with Peak level indicator on each input channel.

■ An Output signal Level controller.

■ One or (preferably two) Headphone sockets, with volume controls. Having two Headphone outputs is useful if you're recording vocals, as both you and your singer can monitor on headphones, and at different levels if need be.

■ A Phantom Power switch for powering condenser mics.

■ A MIDI In and MIDI Thru connection.

■ Eight line outputs for monitoring in up to 7.1 surround sound and/or sending signals out to external processors, or even a hi-fi amp.

■ Two FireWire or USB outputs. I would strongly recommend investing in a FireWire card.

■ S/PDIF outputs for sending 20-bit digital data direct to an external digital recording device.

Expect to pay for your soundcard the equivalent of anything between the cost of an iPod Shuffle and two of the highest-spec iPods on the market .

For many people, the idea of working with digital music and sound via a computer, a mouse, and a GUI (graphical user interface) is counter-intuitive, as music recording is all about equipment that you can see and touch and interact with—mixing desks with knobs and faders, analog controls on synthesizers, effects pedals, and rack units (not to mention musical instruments, of course). Music software—for all its many advantages—can lack a truly human interface.

If you're in the computer-sceptic camp when it comes to music, then there are other options that take digital music away from PCs and Macs, or which bridge the gap between the desktop and more traditional music and sound tools.

Multitrackers

Digital multitrackers and portable integrated studios are manufactured by a broad range of music equipment companies, including Boss, Korg, Fostex, Mackie, Roland, Tascam, Yamaha, and Zoom. Their products range from small, low-cost, digital "sketchpad" devices that allow you to record and mix ideas on the move, to fully-fledged portable studios that offer similar benefits to high-end music and sound software, but within a mixing-desk-style package.

A high-end "studio in a box" console might include:

- 24-track, 24-bit/96kHz digital recording with 24 simultaneous tracks of playback
- a number of virtual tracks per channel (for storing alternative takes and performances)
- motorized faders with total recall (so you can instantly reset the desk to bring up previous mixes)
- a 40GB or 60GB internal drive, to which audio is directly recorded
- phantom-powered XLR inputs and multiple line-ins
- pitch correction facilities
- USB or FireWire connectivity to external processors and expansion modules

- full mixing, routing, and onboard effect capabilities, plus dynamic processors on each channel
- Three- or four-band parametric EQ
- COSM mic modeling, emulating the pickup and frequency signatures of professional microphones
- a large LCD for accessing the onboard software functions.

Such consoles cost about the same as a good-quality mediacenter-style PC or Mac. In some ways, integrated devices are ideal for musicians and engineers, because they put all of a traditional recording studio's controls directly at your fingertips in a self-contained, portable package—and you can burn your work straight to CD using the integral CD writer.

However, there are significant disadvantages—the main ones being that the device locks you into a single, perhaps more limited, way of working; you can't install new software, virtual instruments, or plugins as you can on a PC; you're

obliged to make further hardware choices if you want to add functionality; there's no direct integration with other applications, such as video or animation suites; and your main music and sound tool becomes a depreciating hardware asset.

Control Surfaces

An alternative option is to bridge the gap between the intuitive hardware interface and the expandable virtual studio. While users of Logic, Cubase, Sonar, Tracktion, and other software suites are blessed with an abundance of virtual instruments, soft synths, processors, mixers, and plug-ins, controlling them with a keyboard and mouse can be time-consuming, inefficient, and sometimes frustrating as software tools become both more abundant and increasingly complex. Behringer, Evolution, Mackie, Native Instruments, and M-Audio are among several companies that manufacture control surfaces. These are mixing-desk style pieces of hardware that can be set up to control a variety of functions within your virtual studio, from the faders of your mixer to the various individual parameters of a virtual processor, plugin, or software instrument.

Such controllers offer seamless integration with a broad range of popular software suites (check that your software is supported), together with sliders, rotary panpots, and assignable/programmable controllers.

Workstations

The third option is to explore the world of workstation keyboards. These are typically synthesizers and/or samplers that also include a fully featured onboard 24-track sequencer, pattern editors, multiple drum kits' worth of percussion sounds, and good-quality effects boards. Some can also record audio from a mic, but these functions are usually limited.

Workstations first appeared in the late 1980s, with keyboards such as Korg's M1, revolutionizing home recording for many people. Today, workstations such as Korg's ever-expanding Triton range (the original Triton is pictured here) can be very useful both as keyboards in their own right, but also as writing and arranging tools on which you can multitrack music to master quality, and then burn it to CD. However, all of these functions are available in software form in most good music- and sound-making applications, and it's easier and less expensive to upgrade your software than it is to buy a new workstation keyboard—many of which cost more than a well-featured computer.

1. MULTITRACKERS
Hardware-based multitrackers and portable studios give you all the benefits of a recording studio, but in a portable, mixer-style package. However, all of this functionality is available in software form in applications such as Logic, Cubase, and Digital Performer, without the risk of buying a depreciating asset that's expensive to replace.

2. WORKSTATIONS
Such keyboards revolutionized home recording in previous decades, but are perhaps now an expensive luxury if you're looking to make a one-off investment in a music- and sound-recording system.

AUDIO RECORDING TERMS AND CONCEPTS
AUDIO AND DATA CONNECTIVITY

A/D CONVERTOR
An Analog to Digital (A/D) convertor turns analog data into a stream of bits. Home studio, FireWire, and USB-based A/D convertors are inexpensive and commonplace, operating at 96kHz and 24-bit. (See Soundcards, and Audio and Data Connectivity).

Amplify and Attenuate
Amplify means to make bigger, to increase the amplitude or volume of a signal by increasing its peak in decibels. Attenuate is the opposite, meaning to make smaller, usually in terms of the reduction of a signal's amplitude. Controls to address a signal's amplitude include a mixer's faders, and, in some mixers, also the Gain controls, which amplify a signal at input before further processing.

Beatmatching/Warping
A process within some software programs, such as Ableton Live, whereby prerecorded loops of any tempo and time signature can be mapped to the tempo of a track without changing their pitch. For example, if you import a 90bpm vocal loop into a song that is 123bpm, it can be warped so that the loop now plays at 123bpm, but the pitch and sound of the voice remain unchanged.

Click Track
A function within sequencers and music software in which the tempo of the song (the number of beats per minute, such as 120bpm, within the time signature, such as 4/4) is counted out in audible clicks, metronome-style, so you can play along in time.

Dithering
Intelligent reduction of the bitrate/bit depth of an audio file by adding small amounts of white noise (noise that covers the entire frequency spectrum) to mask any resulting slight deficiencies in the sound. Apogee UV22HR dithering is a standard process adopted by Cubase and other audio production software.

Effects / Digital Signal Processing (DSP)
See pages 56-59.

Equalization/EQ
In audio processing, equalization (EQ) is the process of balancing and modifying the frequency range of a soundwave, or the relationship of multiple soundwaves to each other, via a mixer or an equalizing processor. Changing the EQ of a sound does not modify its fundamental pitch, but the complex mix of frequencies inherent in it. Parametric EQ includes controls to adjust Gain, bandwidth (also known as Q), and the "central" frequency. Shelving equalizers modify a range of frequencies by a fixed amount—a low shelf EQ solely affects low frequencies up to certain point, while a high shelf does the reverse. A graphic

GRAPHIC EQUALIZERS
This seven-band equalizer offers a variety of presets, which are worth exploring. Some graphic EQs, like this one, do not give you the option of editing very low or very high frequencies.

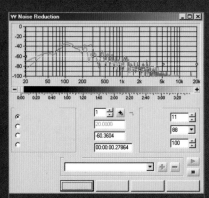

NOISE REDUCTION
Most digital audio systems allow you to remove noise—in this example, in Goldwave (PC), you can remove noise within specific frequency bands. White noise is noise heard across all frequency bands; pink noise is prevalent at mid frequencies, while brown (or red) noise is found at low frequencies.

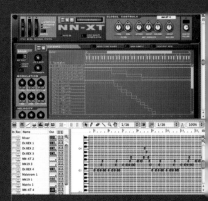

SAMPLERS
Sampling is the heart of all digital audio systems, however a sampler is a dedicated hardware or software device for sampling, editing, and playing back sound clips. Software: NN-XT sampler in Propellerhead Software's Reason.

equalizer allows you to address specific frequency bands within the 20Hz–20kHz spectrum of human hearing, with an independent gain control for each. The graphic EQ in iTunes, for example, gives you 10 editable frequency bands, while the one in Logic has 32 bands. See Mixing, pages 76–85 for more.

I/O
Input/Output. In some devices, sockets can be used as both an Input and an Output. In mixers, such as the one in Logic, the I/O section is where you assign signals to different Inputs and Outputs.

Mastering
See pages 94–95.

Mixing
See pages 76–85.

Normalization
Increasing the volume of an audio recording in software until the loudest peak is 0dB, thus making the track as loud as possible without distortion.

Punch In/Out
When you're recording audio, such as a vocal performance, you may want to re-record just one or two parts of it, while retaining the rest of the track. One way to do this is to play the track and then "punch in" Record at the key moment to replace the mistake with a better performance, and then punch out again leaving the rest of the track intact.

Quantization
This has several meanings in relation to soundwaves, but within sequencing software it means moving musical events so that they fall precisely on certain beats of the bar. For example, if you record a MIDI track in real time, your playing will move slightly in and out of time with the strict beat of the song. If you Quantize the MIDI recording, you will shift all of the out-of-time notes to the exact tempo.

Ripping
The term originated in image processing, but it has come to mean processing any file (such as a Windows Media Audio file) into a different format (such as an iTunes-compatible AAC file). See File Formats, page 96.

Sequencing
In digital audio, a software-based interface for creating and editing sequences of musical events, together with their associated controllers. Some software packages are informally known as sequencers. Sequencing is the process of making and interacting with musical sequences on a timeline. (See Timelines and Sequencing, page 36).

Step Sequencing/Pattern Editing
A specific form of musical sequencing whereby musical events are programmed or drawn onto a timeline or within a pattern-editing window, rather than played by an external keyboard controller. For example, the Matrix Pattern Sequencer in Propellerhead Software's Reason music suite (see picture, page 34, and also pages 48-51) allows you to click on points within a grid to enter musical events and modify them. Hitting Play activates the musical pattern you've just created. If you're not very musically adept, or if you can't play the keyboard too well, this can be a useful way of experimenting with musical ideas.

Signal to noise (ratio), S/N
The gap between the strength of the signal and the noise floor (see below). A higher signal-to-noise ratio is best, as noise will be less noticeable. S/N is measured in decibels.

EQUALIZATION
This is carried out within your mixer, or within dedicated modules. Software shown: Propellerhead's Reason.

Synthesizers

Keyboard musical devices—and now increasingly software programs (soft synths)—for the creation of realistic or artificial sounds by manipulating and editing the constituent elements of a soundwave. There are several types of synthesis, including Frequency Modulation (FM); Subtractive synthesis (in which the elements are subtracted from waveforms of different shapes); Additive synthesis (the inverse of subtractive); Granular synthesis (in which extremely short sound samples, or grains, are layered together to create new sound textures); Wavetable synthesis (in which soundwaves of acoustic and electronic instruments are sampled and layered together); and digital sampling (where real sounds are stored and manipulated using a variety of effects and processors).

THD, Headroom, Noise Floor, and Dynamic Range

Total Harmonic Distortion is absolute circuit overload. Three percent THD is the point at which overload introduces audible distortion. Three percent THD is measured in the number of decibels above 0dB at which this distortion occurs. The gap between 0dB and three percent THD on any audio format is called its headroom, while the gap between the noise floor and three percent THD gives us the signal's dynamic range. The noise floor is the lowest audible element of a signal. The noise floor is the measurement of the sum of all the unwanted signals within an audio system—the system's inherent noise, in other words. It is not possible to measure signals below the noise floor.

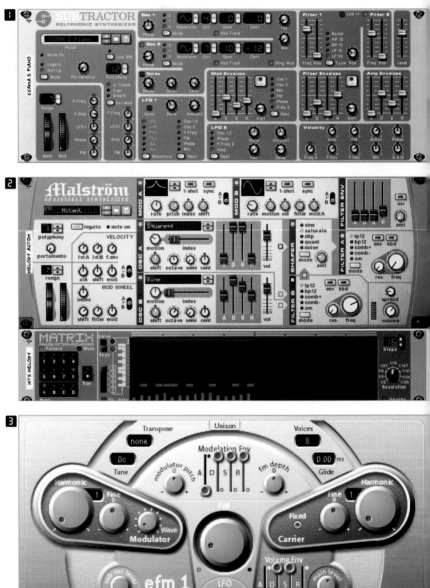

1–3. SOFT SYNTHS (SOFTWARE SYNTHESIZERS)
(From the top) Subtractive synthesis in Propellerhead's Reason music sequencer; the Malström granular synth, also in Reason (with the Matrix pattern step-sequencer patched into it); the EFM1 synth in Logic Pro.

AUDIO CONNECTIONS

When buying audio connections, always invest in a dealer-recommended cable instead of going for the tempting "budget" option. Budget cables won't withstand the rigors of regular plugging and unplugging. Budget cabling is often poorly shielded, which can be a problem in digital audio, especially in "noisy" (in electrical terms) environments–not simply because the quality of the connections may be poor, but also because the cable itself may pick up electrical noise and radio interference. Balanced audio connections are the solution. If you cast your mind back to the introduction to this book, you'll remember that two identical signals (or elements of two signals) can be made to cancel each other out if they're positioned in antiphase. In a balanced line, one wire contains the signal, and another the same signal sent 180 degrees out of phase with the first. The third wire grounds the other two. The noise in the line is effectively cancelled out.

XLR (XLR3)

The rugged, three-pin, balanced-line, analog-audio connection used in professional mics. Your mic will have a male XLR connection of three pins, into which you plug a female XLR. The other end of the lead will have a male connection that fits into your soundcard, breakout box, mixer, or portable studio. Pin 1 is ground; pin 2 is normal polarity (hot); and pin 3 inverted polarity (cold–i.e. positioned 180 degrees out of phase with the signal in pin 2). If you purchase an XLR-to 1/4in jack adapter, ensure that the wiring of pin 2 and 3 matches that of your XLR, otherwise the signal will be lost. Other XLR connections have 4 or 5 pins, and are deployed for stage lighting and other heavy-duty uses.

RCA (US) / Phono (UK)

RCA (Radio Corporation of America), or Phono is a common audio/video/electrical connection in many consumer audio and video devices. An RCA is characterized by a central pin, and a surrounding ring-connector. The pin carries the signal and the ring both grounds the connection and secures it. If you plug RCA connections in while an amplifier is switched on, you'll hear a buzz as the pin carrying the signal connects before the grounding sleeve. Some RCAs are color-coded–yellow for video; red for audio right channel, and white or black for audio left.

1/4in (6.3mm), 1/8in (3.5mm), and 3/32in (2.5mm) "Jack" plugs

The Jack has numerous uses. In audio terms, you'll use a 1/4in jack for electric guitar leads, other electric musical instrument outputs, and some headphone connections. A 1/8in jack is common on many soundcards, MP3 players, and in other headphone designs. Within a Jack plug

there can be various connections, varying from two-connectors (for unbalanced mono sound with grounding); three connectors (TRS, or tip, ring, and sleeve, used for balanced or mono audio with grounding, and for grounded stereo signals). Versions with four or five connectors are used in some audio/video applications, and also in many MP3 players where one or two of the connections may carry a small electrical current.

DATA CONNECTIONS

FireWire

FireWire (A.K.A. i.Link, or IEEE 1394) is a digital interface standard for high-speed data transfer between computers and peripherals, such as digital video cameras, external hard drives, soundcards, and breakout boxes. FireWire is designed to support hot-swapping (connecting or disconnecting components while they're switched on). However, this is not advisable for audio devices. FireWire 400 can transfer data at speeds of up to 400Mbps, while FireWire 800 doubles that speed–a useful standard to aim for if you're purchasing an external hard drive for audio work.

USB (Universal Serial Bus)

Ubiquitous computer peripheral and digital device connection. USB 2.0 devices can transfer data at rates of up to 480 Mbps. FireWire 800 devices are preferable for connections where maximum speed is of the essence. For digital music and sound, use FireWire 800 for transferring and streaming audio, and USB 2.0 for MIDI data transfers, where very high speed is less critical.

MIDI

MIDI connections are becoming less common now that MIDI data is increasingly being sent via FireWire or USB devices. However, your keyboard synth, beatbox, or rack-unit-based signal processor may have a MIDI port. This will normally consist of two or three sockets–MIDI Out, MIDI In, and MIDI Thru. If you're unable to connect your MIDI device directly to your soundcard, you can buy a small, low-cost MIDI hub that links MIDI connections with a FireWire or USB device.

S/PDIF

Sony/Philips Digital Interface Format. System for transferring PCM audio signals via an RCA connection, or via an optical (fiber optic) connection. A common connection on hi-fi CD recorders.

THE STUDIO IN YOUR COMPUTER

TIMELINES AND SEQUENCING

SEQUENCERS THAT CAN RECORD AUDIO

INTEGRATED SUITES

MIDI

MUSIC-ONLY SOFTWARE

LOOPS AND BEATMATCHING

EDITING AUDIO AND MIDI

EFFECTS AND PROCESSORS: TIME-BASED/DYNAMIC

PLUGINS AND VIRTUAL INSTRUMENTS

We've all heard the expression "a sequence of events." What a sequencer does is record and play back just that, with each "event" being a musical or an audio one. All of these events are visible, accessible, and editable within a timeline. "Sequencing" describes the process whereby sequences of musical or audio events are recorded and edited on a graphical timeline.

Timelines are the heart of your music or audio production software—and of any software that enables you to produce creative work that has duration in time, such as video or moving graphics.

A timeline consists of a series of sideways-scrolling, vertical time divisions, and a horizontal row of tracks. When you hit Play or Record, a vertical cursor will run along the timeline and show your current position within the recording. The default vertical time divisions tend to be musical bars (in the sense of "four beats to the bar"), and so the number of divisions through which the cursor moves along the timeline every minute corresponds to the tempo of the song. In multimedia software, you may have the option to view your timeline divided into frames per second (fps) at the appropriate rate, which corresponds to the time divisions used in video and film. In most software you will also see a corresponding readout in Mins:secs:ms, and in some cases be able to check the number of individual samples that each track contains.

There are three types of track:

■ Audio tracks: for the recording, playback, editing, and automation of audio from external sources, such as voices, and instruments that have been miked up or direct-injected (D.I'd) into your recording device. Once recorded, these will usually appear as a waveform within the track.

■ (MIDI) Instrument tracks: as above, but for data sent to internal software instruments, virtual instruments, and so on. In some software suites, these tracks may display the musical notation you've played.

■ External MIDI tracks: as above, but for data sent to and from external MIDI devices, such as hardware synths. You can also record MIDI control data, or other MIDI information. (See page 44).

Every new event you create is visible as either a scrolling horizontal "beam" within the appropriate track on the timeline, or (in the case of software

such as Reason) as individually addressable event markers that appear in the timeline of each track when you hit a note.

You can drag objects—such as prerecorded loops—onto most timelines, and they will appear as smaller boxes, within which is a graphical representation of the waveform, or of the number of musical events within the loop.

Copying, cutting and pasting, and object selection and dragging are all done via the timeline—for example, you could marquee-select any group of objects and move them to different tracks. Any audio track—regardless of its length—is a single object, so if you want to move only a part of it, you need to slice up the track into separate, editable objects.

The window that contains the timeline is known by various software-specific names. In most software, you are given a complete set of tools, including a Pen, with which you can draw events—including control information about the volume of any effect or process you want to apply at key points along the timeline.

Timelines and arrange/event windows are what sets digital music and sound apart from analog recording, in that you can not only hear your recordings, but also see them as sequences of individual events—each one of which can be sliced, diced, and creatively manipulated in any way you see fit. Turn to pages 54-55 for more on MIDI and audio editing.

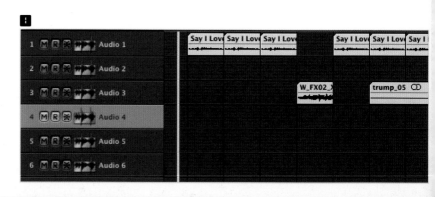

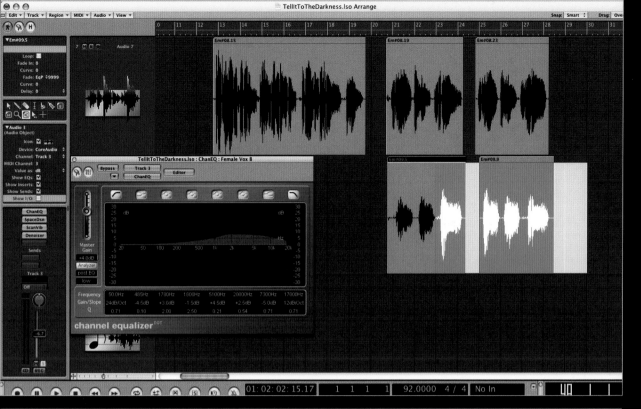

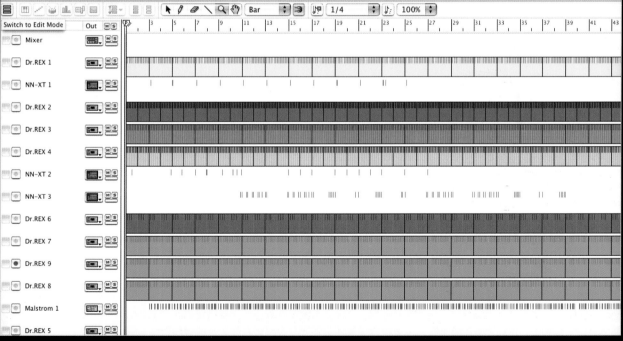

1. SIMPLE OPERATION

Click on an Audio, Instrument, or external MIDI track to record new data onto it.

2. LOGIC ARRANGE WINDOW

A window into each and every element of your recording, where you can edit and arrange your music and sound.

3. REASON

This music-creation tool shows individual events as vertical dashes on the timeline. You can zoom in on these events and edit them in a separate Controller lane, where you can edit volume, effects, and so on.

SEQUENCERS THAT CAN RECORD AUDIO

Today's audio and music production software suites are virtual studios that organize internal instrument tracks, external MIDI tracks, and audio tracks recorded via your audio interface. They are sound recorders, mixing consoles, and effects racks, and many also offer a broad range of integrated virtual instruments, soft synths, and samplers.

Among the packages on offer are Apple Logic Pro (Mac) and Steinberg's Cubase SX (PC/Mac), both of which are also available in "cut down," entry-level versions—Logic Express and Cubase SE, SL, and Cubasis. Other suites include Cakewalk Sonar Producer's Edition/Studio Edition (PC), Cakewalk Home Studio (PC); Cakewalk Project (PC); MOTU Digital Performer (Mac); CoolEdit (PC); and RMS Tracktion (PC/Mac).

Some audio suites can also integrate seamlessly with video and other creative applications and create mixes in anything up to 7.1 surround sound.

MAKING YOUR FIRST RECORDING

We're going to explore how to make a basic audio recording in Logic, but the principle applies to all sound-recording software packages.

- In the preferences section of your software, decide whether or not you're recording in 24-bit and at 96kHz.

- Ensure that your microphone, or your electric instrument, is switched on and connected to your soundcard, and that your soundcard is registering the signal.

- Doubleclicking on audio Track One will bring up the Mixer. Beneath the Level indicator next to your fader you will see a small button with a circle in it. This means the track is in mono. Clicking the button will make the track stereo—a double-circle graphic will now appear.

- Click the R button within audio Track One to enable the track for recording. Until you do this, the track will be safe.

- Hit the Record button in the Transport bar and then hit Play. A dialog will appear saying that your system is recording to a destination folder. Logic will create a horizontal-scrolling bar within the selected track on the timeline.

- Once you've finished recording the performance, click the Stop button. Logic will process the long string of samples you've recorded for a few moments, before presenting you with a graphical readout of the soundwave you've just recorded—ready for editing.

ADDING MIDI INSTRUMENTS

Many of the big sequencing packages give you an array of virtual instruments and music modules. To bring up a new software instrument within your sequencer:

- In Logic, doubleclick on an Instrument (MIDI) track within the Arrange window. This will bring up the Mixer. The track on which you've doubleclicked will be highlighted within the Mixer.

1. YOUR CENTRAL CONTROL CONSOLE
Your audio and music production tool will soon become the central hub of your recording work.

2. PRO TOOLS
This integrated hardware and software suite is discussed on page 42.

3–6. LOGIC OPTIONS
Just some of the virtual instruments and processors available in Apple Logic Pro.

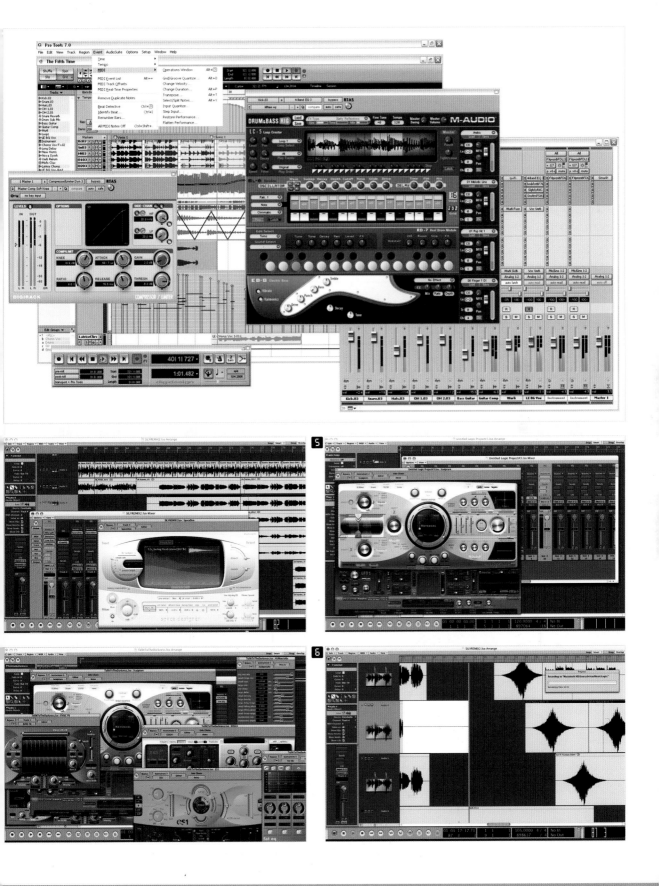

SOME FUNCTIONS WITHIN AUDIO AND MIDI SEQUENCERS

Track Automation: Effects and Controllers

One of the other primary functions of most audio-recording and music-sequencing applications is the ability to automate elements of your mix. All audio and MIDI sequencing packages vary, but in many of them, their automation functions revolve around using the Pen tool in the separate Controller lane of each track (the area where you draw in graphical instructions about how you want a track, or controls within a track, to behave at specific points along the timeline).

Automating Effects

1. In Logic, first bring up the effect you want to patch in by doubleclicking on one of the available Insert buttons within the appropriate Mixer channel. This will open a series of popup menus that will direct you toward whichever effects are available to you—including the effects patches of any plugin virtual instruments you might have added to your application. Select the effect you require, and then play with the controls of the effect window until you hear a sound you like.

2. Go to the View menu within the Arrange window. Scroll to Track Automation (or simply hit "V"). This will create a Track Automation view of the individual track you're working on. (You may find it helps to zoom in on your tracks to get a closeup view within your Arrangement.)

3. Click on the long, horizontal button that has appeared in the Track window. You should now see the Insert effect you've patched in to the track come up as one of the selectable options you can choose from. Select it.

4. A line will now appear that runs along the length of your track. Clicking on this line will create control points that allow you to change the effect's parameters at precise points in the timeline. You can use this same technique to control a huge range of parameters, such as volume, panning, and so on.

- Go to the I/O section of the Mixer within the highlighted channel. Doubleclick in the first of the two tiny, closed windows.

- You should now see a popup menu appear, containing the options Mono, Stereo, and Multichannel.

- Selecting any of these will bring up further menus, each offering a selection of instruments for you to access via your external controller keyboard. In Logic, these include all of the instruments and parameters available within Apple's entry-level Garageband software.

- Any MIDI recording you make on the MIDI Instrument track will trigger the instrument you've selected from this list.

- You could choose, having recorded your performance onto the selected MIDI Instrument track, to change the sound "patch" for a different one, and the MIDI information you've already recorded will now trigger the new sound.

- You might also decide to change the instrument entirely, giving you a completely different selection of sound patches. Again, the MIDI data you've already recorded from your original performance will now trigger (play) the new instrument instead. Remember, with MIDI you're not recording audio, but merely a set of instructions.

- In Logic, going to Window > Matrix Edit will enable you to edit every aspect of your MIDI Instrument Track recording—for example, move notes around, change their length, volume, Attack,

Sustain, and so on. That's the beauty of MIDI. For more on Audio and MIDI editing hints and tips, turn to page 54.

1. HYPER EDIT
Going to Hyper Edit in Logic allows you to draw in a range of different control information across a track with a Pen tool, in a separate window.

2. HYPER DRAW
Alternatively, going to Hyper Draw gives you similar control functionality that you can draw directly onto the track.

3. EDITING AUDIO WITH A CLICK
Doubleclicking on a waveform brings up an Edit window where you can edit small sections of audio.

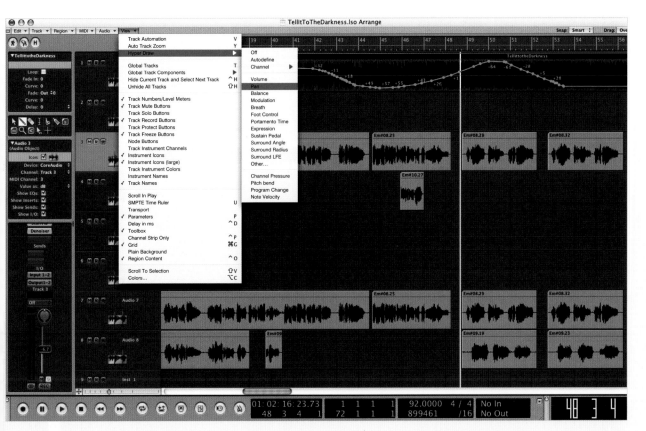

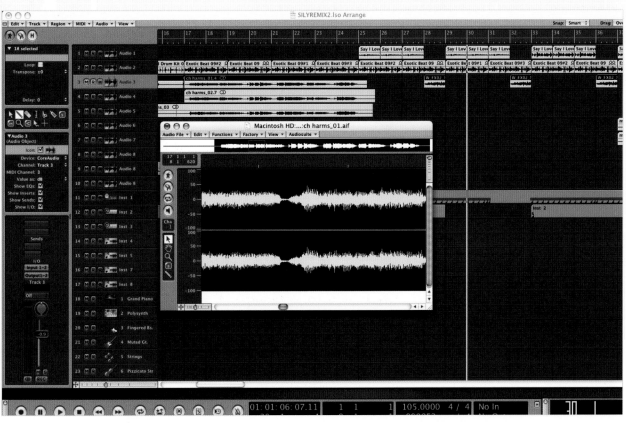

Along with Logic, Cubase, MOTU Digital Performer, Cakewalk Sonar, Reason, and a handful of other sequencers and music-making suites, Pro Tools is synonymous with creating digital music and sound. Pro Tools equipment is made by Digidesign, a division of video technology company AVID.

For most of Pro Tools' existence, what has set the system apart from its peers is that it is both a comprehensive software suite of sequencing tools, virtual processors, effects, and plugins, and a scalable hardware system, offering musicians and aspiring sound recordists an upgrade path from the simplest home setup to advanced production studios.

The entry-level package is Pro Tools LE, which comes bundled with a device called the Mbox. The device is essentially a soundcard/audio interface, but one that is tightly integrated with the LE software.

From the Mbox, the options are scalable all the way up to full-on professional studio and even broadcast facilities—not to mention a crossover into the professional video market and the AVID NLE (non-linear editing) suite, which offers a similar, scalable environment for videomakers to that offered by Pro Tools to musicians.

The intermediary systems are the 001 and 002 interfaces, which are essentially hardware controllers and hard-disk recording systems that integrate

1. DIGI 002 HARDWARE CONTROLLER
Connect it up via FireWire to your Mac or PC and you have an integrated interface to Pro Tools LE software.

seamlessly with Pro Tools software. If having a hardware interface integrated with your Mac or PC-based music software is essential to your work, then it may make sense to investigate one of the Pro Tools systems, instead of opting for a separate sequencer, breakout box, and hardware controller, and then spending both time and energy setting them up to work with each other.

However, Digidesign's acquisition of audio peripherals manufacturer M-Audio prompted a change of tack for Digidesign, with the release of Pro Tools M-Powered— a version of Pro Tools similar to LE, but which will work and integrate with a range of popular M-Audio devices, such as its soundcards and breakout boxes. This makes Pro Tools more widely available to users who are less enthusiastic about being locked into a

single upgrade path, while also making the higher sampling rates of some soundcards over the entry-level Mbox available to people who want access to Pro Tools functionality.

As ever with digital audio, ask yourself what you are trying to achieve, and which functions, tools, and instruments you may need to achieve it. Make your buying decision from there. Pro Tools LE can support up to 32 tracks of sample-accurate, 24-bit/96kHz audio and up to 256 MIDI tracks. In addition, it includes AVID's DV (digital video) Toolkit software and a wide range of audio plugins that allow users to pitchshift, clean up background noise, replace dialog, and change the tempo of audio files. However, the Mbox 2 at the time of writing only supported a sampling rate of 48kHz.

In terms of the choice of Pro Tools hardware, the company is competing with itself in the guise of M-Audio. However, if Apple were to bring out a soundcard or breakout box of its own—as it has long been rumored to be planning—then the combination of Logic, Final Cut Pro, and Apple hardware would be a challenge to Digidesign/AVID's own, very successful version of the Apple business model.

2. DIGI 002 RACK SYSTEM
The rack-mounted version of the Digi 002 hardware controller for Pro Tools LE.

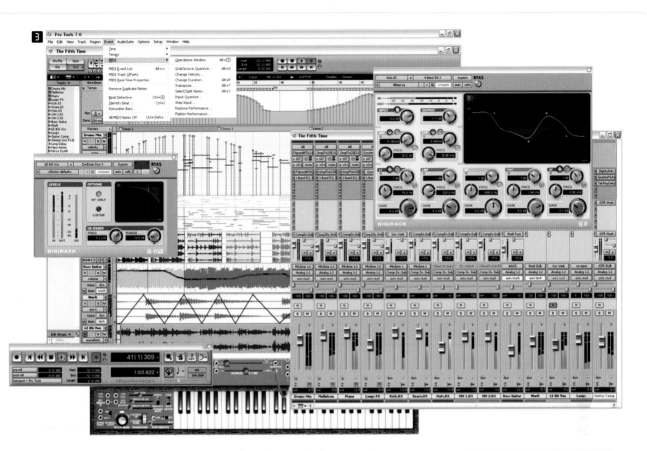

MBOX 2 SPECIFICATIONS

Analog Inputs: 2

Separate source selection and gain control per channel

Mic: XLR with 48V phantom power

Digital I/O

S/PDIF I/O (24-bit)

RCA jacks

Sample Rate: 44.1–48kHz

3. PRO TOOLS LE SOFTWARE
Just some of the virtual instruments, processors, and windows that form Pro Tools LE.

4-5. MBOX 2
Front and rear views of the entry-level interface to Pro Tools LE, which you can use as a portable soundcard and audio interface, the controls of which are integrated with your software's functions.

1. RECORD YOUR PERFORMANCE
Record your performance via an external MIDI device, controlling a virtual instrument on your computer.

2. SELECT YOUR VIRTUAL INSTRUMENT
Any virtual instruments (e.g. soft synths, plugins, and so on) you have will respond to your instructions.

3. SLICE AND DICE...
Once you've captured your performance, you can edit individual notes onscreen in your sequencer.

4. ...OR CHANGE YOUR MIND
You can then assign your performance to any MIDI instrument of your choosing if you wish.

MIDI stands for Musical Instrument Digital Interface, and it is the way in which all electronic and digital music devices "talk" to each other, and can be set up to control each other.

MIDI is a music description language and a standard set of controllers shared by all compatible devices and music-making software packages. In your music-sequencing application, for example, you'll have the option to record MIDI Instrument tracks, and also to control soft synths, soft samplers, and other virtual devices via an external controller keyboard or control surface. All of this communication is done via MIDI.

In a sense, MIDI files are the binary data equivalent of a musical score—a set of instructions about what note to play, how loud to play it, how long the note is held, and so on. If you download MIDI files from the Internet, you're not downloading audio, but merely a complete set of instructions designed to trigger your soundcard's synthesizer. Similarly, if you record a MIDI Instrument track using an external keyboard to control your software instruments, you're generating those instructions as you record. Although you can hear your performance as you play, you're not making an audio recording, but instead compiling data about your performance in real time in

your computer's memory. None of this is revolutionary—after all, if you hit a key on a piano, you're creating a musical event, and if you depress the loud pedal, you're simply activating a controller to add expression to the note. In the digital world, information about such events and controls is stored in a MIDI file, or within a MIDI Instrument track. When you hit Play, the MIDI file will trigger an exact reproduction of your original performance on whatever MIDI device or sound is mapped to that MIDI channel.

Music sequencing packages give you the graphical means of interacting with the MIDI data you've created, slicing, dicing,

GENERAL MIDI PATCHES

This chart shows the names of all 128 GM Instruments, and the MIDI Program Change numbers which select those Instruments. The instruments are arranged into "families"

PROG	INSTRUMENT	PROG	INSTRUMENT	PROG	INSTRUMENT	PROG	INSTRUMENT
	PIANO		**CHROMATIC PERCUSSION**		**REED**		**PIPE**
1	Acoustic Grand	9	Celesta	65	Soprano Sax	73	Piccolo
2	Bright Acoustic	10	Glockenspiel	66	Alto Sax	74	Flute
3	Electric Grand	11	Music Box	67	Tenor Sax	75	Recorder
4	Honky-Tonk	12	Vibraphone	68	Baritone Sax	76	Pan Flute
5	Electric Piano 1	13	Marimba	69	Oboe	77	Blown Bottle
6	Electric Piano 2	14	Xylophone	70	English Horn	78	Skakuhachi
7	Harpsichord	15	Tubular Bells	71	Bassoon	79	Whistle
8	Clavinet	16	Dulcimer	72	Clarinet	80	Ocarina
	ORGAN		**GUITAR**		**SYNTH LEAD**		**SYNTH PAD**
17	Drawbar Organ	25	Nylon String Guitar	81	Lead 1 (square)	89	Pad 1 (new age)
18	Percussive Organ	26	Steel String Guitar	82	Lead 2 (sawtooth)	90	Pad 2 (warm)
19	Rock Organ	27	Electric Jazz Guitar	83	Lead 3 (calliope)	91	Pad 3 (polysynth)
20	Church Organ	28	Electric Clean Guitar	84	Lead 4 (chiff)	92	Pad 4 (choir)
21	Reed Organ	29	Electric Muted Guitar	85	Lead 5 (charang)	93	Pad 5 (bowed)
22	Accordion	30	Overdriven Guitar	86	Lead 6 (voice)	94	Pad 6 (metallic)
23	Harmonica	31	Distortion Guitar	87	Lead 7 (fifths)	95	Pad 7 (halo)
24	Tango Accordion	32	Guitar Harmonics	88	Lead 8 (bass+lead)	96	Pad 8 (sweep)
	BASS		**SOLO STRINGS**		**SYNTH EFFECTS**		**ETHNIC**
33	Acoustic Bass	41	Violin	97	FX 1 (rain)	105	Sitar
34	Electric Bass (finger)	42	Viola	98	FX 2 (soundtrack)	106	Banjo
35	Electric Bass (pick)	43	Cello	99	FX 3 (crystal)	107	Shamisen
36	Fretless Bass	44	Contrabass	100	FX 4 (atmosphere)	108	Koto
37	Slap Bass 1	45	Tremolo Strings	101	FX 5 (brightness)	109	Kalimba
38	Slap Bass 2	46	Pizzicato Strings	102	FX 6 (goblins)	110	Bagpipe
39	Synth Bass 1	47	Orchestral Strings	103	FX 7 (echoes)	111	Fiddle
40	Synth Bass 2	48	Timpani	104	FX 8 (sci-fi)	112	Shanai
	ENSEMBLE		**BRASS**		**PERCUSSIVE**		**SOUND EFFECTS**
49	String Ensemble 1	57	Trumpet	113	Tinkle Bell	121	Guitar Fret Noise
50	String Ensemble 2	58	Trombone	114	Agogo	122	Breath Noise
51	SynthStrings 1	59	Tuba	115	Steel Drums	123	Seashore
52	SynthStrings 2	60	Muted Trumpet	116	Woodblock	124	Bird Tweet
53	Choir Aahs	61	French Horn	117	Taiko Drum	125	Telephone Ring
54	Voice Oohs	62	Brass Section	118	Melodic Tom	126	Helicopter
55	Synth Voice	63	SynthBrass	119	Synth Drum	127	Applause
56	Orchestra Hit	64	SynthBrass 2	120	Reverse Cymbal	128	Gunshot

and editing it to perfection. Because they're simple instructions about musical events, rather than actual audio recordings, you can move notes around, change the notes, stretch them, pitch shift them, or add expression and sustain... there are many choices. In fact, there are 128 separate MIDI controllers that you can apply to any event.

You can also change the instrument from a bass guitar to a sitar or an organ, for example, and your musical performance will be reproduced just as you played it, but on the new instrument. But if you download MIDI files from the Net, how does your soundcard know which are the correct instruments to use to play the track? The solution is General MIDI (GM), which is a set of 128 sound sets, on which all manufacturers of GM-compliant MIDI devices have standardized. You'll find a list of those sound sets above. These sounds aren't exactly the same from device to device, but they are similar.

THE MIDI PORT OR BUS
- In (receives MIDI instructions from an external device).
- Out (sends MIDI data to a device).
- Thru (receives and sends the same MIDI data, as an echo of MIDI In).

The MIDI port can send or receive data on up to 16 MIDI channels. Some devices and interfaces have just two sockets: In, and Out, or In and Thru, while others have dispensed with MIDI ports entirely and now send and receive MIDI data through either FireWire or USB.

Your soundcard or breakout box may include a traditional MIDI port, but will send streams of MIDI data via FireWire or USB. M-Lan is another protocol for linking networked audio and MIDI devices.

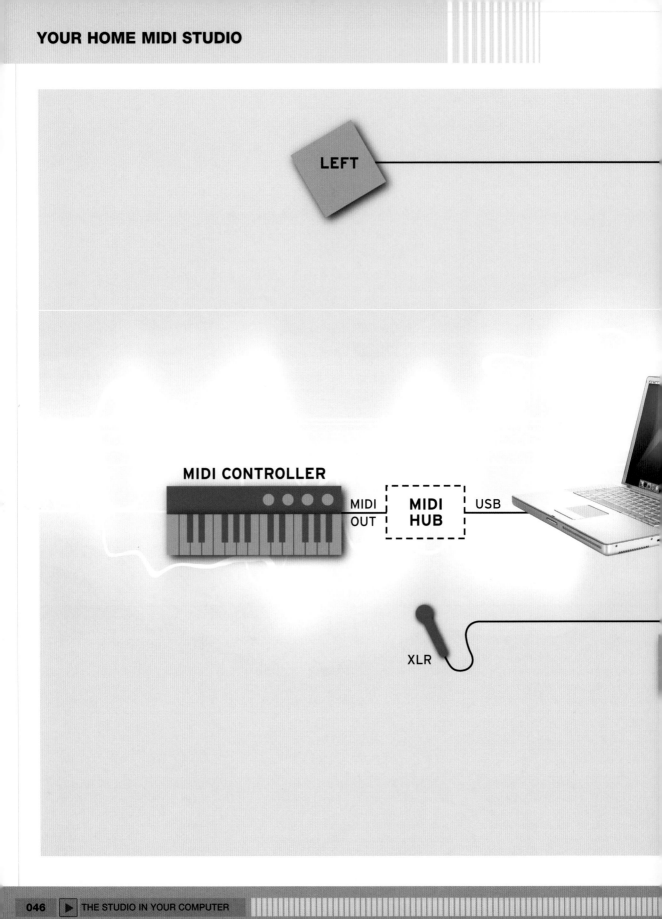

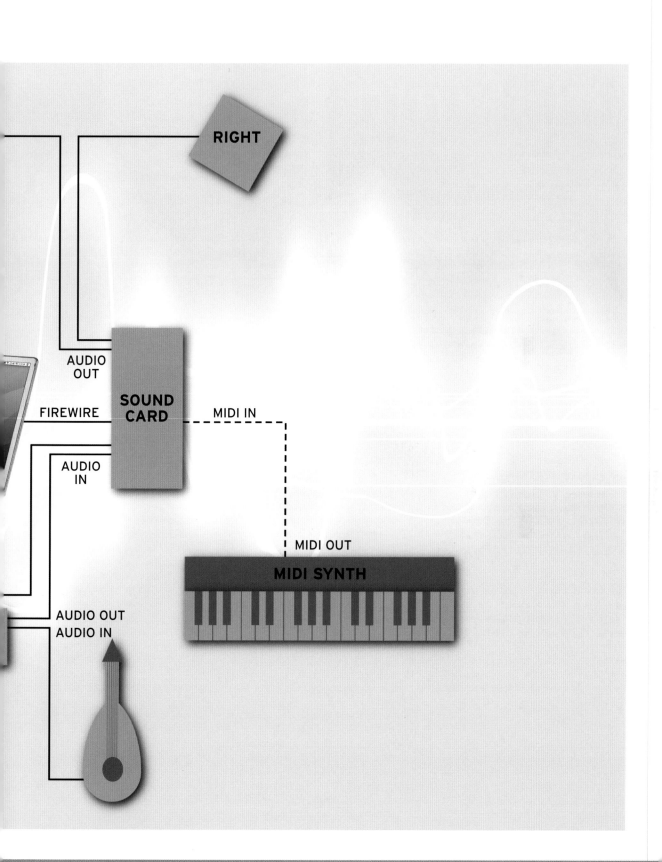

RIGHT

AUDIO
OUT

SOUND
CARD

FIREWIRE

MIDI IN

AUDIO
IN

MIDI OUT

MIDI SYNTH

AUDIO OUT
AUDIO IN

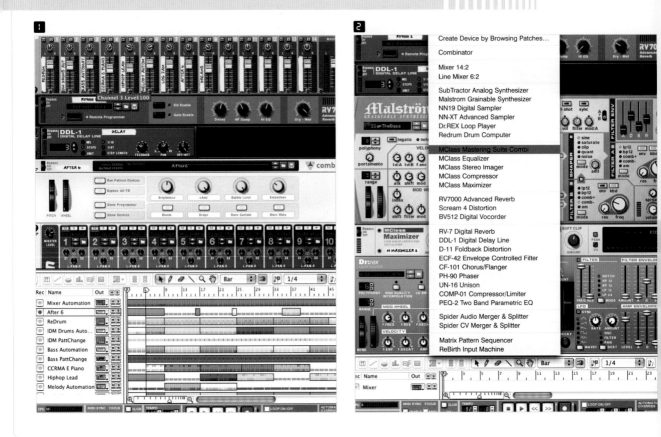

There are numerous music-making software tools available on the market. We'll discuss standalone and plugin virtual instruments and emulators on page 60, but first let's explore some dedicated music-making tools.

Music tools differ from end-to-end applications such as Logic, Cubase, Digital Performer, and Sonar in that they are not designed to record audio from external sources, but rather provide a range of music-only tools, such as software synthesizers, sound modules, effects, drum machines, and so on, plus advanced tools for playing with and arranging loops.

Dance music tools such as Ableton Live and Sony Acid Pro pioneered the idea of time-stretching and beatmatching loops and breakbeats, whereby the tempo of a music clip could be increased or decreased, DJ-style, but without changing the pitch of the overall

sample Suites such as Logic and Cubase—and even Apple's Garageband—allow you to do all of the above to a greater or lesser extent, but many people prefer to use dedicated music tools alongside their main studio software to experiment with ideas, create individual tracks, or even to record complete songs for importing into an audio-enabled suite to add vocals and live instruments.

What appeals to them are the unique sound, dedicated functionality, and ease of use of each music tool. We're going to concentrate on one as an example. Propellerhead Software's Reason suite is a virtual music studio, offering an expandable rack of programmable synthesizers and samplers, mixers, a drum machine/drum sample player, a step sequencer, a loop player, effects modules, signal processors, and mastering tools, together with a comprehensive library of loops and sounds (which is expandable from disks and online resources).

STRENGTHS

Reason is ideal for producing atmospheric instrumental music, especially in dance genres—although classical sounds (pianos, strings, brass) are included in the main library. Reason is also adept at handling rock if you expand the sound library, but the lack of external audio-recording ability means you'll have to add guitars and vocals in another program. Of course, you can always prepare your own samples and import them back into Reason—that's part of the fun.

SEVERAL GOOD REASONS

Reason is popular because, unlike some music-making applications it is fun, intuitive, and very easy to use as well as powerful—despite some people's reservations about the quality of its audio engine. When you open up the software it presents you with a virtual rack—just like the rack of sound modules and effects that a musician might use onstage—onto which you bolt virtual

1. SIMPLE OPERATION

Every track you want to record requires a device to play it. Simply go to the Create dropdown menu and select the device you want. Reason will automatically add the device to the rack, wire it up to the mixer, and create a blank sequencer track. If you click on a track you've already made before creating a new device, Reason will add the new device into the same signal path as other devices in that track.

2. SOME REASON ELEMENTS

Among the dozens of elements Reason offers you are (from top) a 14-channel mixer; a variety of signal processors; a device for editing multiple sounds; a programmable drum machine/drum sample player; and an Arrange window in which you can interact with the elements of your composition in graphical form. You can add as many of these devices as you wish, and in any combination you can imagine.

3. MORE REASON ELEMENTS

Here's a close look at some more creative tools in the program: (from top) a reverb module for creating virtual spaces; a digital delay (echo) unit; a programmable synthesizer (controllable from your external MIDI keyboard); a limiter device for setting the threshold of a signal's volume; and a loop player (for playing and editing prerecorded musical sequences from the library).

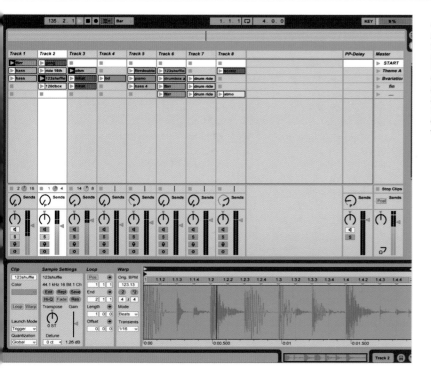

4. REAL-TIME MUSIC SUITE FOR DJS AND VJS

Ableton Live is a different concept in music-making tools, in that it allows DJs and musicians to mix and play arrangements of loops and music clips live. Music clips can be dragged into the vertical columns of each track in real time, and then "warped" (beat- and tempo-matched) so that each loop or sample always matches the tempo of the song/performance. It's a fascinating and fun piece of software, as you can also change the pitch of each sample but without altering its tempo.

instruments and signal processors. Each new track you create in the sequencer window requires a device to play it. The fun part is that you can keep adding as many devices (including synthesizers, mixers, samplers, loop players, and drum machines) as you wish, and then "wire" them up in any combination you can imagine—at least, for as long as your RAM and processor can handle it.

This gives you an almost infinite palette of sounds because any sample or loop you select can be edited, fed into another sound, distorted, spun around, pitch- and beat-shifted, stretched, cut up, or destroyed. For competent musicians, the onboard instruments can be controlled from an external MIDI keyboard, while the less musically adept can either program simple note and chord patterns into a step (pattern) sequencer with a few clicks of the mouse, or play with the library of prerecorded loops.

The downside is that Reason is completely self-contained and it's not compatible with third-party plugins. For some, that is its attraction. Limitations and boundaries should always be seen as a creative opportunity—after all, a four-track tape machine didn't stop the Beatles from conquering the world.

To add audio from an external source you either have to export a complete Reason song (or its constituent tracks) into an audio-production program, or you may be able to synchronize Reason with a compatible audio application using the ReWire protocol. Using ReWire means you can record audio into a package such as any version of Logic or Cubase and synchronize and control Reason via the Play or Record buttons within your audio suite. This saves you the trouble of importing Reason tracks as audio files because you can tweak the mix in Reason to sit in with the rest of your work while keeping both programs open.

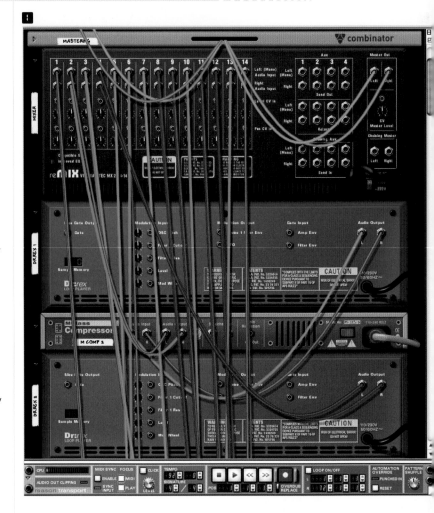

1. REAR VIEW
One of the fun parts of the program is that you can spin the rack around and unplug devices, or patch them into other devices by simply dragging one end of the cable to the input or output you wish to use.

2. SAMPLERS AND EDITING
Reason gives you two different types of sampler (or more accurately, sample players). This one, the NN-XT, can be programmed in minute detail if you click on a tab in the corner of the device. This opens up the sampler so that you can assign different individual samples to each key of your external controller keyboard. Shown at the bottom of this image is Reason's MIDI event window, where you can see all of the individual musical events that have been recorded on the NN-XT device's track. Any MIDI event in Reason can be edited by clicking on it and adjusting it in any way you wish.

3. MAKING NEW CONNECTIONS
If you don't feel confident clicking and dragging the virtual cables on the rear of each Reason device, you can use the dropdown menu to specify how you want to connect each device instead.

4. TIMELINE/EVENT WINDOW (SEQUENCER)
Here is the simplest view of the main Reason sequencer window. Each individual colored block represents a music loop (one from the library, or one that you might have prepared yourself in another program). Each red line (including the red lines within the colored blocks) represents an individual event— e.g. a note that has been struck. When you hit Play, the cursor passes along the timeline and all the recorded musical events play in sequence as the cursor touches them. Any event is fully editable— even one within a prerecorded music loop. This way of working is unique to digital audio: any music or audio event can be edited in any way you wish once it has been turned into digital information.

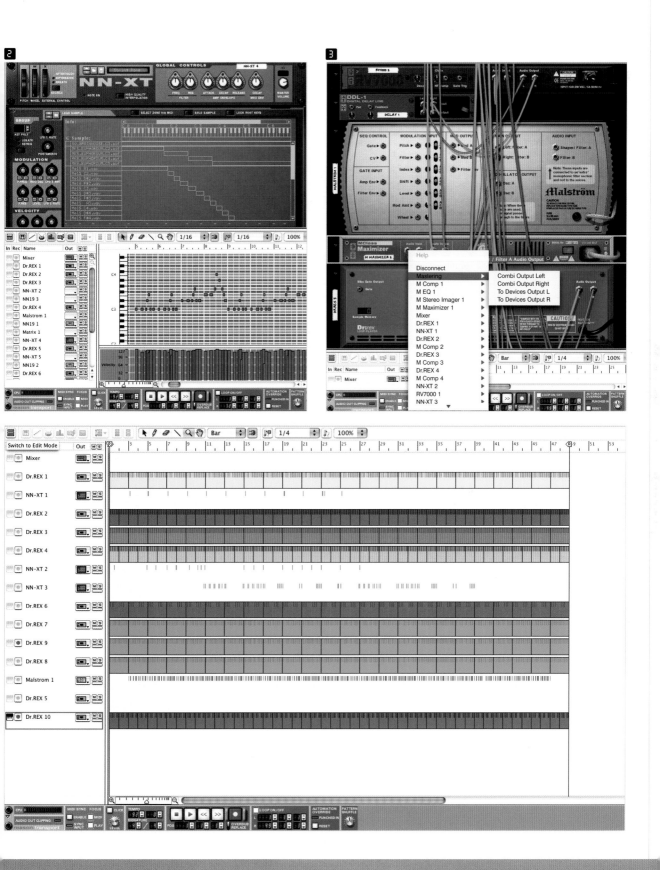

LOOPS AND BEATMATCHING

Loops are prerecorded audio clips that end on precise beats in a musical bar so they can be joined together. If you drag or paste a row of loops into a sequencer track you can create seamless musical sequences—for example, a drum track.

Recording loops for music software and sequencing packages is big business for many companies. Some team session musicians and rare instruments with classic microphones and top producers to create CDs or DVDs of loops in thousands of different styles—from breakbeats and rock guitar riffs to jazz basslines and classical piano chord sequences. If you buy or download such a library of loops and samples, you could take the view that you're buying the services of a session musician for a fraction of the cost of hiring one and a studio. Equally, you could take the view that you're being lazy, using the music equivalent of clip art and royalty-free images. An alternative view again is that it takes a truly creative mind to use widely available raw material in original ways.

Many software packages such as Logic, Garageband, Reason, ACID, Apple Soundtrack Pro, and so on, include onboard libraries of loops (in any of WAV, ACID WAV, AIFF, MP3, RX2, formats) that you can expand until you've built up multi-megabyte collections of your own—and the manufacturers offer huge online resources as well. Other companies, such as M-Audio, Drum Loops, East West, Sonic Reality, Tascam, EMU, IK Multimedia, Propellerhead (maker of Reason), and Steinberg (maker of Cubase), produce sample packs on CD or DVD. In some software such as Reason, you'll need to create the device to play the loop; in others, you can simply drag and drop the loop onto your timeline.

Of course, much of the fun lies in creating your own loops in a wave editor, a sampling package, in a real-time sequencing package such as Live, or even just by cutting up sounds on the timeline of your main audio tool. Assuming both sequencer and soundclip are at the same tempo, then cutting at the end of one of the timeline's time divisions will mean you're cutting to the beat.

There's no doubt that loops can be inspirational, taking your music into thousands of unexplored territories, sparking ideas and collisions of musical styles and genres that might not have occurred to you had you been left to your own devices. For amateur movie and videomakers, there are also vast libraries of sound effects. These can be a boon—Hollywood studios use them, so there's no reason for you not to do the same.

Of course, sampling and mixing musical ideas has been what composers have been doing quietly for centuries, and DJs have been doing more overtly since the days of the earliest Jamaican sound systems in the 1950s. Today, some DJs use CD mixers, or even iPod-based mixers, in their performances, but for most a pair of turntables and a vinyl record box is still what it's all about. However, some are discovering the attractions of in-software mixing, and of making their own loops and samples. The attraction is beatmatching and warping—plus the ability to link with motion graphics (see VJing, page 162).

Until recently, sampling and DJing had an inherent limitation, namely that matching one track/sample with the tempo and/or pitch of another meant speeding up or slowing down the track/sample until the tempos or pitches locked. However, with the advent of software such as Sony Acid Pro and Ableton Live, beatmatching has become easy and commonplace. Beatmatching (see box), or warping (as it's called in Ableton Live), is the technique whereby any audio loop can be processed so that it matches the tempo and even the time signature (e.g. 4/4, 3/4, 7/4, and so on) of your track, but without necessarily changing the pitch of any instrument or voice within the loop. See the box, left, for one warping method.

WARPING (BEATMATCHING) IN ABLETON LIVE

- Open Ableton Live Sequencing Instrument and create a new Live Mix.

- Drag any loop into Track One of your Live mix and set it to Play.

- Now select a loop of a different tempo and drag it into Track Two of your Live Mix, and set this to play as well. Doubleclick in the Warp window toward the bottom of the Live timeline. The tempo of the second loop will now lock with that of the first, keeping the original pitching information of the loop before it was warped—for example, vocal loops will retain the tuning and vocal characteristics of the vocal performance, and not speed up or slow down like a record.

- You can also use the Mode dialog to warp the loop to match the mix's Tones (pitch structure, effectively changing the key of a mix); Texture (self-explanatory), or Repitch (to speed up a sample, or slow it down like a record).

- If you click in the Sample Settings window, you will be able to change the tuning of any loop—you can transpose it up or down in semitones, or fractionally detune it in cents.

Ableton Live is an excellent tool for live sequencing and DJing, but also a useful tool for preparing samples, and also checking their tempo (in beats per minute, or bpm) if your sequencer is not able to do this itself.

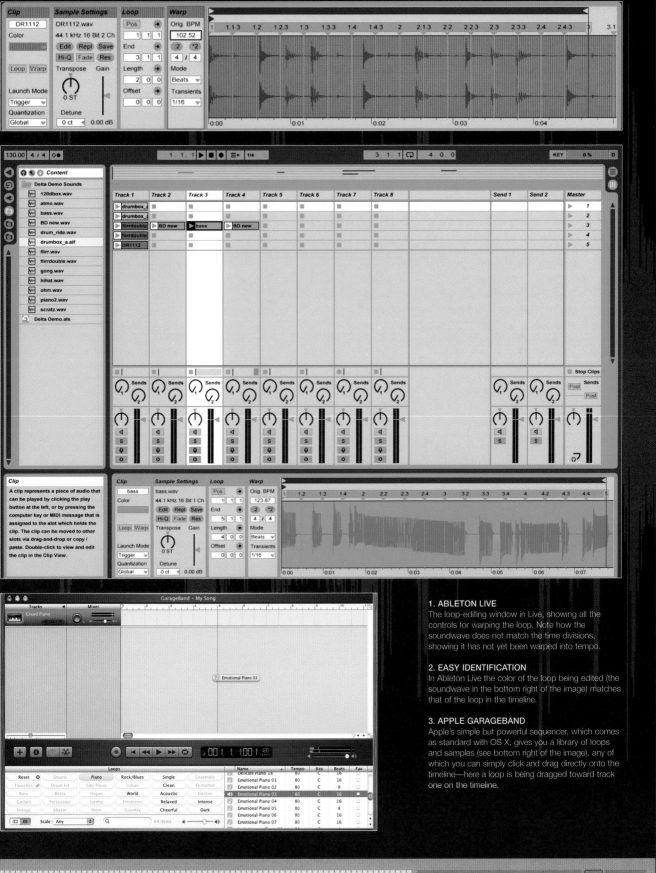

1. ABLETON LIVE
The loop-editing window in Live, showing all the controls for warping the loop. Note how the soundwave does not match the time divisions, showing it has not yet been warped into tempo.

2. EASY IDENTIFICATION
In Ableton Live the color of the loop being edited (the soundwave in the bottom right of the image) matches that of the loop in the timeline.

3. APPLE GARAGEBAND
Apple's simple but powerful sequencer, which comes as standard with OS X, gives you a library of loops and samples (see bottom right of the image), any of which you can simply click and drag directly onto the timeline—here a loop is being dragged toward track one on the timeline.

EDITING AUDIO AND MIDI

REMOVING CLIPPING

Digital recording has an advantage over tape-based recording in that unwanted volume spikes can be individually edited to remove any distortion. Signal clipping is not a permanent artifact of the recording as it can be with tape.

- Locate the spike visually by zooming in on the waveform and looking for the point where the wave pattern hits the full height and depth of the audio track.

- Doubleclick within the track on the part of the soundwave you wish to edit. This will bring up that section of it within a separate edit window. Place your mouse pointer to the immediate left of the spike and then drag carefully to the right to highlight it. The actual spike may be very thin—a hairline, perhaps.

- Now go to the Edit, or equivalent, tab within the window and scroll to Volume/amplitude/level. This may give you the option to reduce amplitude as a percentage of the peak level. Keep reducing the volume in small increments until you've omitted the distortion.

- It may help to "scrub" that section of the track—the digital equivalent of rolling the audioclip backward and forward over a tapehead so you can listen to small sections of the clip.

COMPING TAKES

Many vocals and instrumental performances are compiled from the best parts of different takes. This is good studio technique for any musicians whose style is as much about improvisation as it is about precision. Timeline-based multitrack recording makes it easy to record several takes and edit the highlights together into a definitive performance.

- Don't attempt to punch in and out within the main take. Record a new "patch" take on a different track, and set up the same EQ on both.

- Try muting the main track at the problem point, and muting the "patch" track before and after that point. Listen to whether the two can be joined without too much of an edit.

- If the performance is similar enough for the notes to align, then you can cut out the problem section from take one and paste the new patch into the same space. You can even trim the clip so that a single note is taken half from one take, and half from the patch. Use the Glue tool to create a perfect join.

- If a single note is wrong in an otherwise perfect section, then isolate the note within the waveform and pitchshift it to the correct note in either cents or semitones.

REMOVING NOISE

The graphical waveform within each audio track means that any noise is also visible—particularly in those parts of a vocal where the singer is silent. If you've heavily compressed the voice, then noise will be more obvious.

- You can see noise as the very small peaks in the readout in sections where you know there's no vital information. Highlight each noisy section of the track.

- You can attenuate the signal completely within the highlighted section. Alternatively, erase it, or cut out those elements of the track entirely with the Scissors tool.

- If you do erase or cut out the noise, be careful not to edit the vocal so tightly that you lose natural sounds, such as the singer taking a breath before singing, or (most importantly) the natural decay of a note. Preview or scrub those sections very carefully to ensure you're cutting noise, rather than information.

MIDI EDITING

- When you record a MIDI track, you're recording control information rather than audio—i.e. play this note this loud at this point. As each MIDI event creates an editable icon on the MIDI timeline—for example, within the Matrix Edit window of Logic—then you can drag individual notes to new positions, and also shorten or lengthen each note (and apply any of 128 different MIDI controls to it).

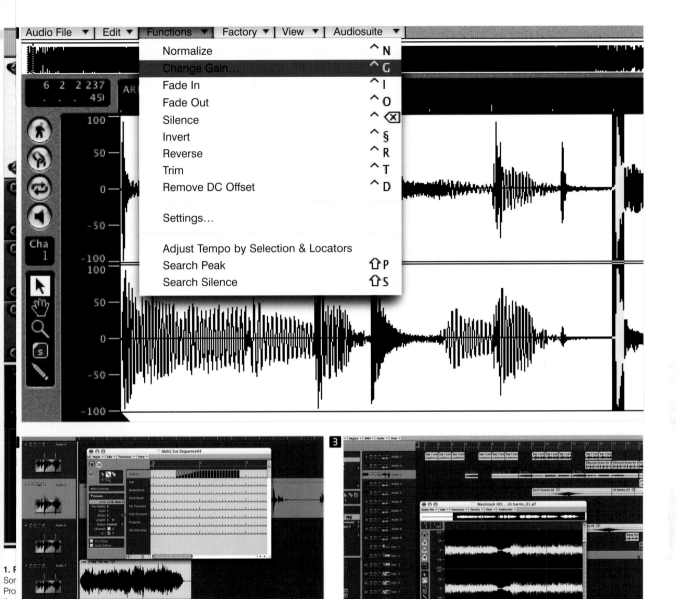

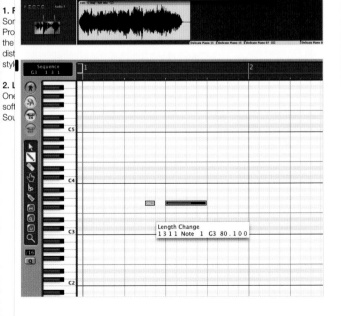

1. REMOVE CLIPPING
Select the overloud portion of the signal. Now go to Edit within the window and select Volume. Reduce in small percentage increments.

2. DRAW CONTROL INFORMATION
In Logic's Hyper Edit window, you can draw in MIDI control information with the Pen tool, creating control curves—such as this volume increase and decrease.

3. SEEING NOISE
In this soundwave, low-level noise is visible in the gap between two notes being played.

4. CHANGING MIDI EVENTS
This close-up of one musical bar shows two notes (both G). The second note has been lengthened from a sixteenth to a quarter note by dragging it.

DYNAMIC PROCESSORS

Some types of sound source, such as certain instruments (by virtue of their construction or performance characteristics) and human voices, are capable of producing a very wide dynamic range—i.e. both very loud and very soft sounds. That means, in immediate, practical terms during a recording session, the risk of unpredictable peaks when the signal becomes too loud ("hot"), and other occasions when the signal may be relatively too quiet.

So-called "dynamic" effects manage these unpredictable elements within fixed parameters so that they can be controlled within the mix. They act a bit like automatic faders, riding the signal and either evening out unwanted peaks, "digging out" passages that are too quiet, or removing some sounds entirely. Dynamic processors therefore relate to a signal's perceived or relative loudness in the mix.

CREATIVE ISSUES WITH COMPRESSORS

People often say that compressors make signals louder; in fact, they simply reduce the loudest parts of a recording relative to the quieter parts. You can then increase the volume of the entire signal, with the effect that the quieter passages are indeed louder in relation to the peaks.

THE FAMILY OF DYNAMIC (RANGE) PROCESSORS

Compressors

Compressors work by proportionately reducing a signal's peak volume when it exceeds a maximum level set by the user, while leaving anything below that maximum level untouched. In other words, they reduce a signal's overall dynamic range by making the loudest peaks quieter. Typical controls of a compressor (and of the wider family of dynamic effects) are:

■ **Threshold**
The user-definable peak level above which the compressor begins to reduce the volume of the signal. In digital systems, the maximum Threshold level will usually be 0dB. The point at which the processor kicks in is known as the "Knee." In some systems the Knee can be set on a scale between "Hard" and "Soft," so the compression either kicks in swiftly (a hard knee), or more subtly (a soft knee) when the Threshold is exceeded.

■ **Ratio**
The amount of volume reduction that occurs above the Threshold, expressed as a ratio—such as 2:1, 4:1, and so on. A 4:1 Ratio, for example, means that the output of any signal above the Threshold is reduced to 25% of the input signal. Some compressors may offer you a compression ratio as high as 30:1, although anything above a Ratio of 10:1 means your compressor is really acting as a Limiter (see facing page).

■ **Attack**
The speed, measured in milliseconds (ms), at which the compressor reduces the volume of the signal when it has exceeded the Threshold. Attack times typically vary from 0ms to 200ms. Fast Attack times should be used on signals that themselves have a fast Attack (e.g. percussion sounds). Slower Attack times will produce a more natural-sounding volume change on musical instruments (including human voices) that tend to have longer note sustains.

■ **Release**
The speed at which the compressor cuts off and restores the original input level of the signal. Too fast a Release time and you will hear artifacts known as "pumping" or "breathing." Too slow a Release time and the volume of the signal immediately after the peak will also be reduced.

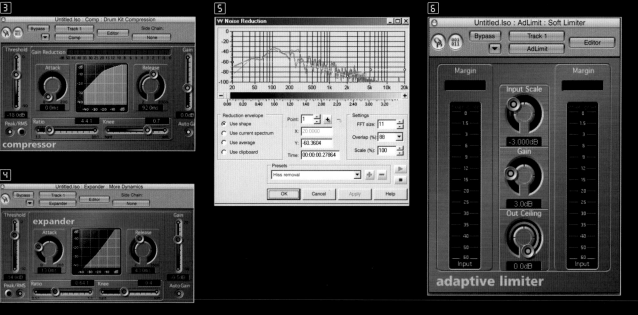

■ Input Gain
The amount of unprocessed signal sent to the compressor.
■ Output Gain
The amount of compressed signal sent to the output.

Multipressors
Some software suites provide Multiband Compressors (Multipressors), which are compressors that are programmable to work across a user-definable frequency range, or group of frequency ranges. This means that you can set a compression Threshold to apply solely or predominantly to signals within a specific band.

Limiters
A Limiter is essentially a more extreme compressor, setting a hard Threshold through which a signal's volume level is not allowed to pass. Limiters are not able to respond instantly (at 0ms), and so to prevent very rapid peaks getting past the Limiter, most Limiters have a Look Ahead control that "sees" the peak coming—in reality, by putting a tiny delay of about 1ms into the signal path to allow it the time to react.

Expanders
These do the opposite of compressors by increasing a signal's dynamic range either above or below a set Threshold, but with similar editable parameters. While expansion might suggest the amplification of quiet details, Expanders actually have the effect of making quiet sounds appear even quieter in relation to loud elements of a signal because the overall dynamic range (the gap between the loudest and quietest points) has been increased. Using an Expander means that the overall signal volume can be reduced to accommodate louder passages.

Noise Gates
These are Expanders that allow signal levels above a user-definable Threshold to pass without any processing, while completely reducing signals that fall beneath that Threshold –in practical terms, they remove unwanted noise.

■ For mixing hints and tips with dynamic processors turn to page 82.

1–6 IMAGES
1. Compressors, in Reason.
2. Choosing Compressor presets in Apple Logic.
3. The compression curve of one of Logic's drum presets.
4. Expander preset in Logic.
5. Noise Reducer in Goldwave.
6. Soft Limiter in Logic.

PLUGINS AND VIRTUAL INSTRUMENTS

Plugins are pieces of software, often developed by third-party companies, that "plug in" to your host sequencer or music production suite and offer additional functionality. Some companies produce bundles of effects and processors for specific tasks—such as mastering—while others design and build fully featured software instruments.

Plugging in a new tool, processor, or instrument to your host application allows you to integrate all of the capabilities of the plugin with those of your sequencer. With some plugin software instruments—many synths and samplers, for instance—you can access individual controls from within other parts of the host application. For example, you may be able to add the instrument's onboard effects to your arsenal of Insert or Send effects.

The vital thing to remember when purchasing plugins is that you choose one that is compatible with your host application, your soundcard, and your computing platform. If you've recently upgraded from Mac OS 9 to OS X, or switched from PC to Mac, and you don't want to lose all of your treasured VST plugins (see box), then fxpansion is one of several companies that produce VST to Audio Unit adapter software.

VIRTUAL INSTRUMENTS AND EMULATORS

Virtual instruments are synthesizers and samplers in software form (soft synths and soft samplers), but you can also buy a wide range of software emulations of other instruments, such as grand pianos, electric pianos, Moog synths, Mellotrons, Theremins, Hammond organs, and even entire orchestras. A number of music hardware companies now produce software emulations of their hardware keyboard ranges. Most virtual instruments will run outside your sequencer as standalone instruments as well, should you wish simply to play the instrument, or use it live.

SIMULATORS AND MODELERS

Another popular plugin type is the simulator or modeler. For example, you can buy software models of guitar amps and microphones, which enable you to plug your guitar or your budget mic into your soundcard and access the sounds of classic amps and speaker cabinets, or the characteristic frequency response curves of classic studio mics.

1. CLASSIC KEYBOARD EMULATOR
Native Instruments' B4 models the sound of a Hammond organ, including its unique "Leslie" rotating speakers.

2. PRESETS
Some of the classic Hammond sounds available as presets within the B4.

3. ADDING PLUGINS IN LOGIC
Go to the I/O window of an Instrument track to bring up virtual instruments, including plugins.

4. A DIFFERENT ENVIRONMENT
Third-party plugins don't work with Reason, which offers a finite selection of virtual instruments.

PLUGIN INTERFACES AND DRIVERS CHECKLIST

Host Software Interfaces

ASIO (PC/Mac): Audio Streaming Input/Output. Software interface and soundcard driver developed by Steinberg, maker of Cubase and Nuendo.

Core Audio (Mac OS X): Standard audio driver for all Macs running upward of OS version 10.2. Integral to OS X.

DirectSound (PC): Windows 98 onward. Latency or buffer settings should be carefully checked.

MME (PC): Standard wave driver for PC soundcards.

Soundmanager (Mac OS 9): Standard Apple wave driver for soundcards.

Plugin Interfaces

Audio Units (AU): Standard format for real-time plugins within Apple OS X, and integral to the operating system. AU plugins will be interrogated by your system to ensure they pass a rigorous quality test. Any that fail may crash your system, but most bugs are being ironed out.

Cakewalk DXi (PCs running Cakewalk Sonar): Interface based on Microsoft's DirectX architecture.

DirectConnect (Mac): Digidesign-made interface to stream audio directly into ProTools.

DirectX (PC): Microsoft plugin standard. Needs DirectX Support. Proprietary versions (Such as Cakewalk's) will run only in specific software suites.

FreeMIDI (Mac): Developed by MOTU for its Digital Performer software to allow mixing of MIDI tracks.

MAS (MOTU Audio System) (Mac): As above, but allows audio routing from a soft synth into Performer's mixing environment.

RTAS (PC/Mac): Real-time Audio Suite. Plugin architecture for Pro Tools.

TDM/HTDM (Mac/PC/standalone): (Host) Time Division Multiplexing. Digidesign architecture beneath its Pro Tools software and hardware.

VST/VSTi (PC/Mac OS 9/OS X with adapter): Virtual Studio Technology (Instrument). Popular plugin standard for effects and virtual instruments.

OFF VIB VIB LOW UP OFF OFF PERC DRV ROT VEL
ON ON ON

SLOW FAST
ROTATOR

01: 00: 00: 00.00 1 1 1 1
1 1 1 1
5 1 1 1

✓ B4 Blues
Scanner Full Bar
Latin 66'
Soft Organ
Theatre Organ
Distortion
Progressive
Deep Scanner
Keyclicker
Velocity
J.B. Percussion
Brasses
A Whiter Shade…
Time of the Season
Emersons Basic
The Cat
Born to B4

Bypass   Instrument 1   Editor
AdLimit   Pres 0

yphony

Options ▾ | View ▾

Global
MIDI
Input
Track
Inst
Aux
Bus
Output

EQ EQ EQ EQ EQ EQ EQ EQ EQ EQ EQ EQ EQ EQ

Inserts ▾ (×14)

Sends (×14)

I/O

Input 1 (×8)
Out 1–2 (×14)
Track 1 Track 2 Track 3 Track 4 Track 5 Track 6 Track 7 Track 8

Off (×8)

No plug-in
Mono   ▸
Stereo   ▸   AU Instruments   ▸   Apple   ▸
Multi Channel ▸   AU Midi FX   ▸   Native Instruments ▸
                  Logic   ▸   [Incompatible]   ▸

0.0 (×14)

M S (×14)
REC (×8)

Audio 1 Audio 2 Audio 3 Audio 4 Audio 5 Audio 6 Audio 7 Audio 8 Inst 1 Inst 2 Inst 3 Inst 4 Inst 5 Inst 6 Inst
1   2   3   4   5   6   7   8   9   10   11   12   13   14   15

Malström
GRAINTABLE SYNTHESIZER

SlapTheBass

MALSTRÖM 1

MOD A
1-shot sync A B
rate pitch index shift

MOD B
1-shot sync A B
rate motion vol filter mod:A

FILTER ENV
inv
A D S R amt

8
polyphony   legato ● note on   VELOCITY

portamento   lvl:A lvl:B f.env   A B
atk shift mod

OSC A
AcoustGuitarSlap
motion   index
shift octave semi cent
A D S R   vol

SHAPER
● sine
● saturate
● clip
● quant
● noise
mode amt

FILTER A
● lp12
● bp12
● comb+
● comb-
● am
mode
res freq

3
range

MOD WHEEL
index   A B
shift filter mod

OSC B
Sine
motion   index
shift octave semi cent
A D S R   vol

FILTER B
● lp12
● bp12
● comb+
● comb-
● am
mode
res freq

spread

volume

Establishing a working space is the most subjective aspect of creating music and sound—the most subjective of creative activities. To an extent, you're limited by the fact that your working space may be (in many cases) perhaps a spare room—a study or home office, perhaps, or a bedroom. However, if you can choose your working space, customize it, or design one of your own, then there are some points to consider. If, on the other hand, it's a case of making the best of what's available, then there are some key considerations here as well.

■ If you're looking for a space in which to record live sounds, such as vocalists or guitarists, then finding a big, open room is a good option. In such a space it's easier to separate sounds, and choose whether to reject the room sound with close miking, or include the ambience in the recording.

■ Rooms that are full of hard surfaces such as tiles, glass, stone, and brick are highly sound reflective. Soft surfaces such as cushions, drapes, carpets, and mattresses "baffle" the sound. Adding soft surfaces in parts of a "live" room will damp the sound in those areas—absorbing it like a sponge. This may be useful for recording guitars, or for isolating the sound of an amp from the rest of a room.

■ Remember that if the room sound is very "present" in a recording, then it will be difficult to remove in the mix. Record a vocal in a stairwell or tiled room, and you won't be able to lose that reverb in the mix. Of course, this may be your intention.

■ Spatial effects applied to MIDI Instrument tracks may have to match the ambience of the physical space in which you've recorded actual sound.

Measure the space in which you're recording performances. As sound travels at a little over 1ft (30cm) per millisecond, then you can work out how long sound will take to bounce off a boundary. Try programming that room size into your reverb unit, and also with the level of the effect.

■ Many sequencer packages include a wide selection of preset reverbs, including stone rooms, wooden-floored rooms, and so on. It makes sense to customize one of these to be a virtual model of your real recording space. Save it and keep it as a preset.

■ If you can, monitor in a separate room from the performance area, especially if the room you perform in is very "live." Noticeable reflections from a very live space will make monitoring difficult; it will be hard to assess how much virtual reverb you've added to a track, for example, if your speakers are positioned in an echoic room, or corner.

■ Bass tends to travel downward. This is the main issue when isolating your room from people living below you. Although it appears less "directional" than other sounds, bass reflections off walls tend to magnify the sound.

■ Sound travels through the air to our ears, so making your recording space as airtight as possible will minimize sound "leakage."

■ Voiceovers, commentaries, and radio shows are often best recorded in very "dead" sounding rooms, as it's best to avoid obvious room sound coloring the voice. Voiceovers should come from "no space," unless you want a specific ambience there for a reason.

■ Building a home studio in a small, windowless room might make sense from a practical standpoint, but it may have a detrimental effect on your work. Some musicians prefer to work in big, bright, open spaces that encourage them to perform "into" the room.

1. COLLABORATIVE SPACES
Wherever you record other musicians, you want your space to encourage collaboration and performance.

2. COMPROMISE SPACES
Advantages here are light, space, and excellent room sound. The downside is sound reflections off windows.

3. LEGENDARY SPACES
Studio 1, Abbey Road—one of the two most famous studio spaces in the world (the other being Studio 2!).

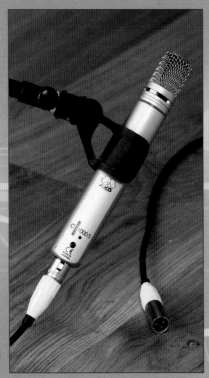

1. SMALL-CAPSULE CONDENSER MIC
An AKG C1000S mic, with XLR connection.

2. LARGE CAPSULE CONDENSER
Chinese manufacturer SE Electronics makes high-quality, low-cost mics.

3. POP SHIELDS
This dynamic mic has a professional pop shield for preventing breaths hitting the mic and causing audible "pops."

MICROPHONES

If you're recording audio from the real world—as opposed to constructing entirely virtual music from samples, loops, MIDI instruments, and so on—then the first device in your recording chain is the microphone (mic). Deriving from the Greek words micro (little) and phone (voice), microphones are small transducers that convert soundwaves into electrical signals, but they have a big impact on your work. Although your mic is step one on the journey of turning analog soundwaves into digital data for you to slice, dice, and manipulate, it really is better to record something well to begin with than it is to spend hours trying to fake a good sound. Here's a one-stop guide to microphone types, uses, and techniques.

Microphone types

There is a huge variety of microphones at every conceivable price point, from a fistful of quarters to a wage packet's worth of dollars. What differentiates mics from each other is their constructions, working methods, sound-pickup patterns, and characteristic frequency responses. As you can probably guess, this means that some mics are better suited for certain types of recordings and sound sources than others. As ever with this most subjective of all media, there are no hard and fast rules—if it sounds good in the track you're recording, then it probably is good.

CONDENSER MICS
How they work

Condenser mics translate soundwaves into impulses by using two electrically charged surfaces—a sensitive diaphragm, which captures the impact of the soundwave hitting it, and a separate backplate. Between them, these two surfaces form a capacitor or condenser. As the soundwaves hit the mic, they force the two charged surfaces together by varying amounts, creating corresponding electrical signals. This is an electrostatic process. All condenser mics have active circuitry, which means they need to be powered, either by a battery within the casing, or by "phantom" power—voltages delivered through a balanced mic cable from your mixing desk or soundcard.

Uses

Most condenser mics are very sensitive and are capable of producing a smooth, detailed response over a broad frequency range. However, because they are active (powered) devices, they can distort at high volumes, so some models have a "pad" switch that slightly attenuates the signal, allowing for the recording of more "robust" sound sources. The bright, sharp sound of directional condenser mics makes them ideal for percussion, such as tom-toms, while large-capsule models are popular as vocal mics. Older valve condenser models (and more recent copies) are highly prized for their warm sound.

4. INVERTED MIC
This can also help minimize pops, and creates a different sound. See overleaf.

DYNAMIC (MOVING COIL) MICS
How they work

Like condenser mics, dynamic mics contain a sensitive diaphragm that captures the soundwaves striking it, but the diaphragm is attached to a tightly wrapped coil of wire suspended within a magnetic field. The vibrations of this spring-like coil correspond to the pressure of the soundwaves striking the diaphragm, and so the coil's movement within the magnetic field creates a varying electrical signal. This is an electromagnetic process. Dynamic mics do not need to be phantom powered, and they are usually rugged and reliable.

Uses

Small diaphragm dynamics are good for live vocals. All dynamics should be suitable for high-volume sound sources, and are noise free. However, they can be less bright at the top end and are less bass sensitive than condensers. Large-diaphragm dynamics can handle very

powerful sound sources, but can produce an equally rugged and less detailed sound, as they have a slower transient response (they respond to changes in the soundwave less quickly) than a ribbon mic, for example.

RIBBON MICS
How they work

Ribbon mics are similar in principle to dynamics, but use a microscopically thin foil ribbon to capture the soundwaves in place of the sturdier diaphragm and moving coil construction. The ribbon vibrates within the magnetic field, producing the fluctuating electrical signal.

Uses

As the ribbon is fragile and highly sensitive, this type of mic is best suited to sound sources that benefit from detail and finesse—sounds that have a reedy timbre, including some voices. They are also favored for string instruments. Ribbons are less rugged than dynamics.

BOUNDARY EFFECT MICS (SOMETIMES CALLED PZMs*)
How they work

This unusual type of mic features a condenser pickup mounted against a coaster-like flat plate, often made of thin steel. The plate, which forms the majority of the mic, is effectively the diaphragm that picks up the soundwaves. When the plate is mounted on something—a wall, a tabletop, the floor—the surface itself becomes the diaphragm, in effect, allowing you to use the wall, tabletop, or floor as the sound pickup source.

Uses

As distant pickups and for capturing room sounds. These mics are fun to experiment with, and some people have even used them with varying degrees of success as studio vocal mics—but this is not a recommended use.

* PZM denotes a range of boundary mics produced by Crown Audio.

Choosing mics

A popular joke among sound engineers is that fat singers need thin mics, and vice versa. The joke has a serious point, though, in that your goal is balancing the sound source with a complementary mic. Trial and error are major factors when making your choice. You may find a particular mic brings out a certain quality in your own voice that appeals to you, or suits it in a particular track, so you can infer from this that what you are really listening for is the mic's **frequency response**.

Microphone manufacturers express their mics' performance capabilities in terms of an overall frequency range. Mics that are said to have a "flat" frequency response are not poor performers, but rather mics that do not color the sound significantly—the frequency response is flat, and therefore more natural, across the frequency spectrum. Other mics have a "shaped" frequency response, which is expressed as a curve. Such mics are designed to capture certain frequencies more strongly than others, creating a characteristic coloring of the sound in key frequency bands. These peaks in the frequency response curve are typically in the 2-10kHz range, and are known as "presence peaks," and can help create greater clarity, detail, and punch.

Directional Characteristics and Polar Patterns

Aside from mics' different constructions and technologies, another factor to consider is their "directionality." The directional characteristic of a mic, when expressed on a circular or spherical graph, is known as its polar response pattern. **Omnidirectional mics** pick up sound from all directions, giving them 360-degree coverage. This makes them of limited use for stage performance, but they are ideal for recording ambiences. Distance affects recording level, but not frequency response.

Bidirectional ("figure of eight") mics

pick up equally from front and rear, thus largely eliminating sound sources that are to either side at right angles.

Unidirectional mics: Cardioid, Supercardioid, and Hypercardioid

Cardioid mics pick up sound most strongly from in front of them, a little from either side, but none from behind. This creates a polar response pattern that is an inverted heart shape (cardioid). Supercardioid mics have a finer front pickup angle, but pick up some sound from behind. Hypercardioid mics have a front angle of pickup that is even narrower than a Supercardioid's, but a wider degree of rear sound pickup.

Directional mics are ideal for live vocals, and for isolating primary sound sources from other sounds in the studio. Hypercardioid and Supercardioid mics are useful for directional sound sources while also recording some of the room sound reflections from behind. How much room sound you capture with directional mics in the studio depends on how far away you place a mic from the sound source, and how you angle the mic to the sound source—and in relation to other mics, if you are using a pair (or more) of them. We'll explore this is more over the next couple of pages.

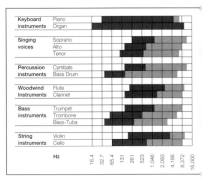

		16.4	32.7	65.4	131	261	523	1,046	2,093	4,186	8,372	16,000
Keyboard instruments	Piano											
	Organ											
Singing voices	Soprano											
	Alto											
	Tenor											
Percussion instruments	Cymbals											
	Bass Drum											
Woodwind Instruments	Flute											
	Clarinet											
Bass instruments	Trumpet											
	Trombone											
	Bass-Tuba											
String instruments	Violin											
	Cello											
	Hz											

INSTRUMENT FREQUENCY RANGES
Use this table to match your sound source with the frequency response of your mic—shaped-response mics will boost certain frequencies for greater clarity.

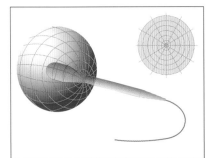

OMNIDIRECTIONAL RESPONSE
Mic picks up sound from all directions.

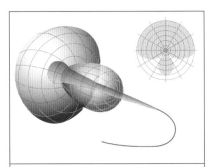

SUPERCARDIOID POLAR RESPONSE
Mic picks up sound from the front, immediately to either side, and a little from directly behind.

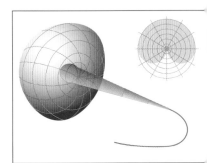

CARDIOID POLAR RESPONSE
Mic picks up sound in a heart-shaped (cardioid) pattern, omitting sound from directly behind.

EXPERIMENT WITH OPTIONS
This mic placement captures a little of the room sound and avoids the proximity effect by angling the mic slightly away from the singer. Note the x-shaped strung "shock mount" on the mic, which prevents noise from the floor or mic stand being recorded on the mic.

THE PROXIMITY EFFECT

Directional mics exhibit a noticeable increase in bass response when the sound source is within 1ft (30 cm) or so of the mic. This is known as the "proximity effect." This can be a problem by creating a "boomy sound."

The human voice is an instrument with a very wide dynamic range, which makes it challenging to record. However, people will judge your track by how well the vocals are recorded.

- There's no right or wrong way to place a microphone to record the human voice, because the possible combinations of voice, mic, and location are infinite. Experiment with mic positions, and with mics that have different polar patterns. Some small condenser mics can be switched between cardioid and hyper- or supercardioid patterns with the addition of a small capsule on the head of the pickup inside the casing. The popular AKG C1000S is one such model.

- Although many people assume you should record vocals with directional mics within a vocal "booth," this technique originated in large studio spaces where the vocalist needed to be isolated from other musicians so the vocal track could be captured "clean."

- Use directional mics in most single-vocalist situations if they sound right, but there's every reason why an omnidirectional mic could be used if you're recording a group of singers, as they can circle the mic and sing with greater openness and confidence.

- Remember, when you record a singer (or musician) to an audio track in your software you're not just recording a well-balanced signal, or some raw material to fix later on; you're capturing a performance that communicates an emotion, a feeling, or an attitude—not to mention a lyric.

- This means you have to create both the right physical environment and the right emotional one. How you position a mic can affect the way a singer performs: put a "big" singer in a claustrophobic space and they might underperform; while other singers may respond better to the enclosed space as they'll feel less conspicuous. 90% of

the art of music production is having good ears and being sensitive to the needs of both piece and performer.

- As we've already explored, proximity to a unidirectional mic will create a bassier sound. One way of avoiding this while still standing fairly close is to invert the mic and angle it slightly away from the mouth. This may create an airier, crisper sound—one that is less colored by the singer's proximity.

- Most large-capsule condenser mics, such as the excellent, inexpensive SE Electronics SE2200A, come with a strung shock-mount, which isolates the mic from the stand supporting it. Any vibrations caused by the singer's movements or noisy floorboards are not picked up on mic.

- As we've discussed in the section on dynamic effects, setting Record levels for either the loudest or quietest parts of the song may cause level problems

elsewhere in the vocal track. So it's worth bringing up a compressor on an Insert to even out the vocal during the recording stage.

■ It's tempting to record vocals in a very "live" space. People like singing in these environments because they flatter the human voice by adding a lot of natural reverb. However, if you record too much room sound, you will not be able to lose it later. Close miking will limit its presence on the track.

■ One technique to "flatter" the voice in the singer's headphones while avoiding problems in the mix is to bring up a reverb within a foldback or monitor channel, so that the singer can hear the effect, but you retain the option to lose or replace it in the mix.

■ If you have the budget, I would strongly recommend buying one good quality dynamic or large-capsule condenser mic for your main vocal inputs, and a matched pair of smaller dynamics, or small-capsule condensers, which you can use individually for recording instruments, or as a stereo pair for capturing room sound during a performance.

■ Experiment with positioning a stereo pair either about 4-10ft (1-3m) apart on separate stands, pointing in the same direction; pointing away from each other by about 30 degrees off axis; or by positioning them together crossways in an x-formation so the right-hand mic points left, and vice versa. Listen to and compare the results.

1. CHOOSING A SPACE
Having a fairly large, open space can be ideal for some singers, and it makes sound separation easier.

2. UP CLOSE AND PERSONAL
Standing in close isolates the singer from the room, and with directional mics, increases bass response.

3. POPS AND BREATH NOISE
Singing without any kind of pop shield risks recording "pops" and bangs on the mic as the breath hits it. Some mics, such as dynamics designed for live work, are much better shielded from breath noise.

4. MONITORING THE VOCAL
Use a directional mic pointing away from monitor speakers, or use headphones. Many singers prefer to have one headphone on and the other off, so they can hear themselves in the room and in the mix.

FUN WITH VOCALS: TECHNIQUES, TEXTURES, AND PROCESSES

- David Bowie's vocal on the track *Heroes* was recorded at Berlin's brittle-sounding Hansa Studios using three mics in a line—one close to the singer, one a few feet directly behind it, and the third a few feet behind that to record the ambient room sound. This third mic was gated so that it only picked up his voice when he sang above a certain level. As Bowie performed the song, the mic opened whenever his voice reached a crescendo, giving extra space to the sound. Listen to the track and picture how it was recorded. Sometimes a little imagination is what separates an average recording from a legendary one.

- Former Abbey Road engineer Chris Clarke once engineered a recording of mine and positioned a pair of mics in a corridor outside the studio to pick up the reverberations from the studio through the open doors. He then mixed this beneath one of the tracks.

- A popular recording technique is to doubletrack a lead vocal by asking the singer to perform the main vocal again and try to mirror the original performance. When mixed beneath the original vocal it fattens up the sound. As the performance is never an exact copy, the shifting phase and harmonic relationships between the two tracks produce a warmer, fuller, attractive performance. (If you cut and paste a copy of the original vocal you'll simply produce a louder track.) As you can waste a lot of time and processing power faking the effect of doubletracking voices in software, why not try it for real?

- Another texturizing technique is to ask the singer to whisper the doubletracked vocal line. Mixing the whispered line subtly beneath the main vocal produces an almost dream-like texture on the voice. A good example is Dave Grohl's vocal on the Foo Fighters' song *Walking After You*. Download the track and listen closely to the vocal.

ANTARES AVOX

There's no limit to what the application of digital theory and knowledge of acoustics and synthesis can achieve if you want it to. Antares, maker of AutoTune, is also behind a very different vocal processing bundle. AVOX brings together a range of different tools.

- THROAT lets you process a vocal through a virtual model of the physical human vocal tract. With it, you can fine-tune some of the characteristics that make your voice "you," which are partly formed by the shape of your mouth and throat. THROAT uses emulations of the way sound behaves in different bodies and maps those characteristics onto your recording.

- DUO The vocal-modeling auto doubler automatically generates a doubled vocal part from an existing vocal.

- CHOIR This vocal multiplier turns a single voice into up to 32 distinct individual unison voices, each with its own pitch, timing, and vibrato variations.

- PUNCH The "Vocal Impact Enhancer" is essentially a souped-up dynamics processor, which has been fine-tuned for vocals.

- SYBIL A "de-esser" that irons out sibilance and related problems.

1. LOGIC PITCH CORRECT
Here a vocal is being corrected within the key Cmin. The readout at the bottom shows the note being corrected was about 20 cents out of perfect pitch—not bad. The response time has been set to 200ms, which is swift, but natural-sounding enough to avoid an artificial effect.

2. VOCAL EQ
Doubleclick in the EQ window of the Mixer in Logic brings up the EQ interface, where you can plot EQ curves and make detailed adjustments. The process is very similar in other software suites.

3. VOCAL EQ PRESETS
Logic provides preset EQs to flatter a range of different voices.

TUNING VOICES (TOP IMAGE, LEFT)

It's a fact of life that some of us may have attractive or fascinating voices but can't hold a tune in a bucket, while even normally pitch-perfect singers can hit a rogue note in an otherwise brilliant performance.

Help is at hand. There are a number of plugins and bundles available for tuning the human voice. Logic's Pitch Correction is standard in the Pro version of the software; Roland's V-Vocal plugin comes with Cakewalk's Sonar 5 and upward; while Akai Pitch Correct is another option for many software suites. However, Antares AutoTune has become the industry standard, and is a worthy investment if you can afford the extra outlay.

You can program most tuner plugins to correct individual notes, change pitching in any major or minor keys, in user-definable scales, and even within specific chords and chord progressions from the jauntiest Maj to the most frustrating 7/b13. Setting an autotuner to respond instantly or very rapidly and then mixing the effect high in the vocal produces the odd, artificial sound used most famously by Cher on the 1999 song "Believe." Slower response times produce a more natural sound.

FEMALE VOICE OPTION 1
Try boosting the mid frequencies, and boosting all of the top end, while rolling off some bass. Listen to how the voice has changed.

FEMALE VOICE OPTION 2
Now experiment with creating a smoother curve all the way from the mid to the top, and slightly increase the bass end. What are the differences?

THE SPOKEN WORD
Try a crisp, radio announcer EQ by creating an upward-sloping EQ curve that rolls off a lot of the bass end, and cuts through at the middle and top.

The guitar is experiencing a resurgence of popularity, but it is also one of the easiest instruments to record badly. However, it should come as no surprise that the digital world has countless sound-shaping tools and effects to offer guitarists, and also some stunning pieces of software that may make purists think twice about any resistance they might have to using computers in their work.

Guitarists, along with saxophonists and violinists, are used to regarding their instruments as extensions of themselves, and so they respond best to tools that they are able to use just as instinctively. Musicians such as Jonny Greenwood of Radiohead have successfully added digital technology to their playing, both live and in the studio. Writing as both an electronic musician and a guitarist myself, I can confirm that the computer can be an excellent way of recording four, six, or 12 strings–and it can be an excellent live tool as well.

1. MIKING AN ACOUSTIC GUITAR
Miking close to the soundhole will give you a bassier sound—but perhaps also a "boomy" one.

USING MICS
Acoustic guitars
If you have an acoustic guitar with no integral pickup or built-in mic, the most popular choices of external mic are dynamics and small-capsule condensers. Placing any mic (especially a condenser) near the sound hole will produce a boomy sound that might need careful EQing to roll off some bass in the mix. If you're monitoring through speakers, you'll also risk feedback problems by miking close to the soundhole. To avoid this, use a directional mic and point it away from the monitors, while sitting at an angle to the speakers so the guitar's soundhole isn't pointing straight at them. (Better still, use headphones!) Miking nearer the bridge will give you a more trebly and incisive sound. The closer you mic the guitar, the less room sound you'll pick up–but the more you'll have to watch your fingers.

2. ELECTRIC GUITARS
A Brandoni custom-made guitar, using an original Eko Vox body.

Electro-acoustic guitars (above)
Some acoustic-style guitars have integral pickups, while others (like this Spanish guitar) also have an internal "shadow system" mic that picks up sound from within the soundbox of the instrument. You may decide to mix the pickup signal with an external mic signal. If you do, consider that the two signals will arrive at slightly different times. If you place the external mic 1ft (30cm) away from the guitar, the speed of sound will mean the mic signal arrives up to one millisecond later than the signal from the pickup–a timelag of 44.1 samples if you're recording at 16-bit. Delaying the pickup signal by 1ms should make the two signals arrive simultaneously.

3. N.I. GUITAR RIG CONTROLLER
This pedal plugs directly into the audio line input of
your soundcard. See next page for more.

4. DYNAMIC RANGE
The potentially huge dynamic range of an amplified
electric guitar is a real challenge for home studios.

Electric Guitars

Amplification, sound separation, and
monitoring are the main problems
when recording electric guitars in home
studios. You might like to record at high
volume to get a real crunch and kick out
of your sound, but this makes it hard to
monitor what you're doing if you're both
guitarist and engineer—and it can be
antisocial! There are several solutions to
the problem, which we'll explore next.

YOU HAVE THREE OPTIONS.

■ Mic up your amp

If you close-mic your amp, then the more centrally you place the mic, the brighter the sound will be, while placing it nearer the rim of your amp's speaker will give you a more subtle, perhaps mellower, sound. If you have two speakers in your amp (or stack) then you may need two mics, or have to place the mic further away.

■ Use a hardware amp simulator

The Line 6 Pod and the Behringer V-Amp are two of the various hardware amp simulators on the market. These are digital boxes that model the unique acoustic signatures and sound characteristics of a wide range of classic amps and speaker cabinets (cabs). If you plug your guitar into the simulator, and then plug the simulator into your soundcard, you can access a huge array of sounds without having to worry about miking up an amp, EQing the sound, or annoying the neighbors. The Pod and V-Amp also include delays reverbs, choruses, and other effects.

■ Buy virtual guitar rack software

One of the most astonishing uses of software to model the real world is the virtual guitar rack. Sound Technology's Amplitube, Line 6's Guitarport, and Digidesign's Amp Farm are some well-known examples, while Logic Pro also includes a virtual guitar rack plugin.

However, one application that's caught people's ears is Native Instruments' Guitar Rig. Like Amplitube, Guitar Rig is an amp modeler in software form, combined with an expandable virtual rack of effects and processors.

It comes with a range of preset setups that imitate both contemporary sounds and the setups of some legendary figures, such as David Gilmour, Jimi Hendrix, Carlos Santana, not officially in every case, but the name of the preset is a strong hint of the type of sound you'll get.

Simply drag virtual amps, delays, compressors, distortion pedals, Leslie rotating speakers, and so on, onto your virtual rack, and you'll gradually set up a unique guitar sound that will exist entirely within your microprocessor, but which will sound like a mix of classic gear miked up in your home studio.

In Guitar Rig and some other virtual racks—such as the one in Logic Pro—you can even select the virtual speaker cab you want to use, what type of virtual mic you want to use, and how you want to mic up the setup. The selections you

make will produce very convincing models of real-world combinations of guitar racks and other gear. To use Guitar Rig, simply plug the Guitar Rig foot pedal into the Audio Input of your soundcard (not the USB or FireWire port)—and that's it.

Some virtual racks work as either plugin or standalone instrument, so you can use them live.

1. SELECT YOUR CABS AND MIC
Choose the cab you want to imitate, pick a virtual mic, and choose where you want it positioned.

2. "GODMOUR" CLASSIC PRESET
This reverentially named preset is an homage to a guitarist prone to big, overdriven, fluid lead sounds. Note all the virtual processors in this setup!

3. DRAG AND DROP
Simply drag your choice of amp, cab, processor, and so on onto the virtual rack, and it will be automatically "wired up." Then assign controls to the pedal.

4. GUITAR RIG AS PLUGIN
Here we're using Guitar Rig as a plugin within Logic.

5. LOOK AT WHAT YOU'VE DONE
Once you've recorded your playing, bring up the soundwave onscreen to make edits.

6. FIX PROBLEMS
Address and edit individual events—here we're reducing the volume of a single note.

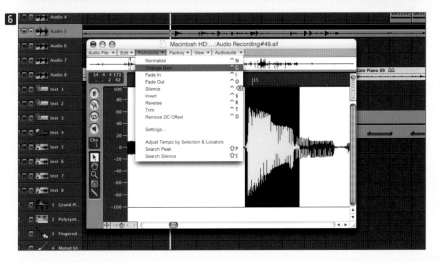

The underlying principle of monitoring is simple: you need a reliable, "known" reference source on which to listen to your recordings, and that source should not "color" your work. Monitors should have as broad a dynamic range as possible, coupled with a flat frequency response (again, "flat" does not mean dull, but a frequency response that is equal across the spectrum, rather than shaped to stress any frequency bands). If you use a set of speakers that has a shaped frequency curve designed to flatter playback by boosting bass, or slicing through the mix with extra-crisp treble, then you will find yourself removing those frequencies, in the belief that it's your recording that's bass heavy, or trebly, and not your speakers.

Nearfield monitors are designed to sit near the listener at ear level or slightly above, allowing you to listen directly without too much additional room sound.

Position the speakers about 4-6ft (1.2-1.8m) apart on stands, and place yourself the same distance away in the middle of the stereo pair. Angle the speakers inward until they are pointing straight at you. You are now in the "sweet spot" of a triangle of sound where you will get the best stereo image.

Avoid placing nearfield monitors directly in corners or too near a back wall, as this will boost apparent bass response—very desirable in a hi-fi, perhaps, but not in a monitor system. Move them about 3ft (1m) away from the wall, and away from any corners.

Farfield monitors are much bigger, more powerful speakers designed to be driven at higher volumes and to sit some way behind, or above, the mixing desk. While nearfield monitors can be either active (powered) or passive (needing a power amp), farfield monitors are usually active.

So can you monitor your work on your hi-fi speakers? It's not advisable. One of the disadvantages of using many conventional hi-fis, for example, is that they are designed to overwhelm the ears with dozens of presets, ambiences, sub-bass settings, and graphic equalizers, while the speakers themselves are also designed to impress. Such a sound system might offer a hardcore listening experience for fans of massive bass or swampy reverb, but what you are actually doing is mangling what a producer, engineer, and mastering engineer have spent weeks crafting. If you genuinely have no other option than to use such a hi-fi, then strip these settings out and add no processing to the playback. If this leaves your work sounding flat and lacking in punch, then perhaps you are hearing the information that is actually there and your recording needs more work. Just as likely, though, is that your ears have become lazy and you have taught yourself to appreciate music that has been processed to death.

A good set of monitor speakers should create transparent listening and leave you confident that you are hearing what is in your recording, and not what has been added by your choice of speakers, amplifier, or additional processing. Get this right to begin with, and you stand the best chance of pleasing the listener—regardless of their own listening environment.

ABBEY ROAD HINTS AND TIPS

Andrew Walter, Remastering Engineer

"Monitoring is something that's terribly important. You need speakers that have a very wide dynamic range and a flat frequency response. What we're really talking about is EQ and being able to judge when and how to boost a frequency here, or subtract a frequency there. That said, it's better to have a cheap set of speakers in an acoustically well-designed room than a good pair of speakers in a poorly designed room. And when you're monitoring a recording, do remember to check mono compatibility by listening in mono from time to time."

1. ACTIVE, NEARFIELD SPEAKERS
A pair of Behringer Truth powered (active) nearfield monitors—a solid budget buy.

2. IN THE SWEET SPOT
You're at the apex of a triangle of sound—but watch those corners of the room and those windows as they'll affect the room sound as you listen.

OTHER MONITORING TIPS

■ Establish a known reference source. Play a favorite CD or download. How does your own work compare on the same speakers?

■ Listen to your work on a range of sources—in the car, on tinny laptop speakers, on a beatbox, on a midrange hi-fi, and on the best sound system you can find.

■ Check out your mix in a spectrum analyzer. How does it compare to your favorite download?

■ Remember to listen to your work both loud, and quiet. The frequencies that "sing" at high volume will not do so when you turn the volume down.

For details about surround-sound recording and monitoring, please turn to page 158.

MIXING CONCEPTS

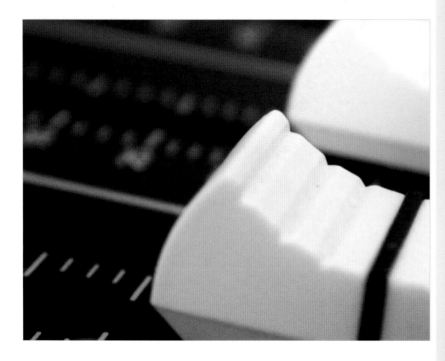

Your mixer is where it all happens. It's where you organize your audio information; route sounds; equalize them, place them in the stereo or surround-sound picture; apply effects and processors; and bring your work to life. Your raw material stands or falls at the mixdown. Record it badly from the outset, and a skilled engineer can fix it to a degree, but no amount of EQ will compensate for poor recordings.

Mixers are central to most music and sound software. The interface may vary, but the principle remains the same: each audio, instrument, or MIDI track is routed through its own channel, and each channel offers controls for modifying and enhancing the information stored on that track—and its relation to other tracks in the piece.

You may choose to work solely in software, but you may also have one or more of the following at your disposal: a hardware mixing desk (analog or digital); a hardware interface to your software (if you're running Pro Tools, for example); or a digital multitracker. If you have these tools, then you may find it easiest to

control the mix from there. However, it's by no means essential—you can create stunning mixes on your desktop alone.

Some mixers have designations such as "16:8:2," which means 16 audio channels, mixing down into eight channels (four assignable stereo groups), and then finally into two channels (stereo left and right). Outside of Reason's Mixer module, most software dispenses with this concept, as you can expand the number of channels on your mixer as and when you need to.

Many software mixers mimic the look and feel of their hardware counterparts—for example, Reason's Mixer resembles a simple multitrack desk. The Mixer interfaces in Logic and Cubase, on the other hand, are gateways to a range of popup windows and menus offering more sophisticated functionality and a variety of routing options.

MIXER CONTROLS

Here's a rundown of some of the basic controls found in each channel strip of some software and hardware mixers.

1. EQ (Equalization): manages the level of different frequency bands, controlling bass, mid, and treble levels. On hardware mixers, EQ controls may be simple pots (knobs); sweepable controls (pots surrounded by an outer ring control that sets the frequency band); or programmable interfaces to onboard software functions. In software mixers, EQ may consist of pots or sliders, or bring up separate windows allowing you to fine-tune equalization using a range of controls, including editable points on a frequency curve.

2. Fader: controls the volume of each channel. Master Faders manage the volume of the entire mix, while Group Faders allow you to control the volume of groups of channels. Most software mixers let you group selected channels together (e.g. all vocals or all drum sounds) via a dropdown menu.

3. Insert: allows you to patch in an effects processor to the channel. Software mixers may allow you to patch in several processors at once (dynamic effects, time-based effects, or plug-ins). Hardware mixers might offer more than one Insert point per channel, each of which routes out to an external processor and back in again to the Insert.

4, 5. Mute (M) and Solo (S): buttons for switching individual channels in and out, or hearing them in isolation.

6. Output Levels: virtual meters, or colored bars alongside each Fader, which rise or fall to indicate the volume of the track. Some are color-coded to show when a signal is becoming too hot (loud).

7. Pan: moves sound between the left and right stereo channels and all points in between.

8. Peak Level: indicates the volume of each track in dB. Some also act as warning lights: green (good); yellow (caution); and red (danger). Many mixers keep the warning illuminated after a signal has clipped (in case you missed it), and retain the dB reading of that peak. Reduce the volume (or investigate what else might have caused it, e.g. excessive EQ).

9. Record Enable: allows you to record on that track. Remember to switch off prior to mixdown.

10. (Aux) Send and Return: Send routes the channel out to a signal processor. Several channels can be sent to the same processor, but the level of Send dictates how much of each signal is sent (so you can assign more or less of the effect to each channel). In software, routing multiple channels to a single processor uses less of your CPU's resources. Return routes the output of the processor back into the mixer.

11. Mono/Stereo: in some software, an option to make each channel mono or stereo.

12. Write and Read: mix automation controls. Write allows you to record a series of actions in real time on a mixer channel (e.g. moving the fader, and so on); Read plays back what you've just done.

13, 14. Surround (see separate image, left): brings up a circular device, within which is a cursor. Move the cursor inside the circle to spin the sound through anything up to 360 degrees. If you set the channel to Write (see above) you can spin the sound in real time and record the panning information.

FADERS DOWN
When you're preparing your final mix, the most important steps are to save a reference mix and walk away, then begin from scratch with the faders down after you've given your ears a rest.

LESS CAN BE MORE
Although most music and sound software lets you add more and more tracks (as far as your processor will allow), it can be useful to limit your options. Why not stick with the 14 tracks of one Reason mixer, rather than add another 14? Does your piece really need more tracks to work?

GENERAL MIXING STRATEGIES: MUSIC

■ Avoid mixing immediately after a long recording session. Leave mixing your track for several hours–perhaps a day or two if time allows. Your ears will have become tired and you will be less alert to the needs of the piece.

■ When you return to your piece try to listen to it with fresh ears. Be hyper-critical. Spend an hour or so fine-tuning the rough mix from the recording session so you have a "performance" of the piece. Then save it as a reference.

■ Make a copy of the reference mix and name it "Final mix." Take down all the faders, take out any EQ, remove all of the effects, and start with a "clean slate."

■ For many people, writing and recording are one and the same process. As a result, you can become focused on irrelevant details, or find yourself creating a mix that "sounds good at the time" because it conveys your excitement with the act of creating it. Listen again later on and you may find the excitement was generated by there being too much going on in the mix, rather than it being a coherent piece of music.

■ Just as you avoid mixing your drinks, avoid mixing with drinks. Alcohol dulls the bass sensitivity of your hearing.

■ Any mix is a performance. Keep searching for the definitive performance and be prepared to abandon everything you've done until you achieve it.

■ In a stereo mix, visualize the stereo image as a physical, three-dimensional stage that exists between and behind your monitor speakers. Imagine each individual track or channel (instrument or vocal) is a performer on that stage. Ask yourself: What have I come to see? What is this performance about? What is the theme? Who or what is the star? Who or what are the supporting players? And where are all the "performers" standing?

■ In some cases the star will be obvious: the lead vocal, or a groove, while the main supporting players might be a bassline or a hook. If you have an obvious star, then it is your job to build the show around him, her, or it.

■ In other pieces, the drama in the mix might come from the interplay between two or more "performers." If that is the case, then set the stage for them and let them fight it out.

■ Consider the perspective of this imaginary, three-dimensional space. It is tempting to turn everything up loud in an attempt

REASON'S MIXER
Reason gives you a simple 14:2 mixer that resembles an analog desk. If you run out of tracks, though, you can simply create a new mixer.

to make the mix sound "big." However, large spaces are defined by distant objects. To create a big sound you need to position some objects at a distance and to create a sense of the relative distances between foreground, middle ground, and background.

■ In other pieces, your central character might be more an atmosphere, mood, or moment that all the elements combine to create. If this is closest to your piece, then as producer or engineer you need to create the right sound environment for that mood to happen, just as a cathedral holds a choir, a comedy club an improv, and a basement bar a jam session.

■ Why is visualizing a mix important? As soon as you imagine that the stereo image is a physical stage with performers standing on it, it makes you realize that you may have no star or too many stars competing for attention; or that one "performer" (an instrumental or vocal line) might be standing in front of another one, or that too many performers are crowded into the same small part of the stage.

■ If two or more performers (channels) are crowding each other out, there may be one of three reasons for this. First, they may occupy a similar frequency range. If so, consider changing

their relative EQ so that the two parts sit better together. Second, they may be in the same part of the "stage," in which case separate them by panning them to different locations in the stereo image. Third, one of them is irrelevant, in which case kick it off the stage!

■ Now compare your mix with your original reference mix. Almost certainly, your new mix has taken the place of your original attempt. If not, rip it up and start again. It may be, of course, that you were right with your original mix... in which case, you've lost nothing.

MAIN MIXER WINDOW STRATEGIES

- Use each channel's main EQ window to equalize the signal; but consider bringing up a Graphic Equalizer as an Insert to dig out, brighten, beef up, or knock back any frequencies that seem hard to isolate in the main EQ window.

- Experimenting with increasing and decreasing each slider on a Graphic Equalizer across a whole song is an excellent way of learning exactly where each element of the song lies in terms of its frequency band.

- It's better to cut than boost. Don't always think of EQ as something to add; think of it as something to subtract to make room for other sounds in the mix. For example, listen to each acoustic guitar, rhythm guitar, or pad keyboard in turn and consider rolling off unnecessary bass or applying a low-shelf EQ. This will give sounds such as kick drums and bass guitars elsewhere in the mix more room to breathe.

- Consider using Preset EQ settings on lead vocals, backing vocals, guitars, bass, and drums—there are numerous studio-designed options in packages such as Logic and Cubase. You can always modify these to suit your taste.

- At the start of your mix, find your feature sound, which may be the vocal. Set the vocal faders just above the middle (e.g. at between -6dB and -12dB), and then set all other faders relative to that. This will give you some room to move.

- A good rule of thumb is to set drums -3dB down from the level of the feature sound, and the bass at -6dB and then EQ from there.

- Use the full stereo image when panning your tracks. (Go back to visualizing the mix: if this were a real band, where would everyone be standing on the stereo "stage"?)

MIXING WITH DYNAMIC EFFECTS

If you've set your recording level to capture the quieter moments of a performance, then a sudden peak will distort the signal; equally, setting the recording level to accommodate the loudest peaks could mean that the rest of the track will be swamped in the mix. This is when to deploy dynamic effects. However, they should be used with care—unless you are aiming for a "brick wall" sound where the signal is slammed against a dynamic effect.

Problems and Solutions

- Signal too hot in places: Compressor / Limiter. If you have one, also consider using an Automatic Gain Control (AGC), of the type used by broadcasters to level out speech by adding gain (increasing volume) to signals below a Threshold, and decreasing Gain above the Threshold, creating a flatter signal. Alternatively, manually reduce the peaks by editing the waveform in your timeline.

- Signal too cold in places: Compressor; AGC; Gain control. Alternatively, manually increase the peaks by editing the waveform in your timeline.

- Unwanted peaks within specific frequency bands: Multiband Compressor (Multipressor).

- Flat-sounding performance: Expander, to increase the dynamic range.

In a mixdown, dynamic effects can be used:

- as Inserts into individual signal paths (channels) on your mixer to manage the dynamics of the channel in relation to other channels in the mix;
- across a signal Bus (see Glossary) if you have grouped together two or more signals and wish to apply the same processing to the whole group;
- as Mastering tools in a soundwave-editing package across the whole of a finished mix, either to fine-tune it for a particular audience/environment—such as radio, a club, and so on—or simply to get the loudest, crispest mix you can.

- On some sounds, such as drum loops or guitar solos, heavy compression can produce attractive, musical effects because the quieter, more nuanced elements are enhanced.

- Conversely, overuse of compression can make recordings sound flat and artificial by reducing the dynamic range of voices and instruments. A lot of modern pop vocal production is heavily compressed and "dry" sounding.

- Do not clip! Don't let signals shoot over 0dB in your software. In analog recording, overloaded signals produce a warm distortion or punchiness that has no correlation with the sharp cracking sound of a clipped digital signal.

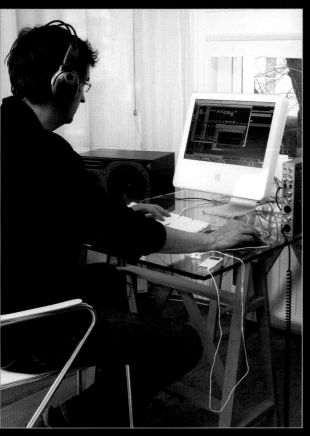

MONITORING THE MIX

■ Now listen to your mix in mono. In mono some instrument levels can appear drastically different, bass frequencies vary, and you might lose some edge or brightness. Listen in mono as your audience might do too.

■ Experiment with preparing the stereo positioning on headphones (cans), but always monitor on your speakers. When you switch between cans and speakers, what has changed and why? Does the vocal seem quieter and less distinct? Have you overcompensated for the bass?

■ Resist the temptation to mix with the monitors at a consistently high volume, as this will dull your hearing, and also fool you as to how dynamic and successful the mix really is. Be bold enough to mix predominantly at low volume and still make the track sound exciting, while occasionally listening louder.

HOUSEKEEPING

■ Mixes rapidly become very complex when you are dealing with dozens of separate audio, instrument, or MIDI tracks, so remember to name all of your tracks. Good housekeeping from the outset is always time well spent. Many software suites give you a menu of graphical icons—e.g. drum kits, guitars, keyboards, stringed instruments, and so on—which you can also use to label each track.

■ Don't make the mistake of assuming that once a loop, audio recording, or sample is in your track you can delete it from elsewhere on your computer. Your computer will still be reading the file from wherever it is stored on your hard disk.

■ If you apply dozens of different Insert processors, effects, and plugins, you're asking a lot of your computer's CPU. Some software includes an optional CPU usage meter. If you have this, watch it carefully—overloading your CPU will bring your recording to a grinding, crackly halt.

■ Very complex mixes within software suites create another problem: latency. On slower systems, for example, the peak level meters might start to lag behind the sound by a noticeable amount, or move in a jerky, jumpy way. If upgrading your system isn't an option, then see the limitations as a hidden advantage—perhaps your mix is genuinely too complex.

MULTIPLE LEVELS

■ If you've recorded multiple tracks of a particular kind—e.g. vocals or strings—or you've recorded each element of a drum kit onto a different track, then it can be difficult to manage all of the faders relating to those tracks individually. On these occasions, it's simplest to group tracks together. Grouping means that all of the tracks assigned to the Group can be controlled via a single Fader, and also be processed collectively. In Logic, click in the window above the track number to reveal a dropdown Group menu. Select Group 1 for the first group. This will bring up another window asking you to name the Group (e.g. "Drums"), and offering a range of further options. In Cubase, right-click (if you have a two-button mouse) on a track to bring up the Track Options menu. Select Add Group Channel Track. Form a stereo Group—you'll notice you can also form a Surround-sound Group.

■ You could also consider Bouncing some tracks together. Bouncing means that a number of individual tracks are merged together to form a single track—similar to flattening separate image Layers in Photoshop. But as with flattening Layers, once you've bounced tracks together you will no longer be able to edit the individual tracks, only the new, composite track. There's no bouncing back!

REVERB

■ If you apply Reverb at an Insert point, then ensure that it is the last processor you apply at that Insert. If you patch subsequent Insert effects into the same track, the reverb will also be fed through subsequent effects.

■ Avoid mixing different lengths and types of reverb together unless there is a very good reason to, as you will create a confusing, splashy mix, as though your music has been played and recorded in dozens of different-sized rooms simultaneously.

■ Reverb types are subject to the whims of fashion. You may date your music with some effects choices—for example, the year 2005 equated to dry, compressed recordings; 1985 to big, spacey sounds.

■ Bear in mind that any loops and samples you use may have their own characteristic reverb contained within the recording.

■ Long "Hall" reverbs will add a slow decay to sounds. Bear this in mind on sounds such as cymbals, as you may begin to blur the boundaries between instrument and effect.

■ Avoid adding reverb to sounds such as bass guitar and bass/kick drums, as these are often best left dry and punchy, and can be fattened up by other methods—with compression, a touch of chorus, and so on.

■ Consider using a single, main Reverb, and apply varying levels of Send to it, and Return from it, within each track.

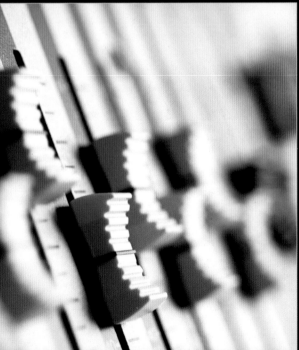

EQ HOTSPOTS

Some useful frequency hotspots and sweetspots to experiment with. These are highly subjective, so season to taste.

Instruments

Bass drum: Boost low at 100Hz; cut at 220Hz; boost at 3–5kHz

Bass guitar: Boost bottom at 50–70Hz; cut low middle at 500Hz; cut high at 500Hz

Snare: Boost at 150Hz; cut at 900Hz; boost at 10–12kHz

Hi-hats: Cut at 800Hz; boost only slightly between 4kHz and 8kHz; roll off any unnecessary bottom end

Rhythm guitar: Boost at 150Hz; boost at 1.2kHz; shelve at 5kHz

Lead guitar: Cut at 5kHz; boost at 1.2kHz (consider separating from rhythm with panning)

Voices

Add high harmonics subtly at 6kHz
Add presence at 3–5kHz
Add body between 400Hz–900Hz

Recently, I was given the opportunity to remix an unusual single. The strategy behind the original track had been to create and professionally record a piece of music in one day, using whatever performers turned up at the studio. The track (written by Jamie and Tim Freeman of Indie band Frazier Chorus) was recorded by engineer Jake Rousham at Metway Studios in the UK.

There are as many strategies and approaches to remixes as there are musicians, so let's explore the issues and ask: **What does a remix look like?**

Archeology

If you're working with someone else's material, then digital music becomes archeology, says Owen Leech, manager of Peter Gabriel's Real World studios. In the days of tape, he says, you simply played the tape, but with digital files you have to sift through masses of data to see and hear what's there, because each track creates a separate audio, instrument, or MIDI file. If those files have been poorly labelled, then it becomes a lengthy, almost forensic process.

Archeology is a perfect analogy. The first thing anyone faces when doing a remix is layers of individual audio tracks, representing dozens of performances recorded at different times of the day—like strata from different periods of history. Unearthing them often means rediscovering things that have been forgotten. It also means analyzing several gigabytes' worth of data. (In this case, the tracks had been recorded through a 48-channel mixing desk and analog outboard gear, onto a Pro Tools Mix Plus system in 24-bit and at 96kHz.)

Jake Rousham was canny enough to record everything that happened during the day, so we had not only the final takes, but also the rejected ones. This opened up the exciting possibility that the remix might not just be a new interpretation of the song, but perhaps an entirely new performance of it by the same people.

The files—some of them as long as the finished track, and others short clips of overdubs, harmonies, or solo instruments, —were labelled, but it was guesswork as to which were the "actual" takes. This is a common experience—and a creative challenge. The files were in Digidesign's Sound Designer II format, so there was a separate file for each of the Left and Right stereo channels of every take.

More than 20 vocalists sang on the original song—four leads, plus what became known as "the mob" of all the other performers. The vocals had been recorded in a live room with four main vocal mics (each one chosen to suit a singer), and also two omnidirectional mics suspended overhead to capture the room sound. This meant more strata still—there was a separate sound file for each of the mics, which also meant the file contained mainly one vocalist's performance.

Strategy

As you can see, strategy is an important element in any remix—it's often vital to establish a working methodology from the outset. I sat with the original producers and previewed the clips in QuickTime. I had not requested the studio's Pro Tools project file, because I wanted to have the option to do anything that sprang to mind. Preselecting the material you work with to whittle it down to a handful of core performances is a subjective process, but often the only practical solution.

Part of my personal strategy was to put back into the song some of the spontaneity of the process that made it. It became clear that my interest lay mainly with the vocals, which had an uplifting, gospel quality in the chorus. I decided to use that as my starting point.

Play

Play and a measure of irreverence can be an important creative aspect of doing a remix, and the first thing I did was purely in this spirit. I dragged the soundclips randomly into Ableton Live, the real-time DJing and sequencing instrument.

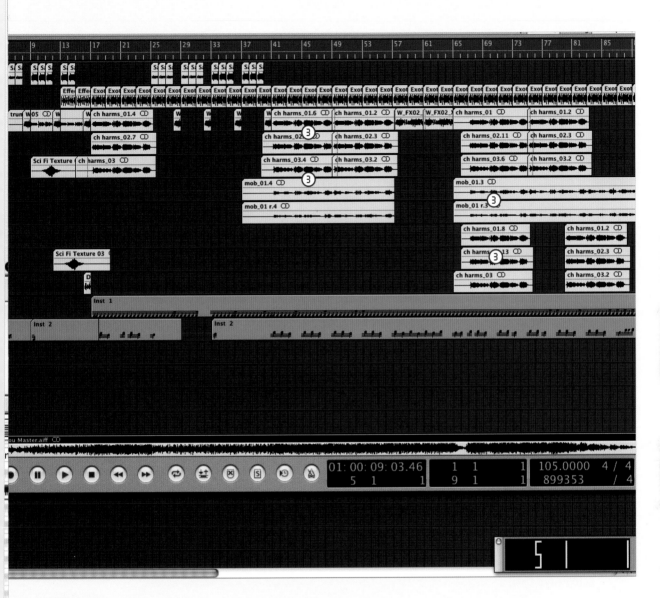

REMIX FEATURES (above)

1. The original guide track (highlighted with the black band) is pasted here purely for your reference. This was originally on Audio Track One.

2. In Audio Track One, you can now see the tiny clips that I made from the Guide track, the waveforms of which I tightly edited so I could position the clips accurately on the timeline at the beginning of the correct bar.

3. The vocal parts edited down from song-length takes so they just contain the chorus. You can see I've also positioned some of these at different points toward the end of the remix, as I wanted the playout to build to a crescendo of cascading vocal lines.

CREATIVE Q&A: HAKAN LIDBO, REMIXER

Swedish composer, producer, and remixer Hakan Lidbo says that he "makes electronic music stretching from totally abstract experimental glitch-and-noise music to straight-up pop." He was recently accepted as a member of the Swedish Composers Association—the first "techno" musician ever to be inducted—and says that he is "working for alternative electronic music being taken as seriously as contemporary art."

Please share your top tips for doing a remix...
"I always spend some time thinking about the track I'm going to remix before I do it. I don't listen to it too many times, but I make detailed plans [about] how to do it and record the ideas by singing into the voice memory in my phone. I try to find the main melody line in the song, and everything I do is somehow connected to that main melody line. If it's a vocal track, I make sure that bassline, chords, and rhythm patterns are all connected to this.

"It's much like arranging classical music where you present the theme with different instruments within the arrangement—sometimes cleverly hidden—but the listener will always have this line to follow and to recognize. I believe that you can only follow one line when listening to music, just like you can only follow one conversation at a party with lots of talkative people, and that line can be represented in the vocal melody, the bassline, or whatever... but only one line, that's the main thing."

Could you do what you do without digital technology?
"No. I'm not even sure I would make music if it wasn't for the technology. I've always wanted to make music that no-one has heard before, and digital technology is totally superior in achieving this. There are absolutely no limits, except those of my fantasy and skills."

What technologies do you use?
"I have a traditional studio with an analog desk, lots of analog synths and effects, and I record on [Apple] Logic. Analog things very often malfunction due to bad leads, humming, and distortion, but those sounds can be used as musical instruments and they will sound different from sounds generated with software. But sooner or later everything ends up in the computer anyway... in the Logic program.

"I truly believe that all the updates, new plugins, and softsynths you can get today aren't moving music forward that much. All these new options make people nervous, and as most people only scratch the surface of each new piece of software, they never get into any depth with it and explore all its possibilities. I'm very often surprised that music doesn't develop faster than it does. I see a lot of people choosing old and strange instruments to make music, simply to find their unique sound. People using Gameboys, C-64s, old Ataris, old synths, field recordings... whatever it takes. And some even build their own digital instruments with Max, Supercollider, or as soundtoys."

What inspires you about what you do?
"Like every human being, I absorb everything that is going on around me. I used to be very impressed with different music, thinking that one day I might be able to do something similar, but nowadays I listen carefully to my own stuff, trying to find out what would be the next logical step. What can I improve? Is this the best I can do? Is this "real," or did I make this music to impress or show off?"

How important is process to you? And what is your process?
"I've been making music for a few years. I've made many records and I've tried many different styles, so I've had the opportunity to reflect on the creative process. I became aware of the presence of doubt very early and learned how to identify that feeling. So, in order to overcome the doubt that stops so many artists from ever finishing their work, I forced myself to finish songs in one day (this was in the mid-80s, long before I started to make records). I'm not saying that I haven't had any doubts since then, but it really helped me to be aware of the doubt that can be so devastating to the creative process."

When you mix or remix a track how do you go about organizing the material and reinterpreting it?
"I normally get everything, and the first thing I do is select maybe one-third of the audio tracks that I like the most, and then I only use those. I want to narrow down my options so I can focus more on what I have.

"Making music on a computer is very much about choice, so if I make a first selection of sound material, I don't allow myself

HAKAN LIDBO
In action as DJ, remixer, and musician, creating a
digital performance.

to go back and look for more. Then I listen to the material that I have, trying to find the essential melody. If it's a vocal track, it's almost always in the vocals. If it's an instrumental–even a minimal or abstract track–I have to look for the melodies elsewhere.

"When I've found the best and most important melody, I arrange everything around that. If the vocals have an interval that is significant for the track, I use that interval in the bassline. If the phrasing of the most catchy vocal phrase has a certain rhythm, I program the drums so it swings with that rhythm. I try to listen to the music like language, catching the most important words so the message is clear."

How do you monitor your work?

"I simply listen to my music over and over, and simply keep or throw away. I almost never regret the way I did a song. I never go back and change it. I'd rather throw it away and make a new one. The only way to mix and produce with no doubt or hesitation is to always believe that I can trust my ears.

"Sometimes I'm wrong, but then I just waste the track and forget I ever did it. I've often found that the mistakes I make can be very musical and interesting, so I often leave some room for mistakes when I make the mix. When I mess up, I simply back up the song and mix the same part again so I can choose between the two–sometimes I end up choosing the one where I did mess up, because it's more musically interesting."

What are your tips for creating and also mastering a good mix (rather than a remix)?

"I give each sound its certain frequency to make sure that sounds don't collide, or that two or more melody lines or rhythm patterns don't phase each other out.

"I listen for the main line of the song—the main line is like a storyline in a script, or a theme in a movie soundtrack. A song is also telling a story, it has its own drama, and I try to make sure that this line isn't interrupted or overtaken by something less important. Clarity is very important. I use my experience as a pop producer when I do experimental or minimal stuff, and look for the main line in those songs as well."

"I LISTEN FOR THE MAIN LINE OF THE SONG—THE MAIN LINE IS LIKE A STORYLINE IN A SCRIPT, OR A THEME IN A MOVIE SOUNDTRACK. A SONG IS ALSO TELLING A STORY, IT HAS ITS OWN DRAMA."

Mastering and remastering are two of the least understood aspects of recording, but also the most talked about in general conversation. So what are they? Mastering is about making your final stereo recording—the result of all those hours you've spent EQing, applying effects, and riding the faders—sound as good as it can. It's like getting the most expert lab print from a digital photo that you've been editing in Photoshop. This might mean mastering a track purely for its own sake, or for a particular market.

There are numerous plugins available for mastering—one example is the T-RackS bundle, which is available in several formats for different sequencers and platforms. This is simply a virtual rack of different dynamic processors. Alternatively, you can choose to master in a soundwave editing package, such as Bias PEAK. However, perhaps the simplest (and least expensive) solution for those on a budget is to create a WAV or AIFF of your final mix, and then import the file back into your sequencer and apply the processors you already have.

Mastering processors might include: a parametric or graphic equalizer for evening out the overall EQ; a Compressor—perhaps a Tube Compressor simulator (which can add a bit of analog-like warmth to your recording); a Multiband Limiter to tweak the dynamic range; and perhaps a Soft Clipping processor (which might be part of your Limiter's functions). Using the latter will get you to 0dB without any obvious distortion.

"Mastering is down to one person's opinion over another's," says Andrew Walter (pictured), remastering engineer at London's renowned Abbey Road studios. Of course, if you've spent hours getting the mix right, why should you then apply yet more effects and processors? "In a professional studio, the mixing engineer has spent ages combining and equalizing lots of different sound sources into two, the stereo signal," says Walter. "The mastering process is about making the finished stereo recording sound good overall."

Mastering came out of transferring lots of separate recordings onto the same disk for an album release, says Walter. It was often necessary to adjust the levels between each song and re-EQ some of mixed tracks until the whole record was consistent.

"Small things can make a huge difference—compression, level, fade up and fade out," says Walter. "It's very subjective—you can take a record to three different mastering engineers and get three different results. At the end of the day, mastering is just another pair of ears. But something magic can happen when a recording goes in front of that new pair of ears—it can add a little sprinkling of gold dust. The more people you involve, the more it drags the standard upward.

"A common problem now is those clients who say 'that sounds better if it's louder.' But in the determination to make recordings as loud as possible—which is a common problem in today's recordings—the heavy mastering, equalization, and compression required often makes tracks sound crunchy and unnatural."

WHAT IS REMASTERING?

Andrew Walter has worked at Abbey Road Studios for 15 years. Now a Remastering Engineer, he specializes in restoring old recordings. "When I joined there were just two computers in the building. What I now do is use Computer-enhanced Digital Audio Restoration [CEDAR]," he says. "When you remaster a recording, you remove the degradations that weren't deliberately recorded, but not to the detriment of the music. None of this technology was around in the 1960s. At the time, when people made edits by physically splicing tape, they weren't audible to the average listener. Today, with our superior monitors and technology, those edits become much more noticeable. We're removing things that you weren't meant to notice in the first place. If we're remastering classic recordings like the Beatles, then we often clean each channel [of noise]. It's like restoring an old painting. With remastering old recordings, people often say they prefer the original. But they don't realize that this is not because the quality was better, it's because it was mastered with the available technology of the day, for the available technology of the day. What I have to tell people now is that, for the very first time, they're hearing what the original tape actually sounded like! You can hear things now that were inaudible to engineers at the time. Digitally remastered recordings are often the first time the public hears the original performance as it really was, rather than the copy of it that was made at the time."

1. REASON MASTERING PROCESSORS
Recent versions of the music suite have added a range of mastering tools.

2–4. COMPRESSION PRESETS
Logic has a range of mastering EQ presets fine-tuned
to bring the best out of different music styles.

So now you've created, mixed, and mastered your work, what next? Here is just a small selection of file formats you may encounter when working with digital music and sound—plus a handful of related acronyms. This is not an exhaustive list.

- **AAC:** Advanced Audio Coding: Web standard developed by MPEG (the Motion Picture Experts Group) as part of its MPEG-4 specification. Supported by Apple's iPod. By default, the compression algorithm used for AAC encoding is MPEG-4 Audio (MP4-A). AAC is a perceptual coding method (relating to how we perceive sound) used to compress digital audio files so they provide sound quality nearly indistinguishable from the original sources, although data have been lost.

- **AAF:** Advanced Authoring Format: Multimedia format developed to exchange data within Digidesign's Pro Tools software. Can be imported by many suites, such as Logic.

- **AIFF:** Audio Interchange File Format (.aif). Standard, cross-platform audio file format for storing high-resolution digital waveform information, which can be read by most audio- and video-editing suites.

- **ACID WAV:** .wav files that have been processed within, or for, music tool ACID, allowing them to be beat-stretched and beatmapped to different tempos (warped), without changing their inherent pitch. Ableton Live will read the .WAV but not the additional ACID formatting.

- **ALS:** a file extension for Ableton Live work. Ensure you use this when swapping files between Mac and PC.

- **ASD:** Within Ableton Live, this is an Analysis file that the software creates when importing a sample (e.g. an .aif or a .wav) for the first time. As a result, you will see files with the suffix ."wav.asd," or ".aif.asd," on any files that Live has processed within the application.

- **ASF:** Media file playable within Windows Media.

- **AVI:** Audio/Video Interleave format. Used to display video in Windows systems, but also readable by players such as QuickTime, Real Player, and Winamp.

- **B-WAV/BWF:** Broadcast Wave format. Developed by the European Broadcasting Union as a "meta format" that contains other media formats for all types of broadcast application.

- **LTC:** A video/audio synchronizing timecode format, short for Longitudinal (or Linear) Timecode.

- **MID/MIDI:** MIDI (Musical Instrument Digital Interface) file format, for sending musical event and controller information between compatible musical devices. See also SMF.

- **MMS:** Multimedia Messaging Service. Protocol for sending text, images, and video via cellphones and mobile devices.

- **MOV:** Apple QuickTime movie format, from which you can extract the audio in most compatible players and audio editors.

- **MPEG:** Motion Picture Experts Group, a group within the International Standards Organization (ISO). It has developed numerous standards for digital audio, video, and related media. Among the MPEG specifications are:

- **MPEG-1:** For digitizing sound at sampling rates of up to 48kHz. contains three Layers (I-III), offering descending levels of quality down to 32-320kbit/s for Layer III (the original MP3 standard).

- **MPEG-2:** Extends the channel capabilities of MPEG-1 and includes enhanced low-frequency sound capability and embraces optional lower sampling rates. (MPEG-2 Layer III, or MP3, therefore embraces a broader range of sampling rates).

- **MPEG-2 AAC:** Provides a superior audio coding standard at sampling rates of up to 96kHz and 48 channels.

- **MPEG-4:** Multimedia standard for next-generation audio and video. In audio terms, it adds the capability to synthesize sound and embrace score-driven sound synthesis and an interface for text-to-speech recognition systems. MPEG-4A is the soundwave element of the specification.

- **MPEG-7** provides new descriptions and description schemes for audio content.

MEDIA PLAYERS

Microsoft's Windows Media formats bundle an audio and/or video codec with Digital Rights Management (DRM, see page 122) capability. Apple bundles Advanced Audio Coding (AAC), with Fairplay, its proprietary DRM system, for iTunes and the iPod.

WINDOWS MEDIA AUDIO (WMA) FILES ON YOUR MAC

If you don't have iTunes, there are other ways of converting WMA files to Mac-compatible formats. One PC-based package can be downloaded at www.dbpoweramp.com, while one Mac-based system can be found at www.easywma.com.

- **MP3:** More correctly known as MPEG-2 Layer III audio encoder and decoder. Legendary compressed audio format for distributing files over the Internet and on media players. Many of the files we download and share are not MP3s at all.

- **OGG:** Ogg Vorbis: An open-source file format. Ogg is an open-source multimedia project, and Vorbis is its audio compression format that promises superior sound quality at smaller file sizes than MP3, and rival quality to MPEG-4A, AAC, and so on.

- **OMF:** Format for data interchange between Digidesign's Pro Tools suite and other applications.

- **OpenTL:** Format for data exchange with Tascam hard-disk recorders.

- **RIFF:** Resource Interchange File Format. Portable format containing whatever mixtures of MIDI, .wav, .aif, and other files you care to create.

- **REX:** (rx/REX 2/rx2) Loop formats developed by Propellerhead Software for its Reason virtual studio and ReCycle suite. The Dr:Rex loop player is the default player for such files inside Reason.

- **RFL:** A Reason ReFill file, containing a library of separate audio files in numerous formats that Reason can interpret and play within its various virtual instruments, players, and modules.

- **RNS:** A Reason song file.

- **SD2:** Sound Designer II format. Standard sound format developed by Digidesign. Files can be formed of combined stereo elements, or separate Left (L) and Right (R) channels.

- **SKD:** Sseyo Koan Design. Native instruction set (seed file) format of Sseyo's generative music composition program, Koan.

- **SMF:** Standard MIDI File format.

- **SND:** A Macintosh sound resource file used within OS9 and below, but still readable within OS X.

- **SNG:** Suffix used separately by various software packages to denote a Song file.

- **SWF:** Macromedia Flash format file for animations, which can be played within numerous media players, such as QuickTime and Windows Media. You can extract the audio from an .swf file (as you can with QuickTime videos, and others).

- **WAV:** Wave file format. The de facto standard audio file format on Windows PCs, supporting a variety of bit resolutions, sample rates, and numbers of audio channels.

- **WMA:** Windows Media Audio format. Standard file format within Microsoft's ubiquitous media player.

- **WMV:** Windows Media Video format.

- **XMF:** eXtensible Music Format. A music-specific evolution of XML (eXtensible Mark-up Language), XML and XMF are metadata (data about data) file types.

EMAILING FILES

If you email audio, video, or any other non-text-based file, use Stuffit (Dropstuff), or Zip the files to ensure they are not damaged in transit. This is particularly true if you are using Web-based mail systems.

CD (AUDIO VERSION)
Sampling rate: 16-bit at 44.1kHz
Dynamic range: 96dB
Capacity: 747MB (74 minutes of stereo audio)
- This means we can calculate that one minute of uncompressed 16-bit audio gives you a file size of 10MB.

SACD (SUPER AUDIO CD)
Offers a frequency range of 2Hz–100kHz. (Human hearing is very roughly 20Hz–20kHz).
Sampling rate: 2.8MHz (2.8 million samples a second)
Dynamic range: 105dB
Capacity: 4.2GB

DVD AUDIO (DVD-A)
The audio version of the format more usually associated with video more than doubles the fidelity of a standard CD. DVD-A offers 400 minutes of stereo at CD resolution (44.1kHz/16-bit); 74 minutes of 5.1 surround sound at 96kHz/24-bit resolution; or 74 minutes of stereo at 192kHz/24-bit resolution.
Sampling rate: 44.1kHz–192kHz
Dynamic range: 144 dB
Capacity: 4.5 GB approx

DVD VIDEO; DVD-ROM; DVD-R; DVD-RAM; DVD-RW
DVD Video: for viewing movies and other visual entertainment. Total capacity is 17 GB if two layers on both sides of the disk are used. DVD-ROM: Similar technology to DVD Video, but used to store computer-friendly data formats. DVD-R has the standard 4.7GB capacity. DVD-RAM: makes DVD into a virtual hard disk, with random read-write access offering capacity of 4.7GB per side. It can be rewritten more than 100,000 times. DVD-RW: similar to DVD-RAM except that its technology features a sequential read-write access. Capacity is 4.7GB per side. It can be re-written up to 1,000 times. DVD Multi will embrace all existing format versions.

HOW ARE CDs AND DVDs DIFFERENT?
Both formats store and read data by reading and writing microscopic spiral grooves with a laser. Tiny reflective bumps (lands) and nonreflective holes (pits) aligned along the grooves represent the ones and zeroes of digital information. DVDs use smaller tracks together with different signal modulation and error correction methods. CD players are unable to play DVDs because the smaller grooves of a DVD require a different type of laser. The emerging high-definition formats, such as HD-DVD and Blu-Ray require a different type of laser again (see below).

BLU-RAY DISK (BD) AND HIGH DEFINITION DVD (HD-DVD)
With the advent of High-Definition TV, and the increasing usage of 24-bit recording in the home there is a need for ultra-high-capacity disk formats. Two main formats are emerging, both of which are written and read by a blue laser rather than the red ones used by CD or DVD burners. Blue light has a shorter wavelength than red, which means that blue lasers can focus on smaller areas of disk and write more data into the same physical space. In one corner of this new standards battle is the Blu-Ray disk (BD), supported by a broad industry alliance of Sony BMG, Matsushita Electric, Hitachi, LG Electronics, Apple, Mitsubishi Electric, Pioneer, Philips, Samsung, Sharp, TDK, HP, Dell, Disney, EA Games, and Twentieth Century Fox. In the other corner is Toshiba's HD-DVD technology, backed by Warner Bros,

---

BURNING A CD (RED BOOK STANDARD)

The specifications for CD audio were set out in the 1980 "Red book" standard developed by the format's progenitors, Philips and Sony, dictating a 16-bit word length and a sample rate of 44.1kHz. At this rate and depth, one second of stereo audio uses 176,400 bytes of disk space.

- You can burn CDs in numerous ways, using widely available Mac/PC software such as iTunes, Roxio's Jam (which will help you compile CDs), and dozens of other free or low-cost utilities. In general it's best to record at 24-bit or higher within your production suite and then export it into a CD burner/compiler where it will be converted down to the Red Book specification. You may wish to use your music or audio production suite to Dither the tracks prior to export into your CD burning and compiling package, which will preserve maximum quality in the bitrate conversion process. In iTunes, Jam, and other applications, you can also Normalize the tracks (iTunes offers its Sound Check facility, which sets the same recording and playback level across all of the tracks you're compiling onto the CD). Remember to set whichever gaps between songs you prefer, and to choose Audio, Data, or MP3 CD options as appropriate. (Many hi-fi CD players will only play Audio CDs, but other players—and your PC or Mac—handle every option.) Remember also to add any text information you also wish to be accessible or displayed.

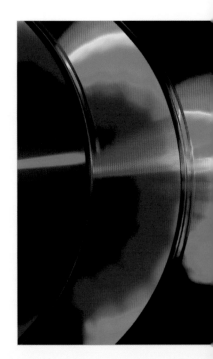

Paramount Pictures, and Universal, among others—a smaller alliance in terms of numbers, but one that packs a punch in terms of the movie business and its associated media arms. Also in HD-DVD's favor is that it is an evolution of the DVD format, which may count with the public.

UNIVERSAL MEDIA DISK (UMD)

Sony's proprietary format for games and other digital content, designed for use on its PlayStation Portable (PSP) device. The disks are like miniature DVDs, with a unique, encrypted copy-protection scheme (which, as is often the case with secure systems, was swiftly hacked). The disks can store up to 1.8GB of data, but are not (at the time of writing) recordable for non-developers.

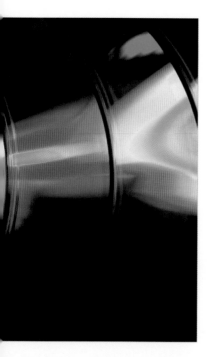

HOW BLU-RAY AND HD-DVD COMPARE

	BD-ROM	HD-DVD-ROM
Storage capacity (single-layer)	25GB	15GB
Storage capacity (dual-layer)	50GB	30GB
Data transfer rate (1x movie application)	36.0Mbps	54.0Mbps (1.5x)
	36.55Mbps	36.55Mbps
Video compression	MPEG-2	MPEG-2
	MPEG-4 AVC	MPEG-4 AVC
	VC-1	VC-1

	BD-R	HD-DVD-R
Storage capacity (single-layer)	25GB	15GB
Storage capacity (dual-layer)	50GB	30GB
Data transfer rate (1x)	36.0Mbps	36.55Mbps
Video compression	MPEG-2	MPEG-2
	MPEG-4 AVC	MPEG-4 AVC
	VC-1	VC-1

	BD-RE	HD-DVD-RW
Storage capacity (single-layer)	25GB	15GB
Storage capacity (dual-layer)	50GB	30GB
Data transfer rate (1x)	36.0Mbps	36.55Mbps
Video compression	MPEG-2	MPEG-2
	MPEG-4 AVC	MPEG-4 AVC
	VC-1	VC-1

Key

VC-1 is Microsoft's Video Codec
MPEG-2 in this regard refers to support for high-definition TV (HD-TV) recordings and DVDs. MPEG-4 AVC High Profile is the highest available standard for video reproduction on disk.

■ Other formats

Minidisk (MD) [PIC]
Sampling rate: 44.1kHz
Dynamic range: 92dB
Storage capacity: 140MB

Digital Audio Tape (DAT)
Sampling rate: 48kHz
Dynamic range: 105dB
Up to two hours of uncompressed audio, depending on the length of tape.

YOUR INTERNET AUDIO MENTOR

INTERNET RADIO

PODCASTS

GENERATIVE MUSIC SYSTEMS: TIM DIDYMUS INTERVIEW

MAKING MUSIC ON YOUR CELLPHONE

DIGITAL RIGHTS, ONLINE COLLABORATION, AND PUBLISHING

We've covered some of the basics of sound, how digital recording works, the technologies and techniques of making music and recording sound, and also many of the file formats and storage systems at your disposal. Of course, the extra dimension of digital music and sound is that it can, like any digital information, be shared, published, consumed, and modified in many different forms—online, peer to peer, including from cellphone to cellphone via Bluetooth, or any superdistributed system (see Glossary). The technologies exist to collaborate online with other creative people in near-real time—you can link your home studio with someone else's on the other side of the globe, and then publish your work to the world. Many artists are doing this very successfully.

So, what are the issues, the technologies, and the creative strategies? Welcome to the world of podcasting, Internet radio, online distribution, mobile music, digital rights, real-time collaboration, and DIY music portals.

YOUR INTERNET AUDIO MENTOR

WHY PUT MUSIC OR SOUND ON MY WEB SITE?

- To provide a richer, more interactive online experience. Rich media content that contains combinations of music, audio, video, animation, and other interactive elements is the main growth area in the online economy, worth billions of dollars.

- To share your work.

- To bring the real world into the virtual one.

- In terms of your own music, it's also a means of bypassing traditional publishing. UK band the Arctic Monkeys found their audience in the virtual world first, then broke sales records with their debut album in the real world. Another band, Nizlopi, had a hit single by building word of mouth online.

WHAT DO I NEED TO CONSIDER FIRST?

- Ask yourself what you want to achieve. Is it a personal or a business Web site? If it is a personal Web site, then your visitors are more likely to appreciate music and sound.

- Visitors to a business Web site are often in offices themselves and may have the sound turned off, or would not appreciate unexpected audio intrusions.

- On a business Web site, keep the audio to an elective section of the site and tell your visitors it is there. Alternatively, give people the option to switch the sound off (or better, on) when they visit, which will alert them to its presence.

- Investigate whether you want to "go it alone" or be part of an existing online community or service, which might provide all the tools you need, drive more traffic to your work, and offer you a money-making framework.

- Check the rights implications of using commercially available music or sound clips (see page 122). Create your own, or consider the use of royalty-free loops and samples—the audio equivalent of clip art.

- If you post your own work online, then you are sharing it with the world and your ideas may escape from you as their creator. This may be desirable, or you may want to take out some form of financial or rights-based protection.

- Just because you can fill your site with rich media doesn't mean you should. Sites such as Google are successful partly because they are simple and uncluttered and don't bombard you with unnecessary elements or force you into making certain choices.

WHAT IS STREAMING?

Streaming media—typically digital music, sound, and video—is heard/seen while it is being delivered over the Internet. Some software media players, such as Real Player, stream digital media (including audio, music, and video) so that when you download a Real Player file you often are downloading a link to a media stream rather than the complete media file itself. Media streams can be "on demand" (stored on servers for access at any time) or live ("broadcast" over the Internet at a specific time). Audio files stream through your computer's processor.

WHAT IS PEER-TO-PEER (P2P) NETWORKING?

Peer-to-peer (P2P) networking is when digital material is sent from client device (a desktop PC, laptop, or cellphone) to another client device, relying on the computing power of the network, which may be configured ad hoc as people join or leave. P2P networks are typically used for sharing digital content. The term covers the sharing of games and music from cellphone to cellphone via Bluetooth and other methods. Usually, P2P is the opposite of the client-server model where communication is to and from a central server, such as one hosting a Web site.

WHAT DOES BANDWIDTH MEAN?

Technically, bandwidth is the measure of the frequency range of any type of waveform, including a soundwave. In a digital system, the bandwidth is the maximum possible rate at which data may be transmitted through the system (such as the baud rate of a modem).

WHAT DOES BROADBAND MEAN?

Broadband refers to the transmission of multiple data simultaneously, either over the same or multiple channels (i.e. voice and data), with the effect that more information can be sent and received more quickly.

■ Not all parts of the world offer broadband Internet access, and not everyone's computer is a high-spec, fast machine with all the latest media players installed. Hope for the highest common denominator, but always consider the lowest.

HOW CAN I USE MUSIC AND SOUND ON A WEB SITE?

■ Discrete audio clips, such as a sound effect, can be added to mouseovers and other navigational elements of your pages, simply by setting a clip to play in your site-building software when a mouse passes over it. Your visitor may regard these as a sophisticated touch, cumulatively as an irritation, or at worst as an annoying intrusion.

■ Atmospheric audio accompaniments could make your homepage more welcoming. This can even be achieved within a program such as Word using the Insert > HTML object > Background Sound command.

■ Music and sound could be the purpose of your Web site, should you wish to set up an Internet radio station, or post tracks, podcasts, or blogs online.

■ For songs and long pieces, music should be in the form of compressed audio files (for example, WMA, MP3, Ogg, AAC), which take up less room on your server and use less bandwidth when downloaded. You can post WAVs of AIFFs as well, but it's not advisable for anything other than short clips as the file sizes will be too large.

■ Alternatively, consider using MIDI, vector audio, or generative music files, which simply tell your soundcard what to play and therefore use minimum download time. See pages 115 and 128.

■ Remember a MIDI file is like a musical score turned into 1s and 0s so your computer's onboard synthesizer can play it. It contains no audio, merely instruction sets.

■ With MIDI files you have no control over the quality of your visitor's GM-compatible soundcard, and so your music may not sound as you intend it to. Most visitors will be unaware of this, and will associate a poor musical experience with your site.

- Vector audio and generative music files (see page 115) are similar to MIDI files, but tell the soundcard how to build the right instrument to play the musical information.

- Audio can be a component of an animation or moving graphic that you direct your visitors toward. You can embed audio in Flash files (see page 126-131), or use specialist Internet plugins such as Koan to play generative music in a Web page. Generative music files (using formats such as .skd) can also generate events that can drive Flash animations. See page 128.

- The easiest way is to create an audio dimension is to upload the file to your Web site and simply create a link to it. If you are using a standard file type, such as MP3 or WMA, then all browsers can handle them.

WHAT OTHER CONSIDERATIONS ARE THERE?
- Does the file need to be in stereo? If not go for mono and keep the file sizes small.

- Your Web site provider may put a monthly restriction on how much bandwidth your Web site can deliver to your visitors. If you are posting big files and getting a lot of downloads, you need to keep an eye on availability and finance.

- If you expect people to check out your site from a cellphone or PDA (personal digital assistant), then keep file sizes down as data transfer costs are expensive.

- Some mobile devices and cellphones don't have the power to play back files at very high bitrates (e.g. 192kbps), or have the space to store very many.

CREATIVE CONTEXT

The 20th century was the broadcast century, the age of mass communication that aimed to reach the widest possible audience with the same core content. The process began electronically with the telegraph over 150 years ago and reached its natural conclusion with terrestrial radio and television. Now many people are realizing that the real boon of the networked 21st century is not putting a local spin on a global message, as so many corporations prefer to do, but making a local message globally available. Paradoxically, "local" is no longer constrained by geographic boundaries as communities of shared interests locate each other across the globe. If homepage is where the heart is, then blogs—personal (Web) logs—and Internet radio and podcasting are the front porch where the conversation takes place.

So how do you become an Internet radio "broadcaster" or a podcaster? What technologies do you need to do it free, on a budget, and on a more ambitious level? What are the technical issues? And most important, what could some of your creative strategies be?

WHAT IS INTERNET RADIO?

Internet radio is essentially audio streamed over the Net from a host server, usually via a dedicated Web site. Stations range from the simplest home set-up to a fully fledged radio studio that allows an ambitious webcaster to mix programmed and live elements. Log onto such a server as a listener and you will hear content that is webcast from all over the world without the geographical and legal restrictions of a terrestrial signal. To listen, you need one of the available media players, such as Windows Media Player, QuickTime, iTunes (on the desktop), Real Player, Audion, or WinAmp. Some mainstream broadcasters, such as the BBC, make their terrestrial and digital radio stations available online (www.bbc.co.uk/radio/), but the technology is there for any creative person to do the same. Although some Internet stations and shows are available on demand, in most cases you have to log on at the right time—just as you tune into terrestrial or digital stations at certain times to hear specific shows.

The only limitations to your ambitions as a webcaster will be the available bandwidth, plus digital rights and intellectual property concerns (see page 122) if you plan to webcast commercially released music. Internet radio is also "radio with pictures," plus any text annotation you make to your files.

CREATE YOUR OWN INTERNET RADIO STATION

To create your own station, you can go for a simple approach by simply compiling playlists of audio files in a standard media player and then uploading them to a specialist host server. However, we're going to explore a more sophisticated approach by looking at software that allows you to add and mix live audio, "tag" your files, and perhaps add video, animations, or live links to your content.

IPODS AND INTERNET RADIO

Your iPod and most other portable media players do not have always-on connections to the Internet. This means that to get Internet radio (as opposed to a podcast) onto your iPod involves recording the webcast and then importing it as an MP3 or MP4A file onto your players. Programs such as RadioLover (www.bitcartel.com/radiolover) allow you to do this dynamically by telling your computer to record the same show or station at the same time each day or week. You can add links to favorite shows to your playlists as normal. However, if you are ripping commercial music to your iPod from a licensed audio stream (i.e. an Internet radio station that pays royalties on any music it plays under the Small Webcasters Amendment Act) then it's worth bearing in mind that this may count as unlicensed content.

Source
Library
Party Shuffle
Radio
Music Store
Purchased Music
90's Music
Bonus Chris-Mas Cracker
Glen Campbell
Recently Played
Tom Cat Soundtrack
ULTIMATE CHRIS-MAS!
untitled playlist
untitled playlist
untitled playlist
untitled playlist 2
untitled playlist 3
untitled playlist 4
CHRIS'S PLAYLIST
christopher rye
christopher rye 2
Prefab Sprout - Steve Mc
untitled playlist
untitled playlist
untitled playlist
untitled playlist
untitled playlist
untitled playlist
untitled playlist 2
untitled playlist 2
untitled playlist 2
untitled playlist 3
untitled playlist 4

Stream	Bit Rate	Comment
▶ 50s/60s Pop		
▶ 70s/80s Pop		
▶ Alt/Modern Rock (43 streams)		
▶ Ambient		
▶ Americana		
▶ Blues		
▶ Classic Rock		
▶ Classical		
▶ Country		
▶ Eclectic		
▶ Electronica		
▶ Hard Rock / Metal		
▶ Holidays		
▶ International		
▶ Jazz		
▶ Public		
▶ Reggae/Island		
▶ Religious		
▼ Talk/Spoken Word (21 streams)		
📡 ACB Radio Mainstream	24 kbps	The Talk of the Blind Community - from th...
📡 ACB Radio Treasure-Trove	16 kbps	The best in classic radio drama and comed...
📡 AM 1710 Antioch	22 kbps	Old-time Radio Shows station
📡 Big Soccer Radio	16 kbps	All the best shows .... Again!
📡 Comedy & Talk RadioNET	32 kbps	The Best Comedy & The Hottest Talk! - A ...
📡 Defcon Radio	32 kbps	Explicit-Comedy on the Cutting Edge! defc...
📡 KCRW World News	56 kbps	News from around the world from KCRW, S...
📡 Khaha.com	32 kbps	The Original .%UNCENSORED%% All Com...
📡 Kid Safe Radio	56 kbps	Safe and fun programming for kids
📡 KZSU2 FM	24 kbps	Free-form radio serving Stanford Universit...
📡 Mystery Play I-Radio	16 kbps	Your #1 station for old time radio
📡 Pirate Cat Radio	56 kbps	Low powered community radio anarchy, br...
📡 RadioPower.org	16 kbps	Talk Radio For The Progressive Mind
📡 Rainbow Soul	24 kbps	Soulful programming featuring Speeches,...
📡 Serious Comedy Radio	32 kbps	Family-friendly comedy with a positive me...
📡 Soldier's Radio News	48 kbps	Army news as it happens, produced daily b...
📡 The Social Crime Radio Ne...	32 kbps	The Social Crime Radio Network: 175 Plus ...
📡 Traders Nation	32 kbps	Talk programming about smallcap stocks ...
📡 WineFairy, Inc.	32 kbps	Wine & Dine Radio
📡 No Holds Barred Radio	56 kbps	The number 1 original adult comedy statio...
📡 No Holds Barred Radio	24 kbps	The number 1 original adult comedy statio...
▶ Top 40/Pop		

82 streams

ITUNES: HOW TO LISTEN IN ON THE DESKTOP (LEFT)

1. Click on the Radio icon in the Source list, and you will see a broad range of stations and genres. Click on any one to listen in.

2. The bitrate should be slower than your Internet connection, otherwise you may find the station is jittery and unreliable.

3. Click Refresh on some visits and see what new stations have been added to the Radio list.

1. YOUR AMBITIONS START HERE...
With digital audio, your station can be as high-tech or as low-fi as you want—you may want to put together a fully featured radio studio and set up your own server.

2. SHOUTCAST
Alternatively, portals such as SHOUTcast exist to broadcast your radio streams to the world. See the following pages for details. SHOUTcast software is designed for PC-based systems, but you can tune in from any computer platform.

Most Popular Stations			Page 1 of 609	[Next]	
Search for	Station, Genre	Go!	or Jump to	Quick Genre ▼	
Rank	Action	[Genre] Description	Listeners/Max	Bitrate	Type
1	▷Tune In!	[Pop Rock Top 40] CLUSTER CLUB 977 The Hitz Channel (HIGH BANDWIDTH) *Now Playing:* Eminem - When I'm Gone	4518/72004	128	MP3
2	▷Tune In!	[Trance Techno Dance] CLUSTER DIGITALLY-IMPORTED - European Trance, Techno, Hi-NRG... we can't define it! *Now Playing:* Corderoy - December 2005 with guest Mike Koglin	3540/86390	96	MP3
3	▷Tune In!	[Ambient Chill] CLUSTER Groove Salad: a nicely chilled plate of ambient beats and grooves. [SomaFM] *Now Playing:* Taylor Deupree - Gen. Sec.	3034/65374	128	MP3
4	▷Tune In!	[80s Pop Rock] CLUSTER CLUB 977 The 80s Channel *Now Playing:* Harold Faltermeyer - Axel F	2758/70080	128	MP3
5	▷Tune In!	[Soft Smooth Jazz] CLUSTER S K Y . F M - Absolutely Smooth Jazz - the world's smoothest jazz 24 hours a day *Now Playing:* Tha Hot Club - I'm Gonna Love You Just a Little More Baby	2709/65367	128	MP3
6	▷Tune In!	[Vocal Trance Dance Pop] CLUSTER DIGITALLY-IMPORTED - Vocal Trance - a fusion of trance, dance, and chilling vocals *Now Playing:* Y Traxx - Mysteryland (Fred Baker And Mr	2704/88842	96	MP3
7	▷Tune In!	[classical easy symphonic] CLUSTER M O S T L Y - C L A S S I C A L - Now on S K Y . F M I - relax... it's good for you! *Now Playing:* Cogliore Innocenzo - I Due Figaro Di Saverio Mercadante - Sinfonia - Elaborazione Per Pianoforte	2654/89606	96	MP3
8	▷Tune In!	[eclectic rock] CLUSTER Radio Paradise - DJ-mixed modern & classic rock, world, electronica & more - info: radioparadise.com *Now Playing:* Muddy Waters - Howling Wolf	2592/67280	128	MP3
9	▷Tune In!	[Pop Rock Top 40 Urban] CLUSTER HitzRadio.com - #1 for all the hits! *Now Playing:* Puddle Of Mudd - Blurry	2443/71166	128	MP3
10	▷Tune In!	[smooth jazz] CLUSTER SmoothJazz.Com - The worlds best Smooth Jazz - Live From Monterey Bay *Now Playing:* Paul Taylor - East Bay Bounce	1781/71164	128	MP3
11	▷Tune In!	[Chillout Ambient Psy] CLUSTER DIGITALLY-IMPORTED - Chillout - ambient psy chillout, check out our trippy flavors! *Now Playing:* Marco Torrance vs. Xenoes - Chillout Avenue Vol. 1	1741/88844	96	MP3
12	▷Tune In!	[TOP HIP URBAN RnB POP RAP] CLUSTER =[:: HOT 108 JAMZ ::]=- #1 FOR HIP HOP - ALL HIP HOP AND R & B LIVE 24/7 @ 128K *Now Playing:* Ying Yang Twins - Wait (Ft Missy E & Busta R) (Remix)	1649/64365	128	MP3

WINDOWS MEDIA PLAYER: RADIO TUNER— HOW TO LISTEN IN...

1. Click Radio Tuner.

2. Click a station name under Featured Stations, My Stations, or Recently Played Stations. Information about the station and programming will appear.

3. Click your selection to begin playing.

To add a radio station to a preset list...

1. Follow steps 1 and 2 in the procedure to listen to an Internet radio station above.

2. Click Add to My Stations.

3. Repeat for as many radio stations as you want to add to your preset list.

To add a radio station to the Media Library

While using the Player to listen to a radio station, click the File menu, point to Add to Media Library, and then click Add Currently Playing Track.

connected to : backboneaudio.com

ON AIR

4:03:38PM
March 7, 2003

0:00:01:25

LIVE

program | on-air

duration : 01 :01 :24 for 16 items +

Random	Name	Artist	Time	Remaining	Time to Air	in	out
☑	Spirits Ahoy	The Bunglers	00:03:13	00:01:25	ON-AIR	00.00	00.00
☑	Snow	The Weather	00:03:56		00:04:05:03p	00.00	00.00
☑	Fire Spatula	The Pet Boys	00:05:07		00:04:08:59p	00.00	00.00
☐	Star Trap	Blimp	00:04:00		00:04:14:06p	00.00	00.00
☐	** NEWS BREAK **	Joe Engler reporting	00:00:10		00:04:18:06p	00.00	00.00
☐	** COMMERCIAL **	Fred Evens Motors	00:03:25		00:04:18:16p	00.00	00.00
☐	** COMMERCIAL **	Chicken-Togo	00:03:25		00:04:21:41p	00.00	00.00
☐	Pizza Theory	Hardly Drawn Boy	00:07:18		00:04:25:06p	05.00	05.00
☐	Lil' Weasel	The Stone	00:02:45		00:04:32:24p	00.00	00.00
☐	Heart Of Kishka	The Cernys	00:04:31		00:04:35:09p	00.00	00.00
☐	Evolution	Nose	00:04:17		00:04:39:40p	00.00	00.00
☐	Steam	The Pipes	00:04:17		00:04:43:57p	00.00	00.00
☐	Lil' Spatula	Irving	00:02:45		00:04:48:14p	00.00	00.00
☐	She Sells Newspapers	Uncle Freaky	00:04:12		00:04:50:59p	00.00	00.00

playlist

delete item

add item

template

audio device [Built-in audio controller]

input [Internal microphone]

stop   play

Add to Schedule

mic gain

Prev Item

Next Item

backbone

BACKBONE
Backbone's ONAir Studio software presents an easy-to-use interface—a rolling playlist, with controls for mixing in your own voice into an Internet "broadcast." The company offers similar software for Internet TV, for any ambitious online videocasters.

ALL-IN INTERNET RADIO PACKAGES: AN INTRODUCTION

Buying an Internet radio package does not mean that your listeners need to download the same proprietary software to listen to your voice or your favorite sounds—they simply need one of the standard media players. In most cases, your listeners probably have the standard players; if not, prompt them to grab the appropriate one by adding a link to a download site. Most hosting companies will do this for you.

So what is the point of buying an all-in-one Internet radio production suite? Essentially, it will give you the flexibility to add a range of sophisticated functionality to your shows and your scheduling by automating and randomizing events based on whatever parameters you set.

■ Remember: your station might broadcast 24 hours a day, but unless you can employ staff, there's no way that you can broadcast all day yourself. Your software fills the gaps when you are unable to broadcast live.

Internet radio software is designed to make it easy to schedule and broadcast all types of live or prerecorded audio online, and—like its counterparts in the worlds of digital audio recording and music production—your Internet radio application supplies you with an interface of tools that mimics the look of real-world hardware.

SHOUTCAST

One of the most popular software suites and online services, SHOUTcast (www.shoutcast.com), provides a suite of broadcasting tools designed for Nullsoft's

downloadable WinAmp player (www.winamp.com), plus an online hosting service. In this way, you produce the MP3 audio, and SHOUTcast webcasts it to the world. Such is the power of the SHOUTcast brand that it acts as a portal through which you can enter a whole world of Internet radio, with stations from Australia to Zaire offering anything from hardcore dance to chamber music and religious content. A quick glance at the "top stations" list will give you an idea of the number of currently logged-on listeners versus the maximum possible simultaneous listeners (a factor of the bandwidth).

CREATIVE STRATEGIES AND TECHNICAL SOLUTIONS

The first and most important thing to do is decide what you want to achieve: what is your station for? What does it play, and

LISTENERSHIP FIGURES AND STATISTICS

One day during the writing of this book I logged on and analyzed the top 10 Internet radio stations on the SHOUTcast network, using its rolling statistics service to see who was listening to what, and when. These statistics show how many cumulative Web page hits were registered with stations using the service over the preceding 30-day period. Obviously, even the next day this survey was long out of date, but it is a useful glimpse of genuine statistics from a service that had not been in the news during that period, and whose listener figures were therefore unlikely to be misleading.

Ironically, one of the advantages of using the virtual world to disseminate music and sound is that you can gather more accurate data from the real world—actual listeners, actual (Web page) hits and downloads. Terrestrial radio stations, for example, gather their listener figures from small but representative groups of people who say which stations they listened to, and at what times of day, during a given period. Similarly, national music charts have historically been compiled from data supplied by select retailers in towns and cities that are deemed to represent a national average. Today, many charts do take into account music download services—but again, only a select few.

Although the Internet is also open to exploitation, the fact remains that, over time, genuine anomalies tend to be ironed out and an online system can be less prone to systemic abuse.

So who was listening to what on this particular Internet radio service? Here is the top 10 for our survey period. (Descriptions are broadcasters' own.)

- 1 Club 977 "The Hitz Channel" (High bandwidth). 3,119,245 hits.
- 2 S K Y.FM "Absolutely Smooth Jazz—the world's smoothest jazz 24 hours a day." 2,335,280 hits.
- 3 Club 977 "The 80s Channel." 2,198,892 hits.
- 4 Digitally Imported "European Trance, Techno, Hi-NRG... we can't define it!" 2,155,244 hits.
- 5 Groove Salad "A nicely chilled plate of ambient beats and grooves. [SomaFM]." 2,094,822 hits.
- 6 Mostly Classical. "Now on S K Y FM! Relax... it's good for you!" 1,849,016 hits.
- 7 Radio Paradise "DJ-mixed modern and classic rock, world, electronicam and more." 1,780,442 hits.
- 8 Digitally Imported "Vocal Trance—a fusion of trance, dance, and chilling vocals." 1,643,938 hits
- 9 Smoothjazz.Com "The world's best smooth jazz—Live From Monterey Bay." 1,518,258 hits.
- 10 Republic of Korea Top Radio. "MUKULCAST.COM KPOP." 1,297,749 hits.

why? Who is your listener? Don't set up a station unless you know the answers to these questions.

You may decide to play your own music or broadcast your own writing and see what response you get—an excellent strategy, as long as you let people know that your station is out there by mentioning it on discussion boards, creating a mailing list, registering your site with an aggregator (see page 110), or setting up an RSS feed (see page 111).

One standard option in most all-in Internet radio packages is Rotation, which allows you to generate iTunes-style playlists automatically based on whatever characteristics you define, such as genre (type of music), priority (the online equivalent of radio stations' A and B

playlists), or tempo. For example, you might want your station to play chill-out mixes in the small hours of the morning, and upbeat music at breakfast time.

Your station might have a range of "signature" tracks that define what the station stands for, and you can specify that these should be played perhaps a dozen times a day. Using this facility means that any audio clip can be assigned other time-based criteria as well, such as start/stop time and date, time-of-day play, and the rate at which priority of play decreases. In other words, you can tell your software to act as the producer of your shows by dealing with the requirements of your chosen playlist and rotating the content within the remit of your station. In radio, what you play is who you are.

BACKBONE AND MULTIMEDIA
Radio packages such as Backbone's ONAirStudio (www.backbone.com) can create playlist templates, which include a modifiable set of broadcast rules. Using these, any type of digital content can be tagged. Tags allow your software to distinguish between different types of audio clip—such as songs, jingles, or station idents—and automatically insert clips that conform to these criteria as and when you would like them to appear.

These can be randomized as much as you wish—for example, your software might run two songs followed by a jingle, then three songs followed by a station ident, and so on. This creates the illusion of content being chosen and played live rather than simply looped and repeated by a machine.

In the 20th Century everyone was famous for 15 minutes, but with blogs and podcasts everyone is famous to 15 people. Well, hopefully more than that if your creative venture is successful!

WHAT IS PODCASTING?

The posting of compressed audio files (usually MP3s or WMAs) on dedicated Web sites so that visitors can download them onto their desktops and media players to listen to at their leisure. The term comes from the ubiquitous iPod.

These audio files might take a similar programmed, professionally recorded form to a broadcast/webcast show, or be a simple personal audio log. The content is neither transmitted nor streamed, but made available in self-contained chunks so that people can download them whenever they want to, and perhaps keep them on their own iTunes or Windows Media playlists.

It's a distinct but related concept to Internet radio, and to many broadcasters' "listen again" services whereby radio shows are made available online for streaming after they have been broadcast. What all of these concepts share is the ability to listen at any time the listener chooses, and perhaps to fast-forward through the broadcast to a specific point, making the original concept of broadcasting meaningless. We are no longer passive consumers.

SO WHAT DO I NEED TO MAKE OR LISTEN TO PODCASTS?

A computer with a broadband connection; some form of MP3 recorder/encoder/player; and access to webspace, or to a dedicated hosting service. And that's it!

A more sophisticated podcasting model is where portable media players can be directed to new audio files by means of a small application on the desktop, or via an RSS feed (see below right). In this way, media players can be dynamically updated whenever new content from your favored podcaster appears.

Although you can download shows directly by visiting your preferred podcasting Web sites, many afficionados prefer to use a podcast "aggregator" service to save them the trouble of logging onto dozens of different Web sites. An aggregator is essentially a portal through which you can subscribe to the podcasts that interest you. These services—have a look at iPodder (http://ipodder.sourceforge.net) or Pod2Go (www.kainjow.com/pod2go)—automatically download and collate podcasts you have subscribed to via the service and create playlists for you.

As there are as many types of podcast as there are people, let's look at just one venture and explore some creative strategies and technology issues that arise from how it is set up.

CREATIVE CASE STUDY: 21C VOX

This is an experimental talk- and music-based "station."

Technology

21C Vox is currently using a portable MP3 recorder on location; an ambient mic; iTunes; and the Liberated Syndication (Libsyn) hosted service (www.libsyn.com). It's moving toward creating some extra, more "professional" sounding content in a Apple Logic-based music studio to complement the "low-fi" location-based recordings. "It's about a networked conversation as opposed to a 'broadcast' channel," explains Neil Gibb, co-founder (with friend Andy Darling) of the podcasting venture, in which "digital thinker" and entrepreneur Andy Hobsbawm has an editorial advisory role.

"What we aim to do is create content that has a very clear 'place in the world,' that is both 'from somewhere' and 'about something,' but aimed at niche groups that may be geographically dispersed."

21C Vox is short for "21st Century Voices" and there is a reason for that, says Gibb. "A lot of people are talking about how the Net has changed the way the world works, but in many ways it has returned the world to the way it used to work: it's about people, connecting with each other, creating small, rich, vivid communities that participate in the creation as well as the use of content."

CREATIVE TIPS: STARTING OUT

You will find all manner of expensive podcasting starter kits online—these are essentially bundles of often very expensive audio hardware that are targeted at would-be podcasters. The fact is, you probably don't need them: you can podcast for next to zero financial outlay using readily available technology and a hosted service. Good advice would be to experiment with this approach first before considering what equipment you really need to put together more professionally recorded content.

"THE BEST THING ABOUT PODCASTING IS THAT TRULY NICHE SHOWS BECOME VIABLE. IF YOU ARE ONE OF THE 90 MILLION AMERICANS WHO DRIVE TO WORK YOU CAN LISTEN TO A PODCAST ON ABSOLUTELY ANYTHING THAT INTERESTS YOU, WHETHER IT'S FISHING, OPERA, HUNTING, TECHNOLOGY, RELIGION, OR AN OLD LADY TAP-DANCING IN NEBRASKA."

RSS

Really Simple Syndication (RSS) is an easy-to-use tagging system that allows you to syndicate news stories, or updates to your personal blogs and podcasts via any aggregator services you are registered with. Likewise you can use it to receive alerts about your favorite content. Set up an RSS feed with one of the aggregators (you will find instructions on how to do this on many podcasting sites), and watch the hits roll in whenever you podcast new content. It's a simple way of reaching your listeners by pushing content to them in the same way that broadcasting does, while still retaining the "pull," non-broadcast model of the Internet.

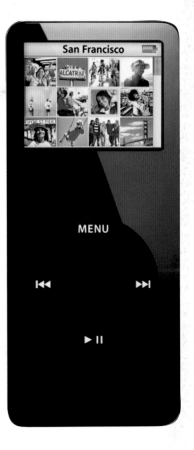

Gibb noticed that most of the "real" conversations and traffic on the Net are in places where the emphasis is not on design, but on facilitation—such as discussion groups, Instant Messenger, and so on, so he focused on what he terms "content and connection." "We didn't want to get caught up in the process of making a Web site but instead just concentrate on creating great content," he says.

PODCASTER ADVICE

For creative people wanting to set up a similar service, Gibb outlines a simple, low-cost strategy. "We keep it simple, using Libsyn service. Technically it couldn't be easier. It [Libsyn] is an audio blog-based service—it's simple, stripped down, and allows you to post and host MP3s. But the killer feature is that it offers unlimited bandwidth—which is vital if you want to serve big files and grow your audience.

"We have been deliberately 'lo-fi' for two reasons. One, it is cheaper, and two, we want to keep it 'real,' capturing the ambience of who and where we are. The aim is to create an atmosphere where people feel they are actually there with us. We just use a portable MP3 recorder that is about the size of a cellphone, plus an ambient mic—like the ones used in conferencing facilities. It captures the whole space."

KEEPING IT SIMPLE

A typical podcast in the earliest, experimental stages of the venture involved two friends sitting in specific locations and arguing passionately about music, politics, and other subjects. Such an unfiltered "fly on the wall" approach proved extremely effective in an age when so many people use new media to imitate old media production standards and content, rather than try something suited to the new medium.

> "THERE IS A QUALITY VERSUS AVAILABILITY TRADEOFF WITH PODCASTING, BUT I LIKE THAT, AS EVERY CONSTRAINT BEGINS A NEW CONVERSATION." Neil Gibb

---

ONLINE MEDIA PLAYERS

Many online media players (jukeboxes) and music download services are branded plugins to Microsoft's Windows Media service. These provide access to thousands of downloadable tracks, live music services, podcasts, Internet radio services (programmed playlists for online streaming), and more recently videos and TV programs. Many services are hosted by, or link to, digital media distribution services, such as Vitaminic and the UK's OD2 (On Demand Distribution), co-founded by musician Peter Gabriel. With most other jukeboxes and MP3 players standardized on Windows Media and its associated audio and video formats (WMA and WMV), this leaves Apple's generation-defining iTunes service and iPod in the familiar position of being "the only one marching in time."

Microsoft's proprietary Windows Media formats bundle an audio and/or video codec with digital rights management (DRM, pages 122-125) capability. Apple's approach is to bundle an open, wideband MPEG-4 standard (Advanced Audio Coding, AAC), with Fairplay, its proprietary DRM system. This turns an MP3 or MP4A (audio) file into an M4P (protected) file. It then applies licensing and usage terms associated with a customer's unique identity.

Apple's success and Microsoft's market muscle suggests the sustainability of two overarching formats—both of which can be built on to add multimedia capability. These are Windows Media DRM, and MP4/AAC Fairplay (M4P). Apple's iTunes can rip Windows Media files, and then convert them into the iPod playable format. Sony's digital players were originally compatible only with files stored using its preferred Atrac compression algorithm, but are now compatible with most formats aside from Apple's proprietary approach.

However, these are not the only file formats in the frame—there are numerous other MPEG standards, such as MP3PRO, which offers high-quality audio. Also available are open-source audio formats, such as Ogg Vorbis, which are readable on Linux-based systems. However, next-generation optical storage media, such as HD-DVD and Blu-Ray disks, will spur the ability of next-generation hardware players to handle large, uncompressed file sizes.

That said, Gibb aims to begin using a local musician and sound engineer's Logic Pro-based studio to record and edit a small amount of core content, creating a professional-sounding "home" around which the location-based, handheld recordings can revolve.

ADVICE ON FORMAT AND BITRATE

"We record in .wav format and then convert to MP3," he says. "We are still experimenting with the optimum bitrate. The main thing is we want to keep the file sizes manageable. We keep shows to 30 minutes and aim for file sizes of about 30MB max. All listeners need is a broadband connection and a pair of speakers."

As we've explored, Internet radio (like all digital content) presents creative people with the age-old challenge of the quality vs. availability tradeoff: the higher the quality (resolution) of the file, the longer the download time. The concomitant of that is that fewer people can access it simultaneously. Is that the same with podcasting?

"There is a tradeoff, but I like that as every constraint begins a new conversation. The main issue we have at the moment is we get spikes when people hit the site as the new show is posted, and sometimes that means people can't download it when they want to."

1–3 LOCAL GOES GLOBAL
Here's just one of thousands of podcasts on the Libsyn service—posted as an MP3 file once a week, this local UK service, "Brighton Calling," attracts emails and correspondence from all over the world.

This is Brighton Calling

A little bit of love from the city by the sea.

Tue, 3 January 2006

This is Brighton Calling 2006

Brighton calling will be switching to a Saturday in 2006. Thanks to all of you who participated in 2005: After a stuttering start we saw strong audience growth in the second six months, and go into the new year with a sense of verve and purpose. The first show of the new year will be with you at the weekend and watch out for some new shows and content.

As a taster here's something to listen to meanwhile - an up-until-now unreleased re-mix of SAY I LOVE YOU from the Brighton gothic enigma that is Christopher Rye.

(Copyright: This song is released under a Creative Commons license, meaning you are free to keep it, play it, or pass it on - but not to alter it or use it for any commercial pupose. Details of the licence can be found at: http://creativecommons.org/licenses/by-nc-nd/2.5/)

Direct download: Say I Love You Midnight Massive Remix.mp3
Category: podcasts - posted at: 9:50 AM

Categories

podcasts

Syndication

RSS 2.0

Keyword Search

[Search]

Archives
Jun 2005
Jul 2005
Aug 2005
Sep 2005
Oct 2005
Nov 2005
Dec 2005
Jan 2006

Mon, 12 December 2005

Brighton Calling: It's Christmas for crissake...

This is Brighton Calling on Monday 12 Dec 2005. It's Christmas, and as fights break out across the land over X-Boxes, we step through the drunken bodies of binge drunk office party casualties, pass ladies shreaking, toss the Sugar Babes CD towards the sea, and look at what people are really listening to...

Direct download: s.mp3
Category: podcasts -- posted at: 7:39 AM

Comments[0]

Thu, 8 December 2005

Brighton Calling: From the Cure to Only - The glorious legacy of romantic English Goth

This is Brighton Calling on Monday 5 Dec 2005. The re-emergence of romantic English gothic music. From The Cure to Only - we explore the glorious legacy of a troubled English soul.

Direct download: Brighton Calling 5 Dec 2005 copy 1.mp3
Category: podcasts - posted at: 5:21 AM

Comments[0]

Mon, 28 November 2005

Brighton Calling: The Say I Love You interview

This is Brighton Calling on Monday 28 November 2005. The 'Say I Love You interview

liberated syndication
podcasting made easy

★ Class of 2000: You've come a long way baby.

username: [   ]
password: [   ]

forgot password

[Login]

sign-up for service

Start Podcasting.

Welcome to the revolution. Podcasting is a means to publish audio and video content to the world via the Internet. Listeners are able to subscribe to their favorite shows and automatically receive the latest episodes in iTunes or similar client. Creating a podcast of your own is almost as easy as listening to one. Grab a mic, record an MP3, get on your soapbox, and let us take it from there!

You've created your podcast. Now let the whole world hear it.

Liberated Syndication is a premiere media distribution service built from the ground up with DIY content creators in mind. Libsyn is the first full featured provider tailored specifically for all-media self-publishing and Podcasting with pricing models that make sense for this new generation of content creators.

Love is all you need.

XML sound-off

So has Gibb considered moving the whole venture onto a more professional footing, in terms of its production values? "We want to make the whole thing 'more professional' without losing its authenticity," he says. "The challenge is creating the space to capture the sound. But we don't see broadcast-type content as something to aspire to. The blandness of broadcast is why we're doing this."

Of course, the unique thing about this creative model is the direct relationship you can create with your listener. "The great thing about the Net is statistics, in that you can see exactly how many people listen to each show—so we can see what worked, and what didn't," says Gibb.

"But the real measure of success is the e-mails, calls, and people who get in touch with ideas, thoughts, contributions, and—all too frequently—rants."

"The best thing about podcasting is that truly niche shows become viable," says Gibb. "If you are one of the 90 million Americans who drive to work you can now listen to a podcast on absolutely anything that interests you, whether it's fishing, opera, hunting, technology, religion, or an old lady tap-dancing in Nebraska."

WIDGETS!

Various companies make mini applications for the iPod and for iTunes; these add new functionality to the system. Among these are apps that display album cover artwork, information about whatever track is playing on a podcast, and links to Web sites and music download sites.

The iTunes interface showing the Comedy 365 podcast page.

iTunes

Account: chris@darksome.net

◄ ► ⌂ Podcasts ⟩ Comedy 365

Comedy 365
www.comedy365.co.uk

Please upgrade to iTunes 4.9 to download and subscribe to podcasts.
Upgrade now ➲

Total:20 episodes
Category: Comedy
Language: English

Podcast Description
Now with over half a million subscribers, Comedy 365 is an iTunes Top 10 podcast in the United States, Canada, UK and Ireland. Recently Time Out Podcast of the Week in London: "Very slick... a brilliant showcase". Sowerby & Luff present the world's "funniest daily download". Comedy 365 is currently syndicating award-nominated comedy DJ Chris Skinner, hilarious spoof pop band Dogs Must Be Carried featuring Richard Cray, Figgis & Kruup, Resonance FM's John Dredge, Stratton & Eady, Fetto & Palmer, Data Radio, Rosie Koonunga-Hill and top-rated talk shows "The Big Squeeze" and "The Rush". To help Comedy 365 secure a major podcast sponsor for 2006, please complete our listener survey at www.comedy365.co.uk

Website ➲
Report a concern ➲

Customer Reviews NEW
Be the first to write a review ➲

	Song Name		Time	Artist	Album		Genre	Price	
1	Big Squeeze Week – Brian...	EXPLICIT	Not av...	studio@comedy36...	Comedy 365	☉	Comedy	Free	GET
2	Big Squeeze Week – Dres...	EXPLICIT	Not av...	studio@comedy36...	Comedy 365	☉	Comedy	Free	GET
3	Big Squeeze Week – Most...	EXPLICIT	Not av...	studio@comedy36...	Comedy 365	☉	Comedy	Free	GET
4	Big Squeeze Week – with ...	EXPLICIT	Not av...	studio@comedy36...	Comedy 365	☉	Comedy	Free	GET
5	Dog In a Manger – The D...	EXPLICIT	Not av...	studio@comedy36...	Comedy 365	☉	Comedy	Free	GET
6	Most Wanted – Brian Luff'...	EXPLICIT	Not av...	studio@comedy36...	Comedy 365	☉	Comedy	Free	GET
7	Most Wanted – Sowerby a...	EXPLICIT	Not av...	studio@comedy36...	Comedy 365	☉	Comedy	Free	GET
8	Sowerby and Luff – The E...	EXPLICIT	Not av...	studio@comedy36...	Comedy 365	☉	Comedy	Free	GET
9	Sowerby and Luff's Big Sq...	EXPLICIT	Not av...	studio@comedy36...	Comedy 365	☉	Comedy	Free	GET
10	Sowerby and Luff's Big Sq...	EXPLICIT	Not av...	studio@comedy36...	Comedy 365	☉	Comedy	Free	GET
11	Ten Pairs of Pants (Day 4)...	EXPLICIT	Not av...	studio@comedy36...	Comedy 365	☉	Comedy	Free	GET
12	Ten Pairs of Pants (Day 5)...	EXPLICIT	Not av...	studio@comedy36...	Comedy 365	☉	Comedy	Free	GET
13	Ten Pairs of Pants (Day 6)...	EXPLICIT	Not av...	studio@comedy36...	Comedy 365	☉	Comedy	Free	GET
14	Ten Pairs of Pants (Day 7)...	EXPLICIT	Not av...	studio@comedy36...	Comedy 365	☉	Comedy	Free	GET
15	Ten Pairs of Pants (Day 8)...	EXPLICIT	Not av...	studio@comedy36...	Comedy 365	☉	Comedy	Free	GET
16	Ten Pairs of Pants [Day 1]	EXPLICIT	Not av...	studio@comedy36...	Comedy 365	☉	Comedy	Free	GET
17	Ten Pairs of Pants [Day 2]	EXPLICIT	Not av...	studio@comedy36...	Comedy 365	☉	Comedy	Free	GET
18	Ten Pairs of Pants [Day 3]	EXPLICIT	Not av...	studio@comedy36...	Comedy 365	☉	Comedy	Free	GET
19	Ten Pairs of Pants [Day 9]...	EXPLICIT	Not av...	studio@comedy36...	Comedy 365	☉	Comedy	Free	GET
20	Ten Pairs of Pants [Day 1...	EXPLICIT	Not av...	studio@comedy36...	Comedy 365	☉	Comedy	Free	GET

Source
- Library
- Party Shuffle
- Radio
- Music Store
- Purchased Music
- 90's Music
- Bonus Chris-Mas Cracker
- Glen Campbell
- Recently Played
- Tom Cat Soundtrack
- ULTIMATE CHRIS-MAS!
- untitled playlist
- untitled playlist
- untitled playlist
- untitled playlist 2
- untitled playlist 3
- untitled playlist 4
- CHRIS'S PLAYLIST
- christopher rye
- christopher rye 2
- Prefab Sprout – Steve Mc
- untitled playlist
- untitled playlist
- untitled playlist
- untitled playlist
- untitled playlist
- untitled playlist
- untitled playlist 2
- untitled playlist 2
- untitled playlist 2
- untitled playlist 3
- untitled playlist 4

20 songs

1–2 ITUNES ACCESS
If you have iTunes on your PC or Mac, you have easy access to a world of local and international podcasters. Big names and rising stars all have equal market presence.

CREATIVE TIPS: EVOLVING YOUR PODCAST

■ Don't try to emulate "big media", as there are thousands of people doing that very well (or very badly) already.

■ Podcasting is one area where good ideas will succeed more readily than something slick and empty, just as a useful Web site will retain more unique visitors than one that merely looks beautiful, and simple discussion boards attract more passionate debate than corporate portals.

■ Try creating something that is about you, where you're from, what motivates you, and what you want to share.

■ Spend time scripting something you are proud of; alternatively, get out and about and record real events as they happen, or try to get your community involved.

■ The "stars" of podcasting will be those people who recognize what the medium can do that is different, separate, and distinct from other media, and how it can give a public voice to anyone who has something to say.

GENERATIVE MUSIC

If you have ever mused that there might be more to digital music and sound than mixing audio loops and MIDI sequences, then generative music systems may be of interest. Composer and sound artist Tim Didymus (www.shingtactical.com) and the author explain generative music systems, and what they can do for your creativity.

Music has always been at the forefront of available technology, from the earliest, drums to the most advanced virtual instruments. Musical inspiration and compositional processes invariably relate to technological breakthroughs, and each breeds a change in behavior.

In the mid-1990s a number of people began experimenting on PCs with the idea that computers could be music and sound-generators and improvisers, and not just "reproducers." The concept of auto-composition may be challenging, but the field of generative art is becoming increasingly important to many musicians on the one hand, and Web designers, cellphone networks, and multimedia designers on the other. So what is generative music and art? In many ways, the hugely popular computer game The Sims is a generative system. Now imagine that Sims characters you create are sounds and musical ideas.

Perhaps a better analogy is to liken generative music to the process of planting seeds—growing and cultivating first individual plants, and then a garden.

You might know what seeds you have, but you can never be sure how the plants will grow—but selecting them, watching them, and tending to them is the pleasure. With generative music, you create the "seeds," (in fact, seed files) plant them, specify the conditions in which you want them to flourish, and then listen to your sound garden grow as each "plant" (a musical sequence, tone, texture, rhythm, sample, effect, or process) matures and intertwines with others you've planted.

Generative systems are not about chance; rather they can be thought of as being scalable between the sequenced form of sound reproduction on one hand, and live, improvised music on the other. We're not talking about ceding control of music composition to a microchip (unless you want to). Rather, you can compose music that evolves so that it is never quite the same each time you listen to it.

GENERATIVE MUSIC ENGINES (PC)

The best known generative music engine is Sseyo's Koan Pro, which offers many rich and complex real-time musical controllers (parameters). It is also designed to playback pre-prepared, imported MIDI sequences, to which you can ask the

computer to apply controlled mutations. The idea of the self as composer remains absolutely central—perhaps even more so, as you have to think in terms of scales of uncertainty within your music to get the best out of the process. You also allow movement into the composition—something that has been lost to a degree in the cut-and-paste culture of the sequencer. Unusually, this makes your normally passive computer receptive and active—the software is always throwing new ideas at you, and that's a valid compositional tool.

Perhaps it's inevitable in the days of increasingly programmed content that digital media will become less certain in outcome. The randomizing "Shuffle" function on your iPod is a form of generative system. You've handpicked the Playlist, you've sorted it into files, but the end result is only predictable in the sense that it is playing music you like.

GENERATIVE MUSIC AND THE WEB: KOAN PRO (PC)

How does it work?
Use the Koan system to create "seed" developer files, which store your compositional rule-set for each idea. The developer files need the software to interpret them.

Does the listener need the software?
Yes, they'll need both developer file and player. The player is the vital part, as it contains the music engine. This performs the instructions from the "seed" developer file you've planted in it.

How can this work online?
Because the developer files can be simple instruction sets for your soundcard, they are often very small and are swiftly downloadable online. Give people access to the player, and you can create a rich sound environment for them on a Web site. With larger files that use samples, MP3s, and so on, broadband connections are ideal.

What is Vector Audio?
A concept used in generative systems and an increasing number of music-making packages. If a MIDI file is a simple set of musical instructions, then a Vector Audio file builds the virtual instrument to play it.

THE BIG QUESTION

Does the fact that music is so widely available on the Web begin to devalue it?

"I do think there will probably be something of a backlash against ubiquitous computing ['ubicomp']. For example, the rise of things that are deliberately not available 24x7, anywhere, anytime, anyway. In a 'post-scarcity' world some brands will make capital out of being less easy to find. But in terms of music I think it's about accessibility. As someone once said, the future isn't about copyright, it's about access right. Also, when you talk about 'value' it depends on whether it's the economic value of the producer or the perceived value of the consumer. Yes scarcity translates into greater demand than supply, which means the people who hold the information can charge a premium for it. When you break that information monopoly the price goes down. When records were invented, did the infinitely greater number of people who could now hear a singer without having to be within physical listening range enjoy the music any less?"

Andy Hobsbawm, Internet entrepreneur

1–3. PLANTING "SEEDS" IN KOAN PRO

Creating a Koan generative music composition can be as simple or as complex as you like. When you first plant sounds into the system, you select a voice, a sample, a texture, a rhythm, a synthesizer patch, and so on. You then ask the computer to modify that patch, how it behaves, and the way it relates to other sounds and musical ideas in a whole variety of programmable ways. Next, draw in curves and control information; and also melodic and chord progression information, specifying how strictly you want these rules applied. The end result is something that you've composed, but which is also surprising, unusual, and improvisational. As Koan "seed" files can be extremely small, they are easily shared and published online. Your listener simply needs the player.

MAKE MUSIC ON YOUR CELLPHONE

"THE CELLPHONE IS THE NEW ELECTRIC GUITAR; IT IS THE CONNECTED MUSICAL INSTRUMENT FOR THE EMERGING GENERATION OF MUSIC-MAKERS, CREATIVES, AND HOBBYISTS."

Tim Cole, Bafta-Award-Winning, music software maker

"The cellphone is the new electric guitar," says Tim Cole, double-BAFTA-award-winning head of audio at the Tao Group. In this exclusive interview, Cole explains how and why he believes the cellphone may become the device of choice for music making, as well as new music consumption, sharing, and usage models."

Why do you say the cellphone is the new electric guitar?

"It is the connected mobile musical instrument for the emerging generation of music makers, 'creatives,' and hobbyests. Musicians can already create music from scratch entirely on a computer, using a sequencer, audio plugins, samples, MIDI editing, and so on. Phones are five years behind computers in terms of their computing power, but people have been making music on computers since the late 1970s.

"Phones have an extra dimension: their mobile and 'connected' elements. By 'mobile' I mean something that is handheld, like a guitar. 'Connected' means a device can be used to exchange

information in real time or offline. That information can be voice, riffs, loops, songs, or complete recordings such as podcasts. That means collaboration on a local or a remote basis, such as via Bluetooth, WiFi, or WiMAX [wireless data transfer systems], or even over the mobile network.

"miniMIXA is just one of an emerging generation of mobile music tools suites that people are using to make, mix, and remix music, build new applications, and share their creative output in our connected world."

What is the technology behind miniMIXA and how does it work?

"It's built on Tao intent, a mobile middleware platform that can run on many computing platforms—such as Windows desktops or a mobile device running Windows Mobile or Symbian [operating systems]. We chose to create a truly portable mobile music mixer so that the user didn't have to worry about what computing platform or operating system they have. "With mobile music applications you can mix MIDI, audio,

compressed audio, software-synthesizer sounds, and generative music together in any combination and then record the results as a finished track, or as a rich form of ringtone, for example. Of course, you don't have to record it—you can simply have fun in real time."

What are the creative differences in using cellphones to make music?

"The number-one device that people carry around with them is their cellphone. If their favored mobile device can make music—and I mean rich, hi-fi-quality sounds—then they can create anytime, any place. This technology has already been used by songwriters to capture ideas, and by composers to mix and build up tracks. Two composers—Drew Hemment, founder of the Futuresonic music event—and Tim Didymus have already performed live concerts using this technology on their cellphones.

"Of course, being connected means easier collaboration with others, too. What can be done comes down to interfaces, but there will always be those

---

SUBSCRIPTION-BASED MUSIC ON PHONES AND PLAYERS

Cellphone network Vodafone has a streaming music service that allows customers to create and personalize their own music "station." Vodafone Radio DJ ties in with Sony and works by allowing Vodafone customers to choose from a range of preset genre music selections (effectively playlists). By indicating a like or dislike for a song, the "station" saves your preferences and gradually builds up a playlist that reflects your taste. The service can also be accessed via PCs with a broadband connection for a subscription fee. This move reflects Microsoft's own strategy with its "Urge" service and music player, which competes for Apple's iTunes dominance with a subscription-based model rather than a fee per download.

MINIMIXA MINIMUM DEVICE REQUIREMENTS

Microsoft Windows Mobile: Smartphone 2003/5.0; Pocket PC 2002/2003/5.0

Symbian: Symbian 8 and Series 60/UIQ2.0

Windows XP/2000

(Others platforms supported include WinCE, Linux/Embedded Linux)

6MB RAM, 120MHz processor

who know how to coax the most out of it, and those who will play it like the instrument it is."

What are the wider implications of a switch to mobile music-making?

"Huge. It offers great experiences for the occasional, casual user right up to the music professional. Music consumption is changing. Fans want more interaction with bands and artists, to feel more

TECHNOLOGY BACKGROUND

Powered by the intent Sound System (iSS) from Tao Group, miniMIXA draws on the full complement of advanced audio technologies within the iSS. These software technologies include comprehensive audio and MIDI frameworks, modular synthesizer, wavetable polyphonic MIDI synthesizer, generative music engine, audio effects plugins, visualizers, and a range of codecs for standard and emerging media formats.

TIM COLE
BAFTA-award-winning head of audio, Tao Group.

SUPPORTED FILE FORMATS

SSEYO miniMIXA supports the widest range of audio and music formats, from WAV, AU, and Ogg Vorbis through to MIDI, and XMF. It also supports the SKM (SSEYO Koan Mobile), SKD (SSEYO Koan Design), and SKA (SSEYO Koan miniMIXA) formats. As well as supporting XMF-like possibilities, the XML-based SKM format allows the inclusion of synthesizer network descriptions (sound generators), effects settings, and generative music files.

This means that a mix can include material in a range of formats, and so miniMIXA is in many ways "content fluent."

**www.sseyo.com/products/
miniMIXA/index.html**

www.minimixa.com

involved. It is not a big leap to see how remixing commercially released tracks will be immensely popular. And, it is possible to see how it could become very fashionable to have your own mix of a track as a ringtone.

"For record companies, releasing music that can be remixed on cellphones will be the big opportunity for the rest of the Noughties and beyond. Certainly hobbyist, amateur, and pro musicians want to do it–and there are plenty of them in the world!"

Can you put this in the wider context of other developments in digital media?
"There is also another huge trend happening now, and that is DIY content, or what I like to call 'social media.' Users are creating and uploading/posting content they have made–be that text, pictures, videos, karaoke, or music mixes. This kind of content is even finding its way into mainstream news.

"There are already a large number of places to find the earliest forms of social media, such as blogs and podcasts, and there are many companies scrambling to try to become destinations for it by

building communities around it. Much of this content is created already on mobile devices, and the quality of it will increase as capabilities increase.

"One of the big areas for technologies like this, therefore, is for them to be extended to give greater facility to making podcasts, and also to evolve into general purpose media mixers–for example, mixing music with video clips."

How do you use it to remix tracks?
"Simply add them to the mix and use the keypad (or navkey or touchscreen if you have one) to turn them on/off. Saving keystroke recordings (mini-automated mixes), making ringtone recordings, or even saving the mix files themselves is very easy."

What else can you do with this type of technology?
"One of the things you can do with miniMIXA is to make your own microphone recordings and then add them into a music mix you have put together. When you see how easy it is to do this, it is liberating and entertaining at the same time–it could be your first mini podcast recording. You can use mixes as

personal ringtones, or DJ live from the phone. If you want to send on your mix recording, then miniMIXA (content rights permitting) presents the option to e-mail it (device dependently) when you have made it. Future versions of the software will be extended to allow other means of uploading."

ELECTROPLANKTON

ElectroPlankton is a mobile game created by Japanese artist Toshio Iwai. The game is based around ten environments where you can play around with music, create sequences, record your voice, and sample sounds.

www.electroplankton.com

"ONE OF THE BIG AREAS FOR TECHNOLOGIES LIKE THIS IS FOR THEM TO BE EXTENDED TO GIVE GREATER FACILITY TO MAKING PODCASTS, AND ALSO TO EVOLVE INTO GENERAL-PURPOSE MIXERS–FOR EXAMPLE, MIXING MUSIC WITH VIDEO CLIPS"
Tim Cole

Demo5					0:18		Stop
☰	✓	■	●	136	○	⊞	
Drum	1		(beat_beat_beat_beat_)				
Drum	2	✗					
Bass	3		(bass_		bass_		fill
Bass	4	✗					
Chord	5		(0-cho				re
Chord	6		(0-cho				
Chord	7	✗	(				
Lead	8		(riff_k	riff_k	riff_k		ch
Lead	9		(riff_k	riff_k	riff_k		
Lead	10	✗					
Custm	11	✗	(				
Custm	12	✗	(				

◀··· 🗎 ◀▶1 ◀▶2 ◀▶3 ◀▶4 🔧 ⊞

Mon_Amore			0:00	Track Volu
☰ ✓ ▶ ● 130 ○ ⊞				
▬▬	1		(beat_beat_beat_beat_)	
▬▬	2	✗	(beat_	
▬▬	3		(bass_bass_bass_bass_)	
▬▬	4	✗	(bass_	
▬▬	5		(chord chord chord chord)	
▬▬	6	✗	(chord	
▬▬	7	✗	(chord	
▬▬	8		(riff_ri riff_ri	
▬▬	9	✗	(4-riff	
▬▬	10	✗	(riff_ja	
▬▬	11		(spots spots spots)	de
▬▬	12	✗	(	

◀··· 🗎 ◀▶1 ◀▶2 ◀▶3 ◀▶4 🔧 ⊞

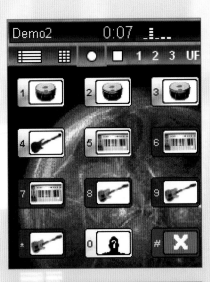

Demo2　0:07　.‖..
☰ ⊞ ● ■ 1 2 3 UF

Tap when done	0:21	Key Function
1 Keys - Normal		
2 Keys - Select Content		
3 Keys - Track FX		
4 Keys - Mic Record		
5 Master Volume		
6 Track Volumes		
7 MIXApaks - Tempo/Pitch		
8 Stop		
9 Equaliser		
0 Visualiser		
Show Button Pictures: Yes		

Club　0:00　Equaliser FX

1	2	3	4	5

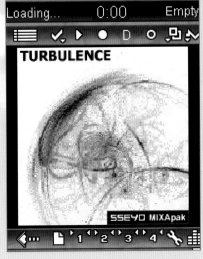

Loading...　0:00　Empty
☰ ✓ ▶ ● D ○ ⊞ ♪

TURBULENCE

SSEYO MIXApak

◀··· 🗎 ◀▶1 ◀▶2 ◀▶3 ◀▶4 🔧 ⊞

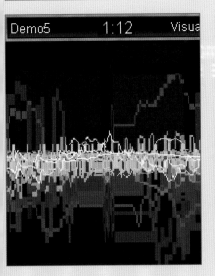

Demo5　1:12　Visua

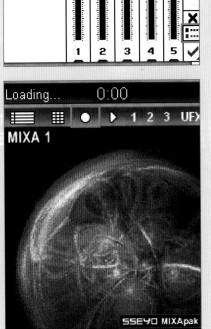

Loading...　0:00
☰ ⊞ ● ▶ 1 2 3 UFX

MIXA 1

SSEYO MIXApak

THE POCKET MUSIC ENGINE
Cellphone screens showing some of the deep functionality hidden in this apparently simple program. Your phone's connection to the cellphone network and ability to handle different media types mean a promising future for mobile devices in creating digital music, sound, and related media.

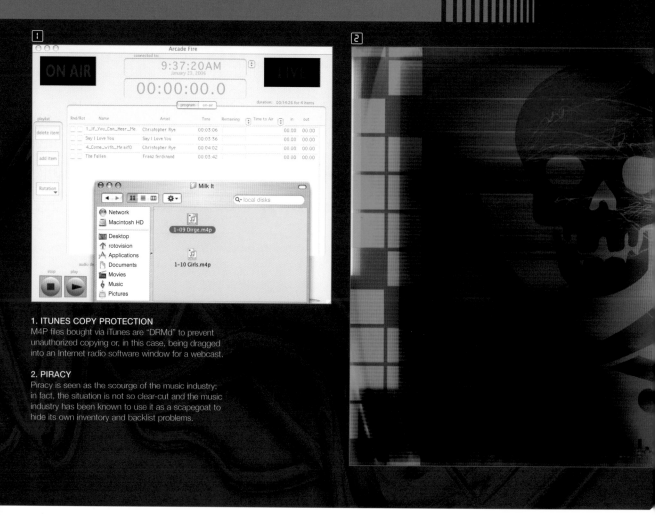

1. ITUNES COPY PROTECTION
M4P files bought via iTunes are "DRMd" to prevent unauthorized copying or, in this case, being dragged into an Internet radio software window for a webcast.

2. PIRACY
Piracy is seen as the scourge of the music industry: in fact, the situation is not so clear-cut and the music industry has been known to use it as a scapegoat to hide its own inventory and backlist problems.

DIGITAL RIGHTS, FAIR USE, AND THE FUTURE OF DIGITAL CONTENT

Many of us have grown up in a culture of free downloading—free in the sense of low or zero cost, and free in the sense of unlocked and able to move at will. Clearly, the latter is what many of us want. Music has always been portable, in the sense that songs stored on a physical format can be played wherever there's a machine on which to play them. Despite this, the error that some in the music industry made not long ago was to attempt to impose the same usage and licensing limitations on music that applied to desktop software applications, for example—such as "locking it up" on a single device. Many critics saw that as imposing restrictions on music consumption that had never existed before—something that was always going

to anger law-abiding consumers and please opportunistic pirates, making file-sharing services seem like a desirable alternative to both.

One curious aspect of the digital age is the phenomenon of limitless choice. When this was combined with pressure from industry to restrict portability, the result was tension in the market for digital music that was only relieved by consumers searching for a way around the industry's legal obstructions. Law-abiding consumers don't like to be thought of as criminals.

The model by which the music industry sells the rights to consume its intellectual property had for a century and a half been based on shifting units. In other words, its business model, legal

framework, and distribution network was all about selling goods in a physical format—and then reselling them in a different format. In the Internet age, this idea met its mismatch: digital content could be "stolen" an infinite number of times while still leaving the owner in possession of the original article. Pop music was, and remains, uniquely suited to filesharing and digital downloading, since it is available in the byte-sized chunks of three- and four-minute songs (a partial artifact of the analog age).

The music industry—80% of which is just four multinationals—for a long time saw filesharing as a catastrophic failure of policing. Of more concern, it saw it as a technology problem that could only be remedied by more technology. However, evidence from consumers suggested that

the music industry and other industries that faced the on/off digital future were suffering from a new phenomenon: catastrophic success, combined with an outmoded business model. Arguably, the original Napster and other filesharing services had actually saved the music industry billions of dollars in R&D (research and development costs) by proving and building demand for the download market we enjoy today.

So what is DRM? Digital Rights Management (DRM) is a generic term for those security technologies that govern the licensing terms embedded in digital content (such as music bought via download services such as iTunes, and on some CDs). It authorizes you and your device to use what you've paid for. In recent years, DRM has occasionally been used as an umbrella term for all trust-assurance technologies, from content authentication applied at the mastering stage in DVD authoring suites, through digital watermarking processes, to the systems that deliver paid-for digital content to an authorized PC, Mac, cellphone, or media player. To some people, however, it's also become a means of limiting their freedom to share things—not to mention tracking content use and invading privacy.

Put another way, DRM can be regarded as the application of technology to a company's policy objectives—and some people dislike certain companies, and therefore dislike the technology they use to do business. The concept of fair use of digital content (and, in Europe at least, of personal privacy) has also presented a challenge to many DRM systems. This is partly because fair use conventions are established case by case, and partly because local conventions among individuals and cultures are hard to turn into computer code.

However, DRM isn't going to go away. It's central to the way companies want to deliver licensed digital music, video, games, and multimedia content to the rest of us online, on our mediacenter PCs and Macs, and also on next-generation optical storage disks such as Blu-Ray disks and HD-DVDs—all of which are part of what's called the "digital home." As digital content creation, consumption, and services increasingly become one and the same thing, it's inevitable that DRM will become proactive and embedded into more

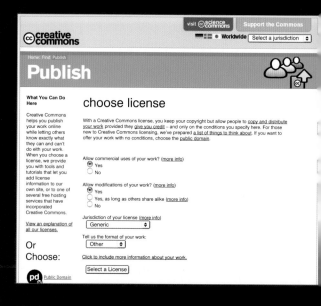

CREATIVE COMMONS
This licensing scheme is proving popular on the Internet as a means of encouraging sharing and fair use of files, while maintaining a degree of copyright ownership. However, many broadcasters don't understand the licenses.

and more services and technology specifications (just as it has with Apple's iTunes and the iPod). It will become the invisible bridge between the content, the format, the platform, and the payment mechanism—whether some of us like it or not. On cellphone networks, DRM schemes will encourage us to distribute content to our friends and receive loyalty or incentive points.

The cellphone environment in particular has thrown up the phenomenon of the ringtone, which signals the direction that the mainstream digital publishing industry and DRM systems may take. Ringtones suggest that content will evolve into a variety of new forms that are no longer restricted to audio content—amalgamations of music, video clips, animations, games, do-it-yourself remixes of commercial songs, advertisements, interactive elements, incentive schemes, and vector-audio elements.

At the other end of the spectrum, it's likely that as high-definition content becomes available on storage media like Blu-Ray disks and HD-DVDs, the music industry will see "the album" being reinvented as a mix of master-quality audio, plus videos and animations. If this happens, MP3 downloads will take on a relationship with albums that is similar to today's ringtones' relationship to the songs that inspired them—poor-quality imitations of the original.

Companies such as Apple, Sony, and Microsoft are in the vanguard of merging content creation and consumption. Buying into their visions turns all of us into content creators (which is why you're reading this book)—and that means growing opportunities for any individual to license his or her work securely online with the same advantages that mainstream publishing and distribution supply. Consumer DRM portals offering

the chance to make money by selling your work to the world are already appearing. One organization that shares this view is MUDDA (www.mudda.org), the Magnificent Union of Digitally Downloading Artists. This is another venture by the musician and entrepreneur Peter Gabriel, whose track record includes co-founding Europe's largest business-to-business music distribution service, OD2. MUDDA takes as its departure point the notion that traditional licensing structures are unworkable online and seeks a new approach to the music industry that frees content creators from restrictive and punitive contracts, allowing people to treat their own works as a service rather than as part of a packaged format.

At the consumer end of the market, a venture called Brightskies (www.brightskies.com) is one of many portals allowing unsigned acts to license,

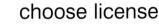

✓ Select a jurisdiction
Argentina
Australia
Austria
Belgium
Brazil
Bulgaria
Canada
Chile
Mainland China
Colombia
Croatia
Hungary
Denmark
Finland
France
Germany
Ireland
Israel
Italy
Japan
Jordan
Korea
Malaysia
Malta
Mexico
Netherlands
Nigeria
Philippines
Poland

Publish

What You Can Do Here

Creative Commons helps you publish your work online while letting others know exactly what they can and can't do eith your work. When you choose a license, we provide you with tools and tutorials that let you add license information to our own site, or to one of several free hosting services that have incorporated Creative Commons.

View an explanation of all our licenses.

Or Choose:

choose license

With a Creative Commons license, you keep your copyright but allow people your work provided they give you credit – and only on the conditions you new to Creative Commons licensing, we've prepared a list of things to think offer your work with no conditions, choose the public domain.

Allow commercial uses of your work? (more info)
- ● Yes
- ○ No

Allow modifications of your work? (more info)
- ● Yes
- ○ Yes, as long as others share alike (more info)
- ○ No

Jurisdiction of your license (more info)
[Generic ⬍]

Tell us the format of your work:
[Other ⬍]

Click to include more information about your work.

---

rights-manage, and content-protect their works securely, earning money from each download of their work.

Others take a more community-spirited approach to licensing. Creative Commons (www.creativecommons.org) is an organization that aims to create a layer of "reasonable copyright" within licenses, under the principle that "some rights are reserved." It aims to encourage the sharing of different types of material—including music, video, photography, coursework, and even speech—but within reasonable licensing restrictions that do not neglect the creator of the work.

In this way, the organization forms a philosophical bridge between the opposing forces of the proprietary copyright industries and the so-called "copyleft" community, which believes that the notion of intellectual property has no place in the online world.

The organization says, "We use private rights to create public goods: creative works set free for certain uses. Like the free software and open-source movements, our ends are cooperative and community-minded, but our means are voluntary and libertarian. We work to offer creators a best-of-both-worlds way to protect their works while encouraging certain uses of them."

2 ▼ Library - MuteNoiseToy1.fla
152 items

Name	Kind	Use Count	Linkage
SoundsNew	Folder		
Dream On 1_...	Sound	-	Export: mute1
Dream On 6 0...	Sound	-	Export: mute2
Dream On 60...	Sound	-	Export: mute3
erasure 2 001...	Sound	-	Export: mute4
laibach laiwer...	Sound	-	Export: mute6
LUKEALEX1 0...	Sound	-	Export: mute5
maths 001.aif	Sound	-	Export: mute7

3

Sounds5	Folder	
SoundsNew	Folder	
Dream		
Dream		
Dream		
erasu		
laibac		
LUKEA		
maths		
moby		

Rename
Duplicate
Move to New Folder
Delete
Edit
Edit with…
Properties…

4
```
function mysoundobj(idname) {
    mysoundobj = new Sound(this);
    mysoundobj.attachSound(idname);
    mysoundobj.start(0, 0);
}
mysoundobj("mute1");
```

Just as worlds are colliding in terms of live DJ and VJ experiences, with artists blending digital moving graphics with music and sound in real time, so even the normally static, print-based world of graphic design is also moving into other realms of the senses. Paul Farrington of Studio Tonne is perhaps the best-known person rewriting the definition of what it means to be a graphic designer when digital media collide, mix, and morph on the desktop, and when graphics are just as likely to be consumed online, on iPods or cellphones, or within video ringtones as they are on the page.

In recent years, Studio Tonne has been commissioned by multimillion-selling artists such as Moby and Depeche Mode to play with the interface between digital music and sound and other media. In this section

Paul Farrington helps us explore how to use music and sound within digital animation program Flash. We'll then have a look at the workshop process behind two interactive projects using digital music and sound in Flash—two online sound toys, one for Mute Records, and the other for the band Depeche Mode.

BUILDING A SIMPLE SOUND TOY
1. The brief
Music label Mute Records invited designer Paul Farrington to concept-design a series of "noise toys"—online interactive virtual toys that blend music and sound with graphics and animation—that would go into the "Distract" area of Mute Records' Web site. The brief was that the toys simply had to be fun to play with. Farrington says, "For me I have always designed sound toys that allow the user

to build a piece of music from scratch. Most of the toys are like remixers and sequencers that allow music to be visualized and played with.

"The design of this particular toy works differently in that it plays all the samples as soon the toy is loaded, so the user then has to turn off all the sounds—in other words mute them, a play on words with the name of the label."

Mute provided Farrington with a couple of CDs that contained a variety of tracks from Mute's back catalog: Plastikman, Depeche Mode, Erasure, Nick Cave, and Speedy J.

2. The Flash build
The toy was originally designed in Freehand MX, and then these elements were rebuilt in Flash. "The design

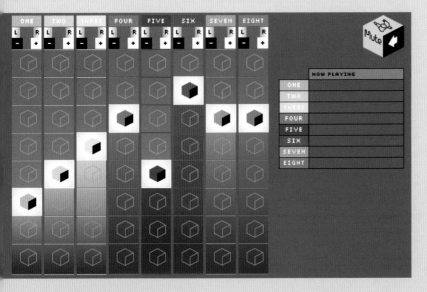

1. **LOADING SCREEN**
The screen that users see as the toy loads up.

2. **THE FLASH SOUND LIBRARY**
All the sounds in the project, with associated links.

3. **LINKING IT UP**
Assign sounds to an action script within Flash.

4. **CODING THE CLIP TO PLAY**
Tells the clip to play once.

5. **THE SAMPLE LANE**
Where users can play with samples in separate lanes.

6. **TRIGGERING THE SAMPLES**
Add audio to a frame in the timeline, or link library sounds to a script.

7. **WARPING IN ABLETON LIVE**
Beatmatching samples before importing into Flash.

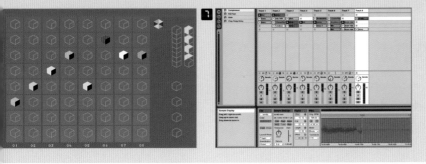

developed from something that was very simple and in black and white (as in on/off) to something that was much more in keeping with the Mute logo identity," says Farrington. "It also developed visually and functionally through the programming process, which was as playful as the toy itself."

The structure of the toy is made up from six elements, one HTML, and the others .swf (Flash) files.

1. index.html, the file that will be read by the browser.
2. loading.swf, the loading screen.
3. MuteNoiseToy.swf, the container that houses the design.
4. MuteNoiseToy1.swf, sample bank 1.
5. MuteNoiseToy2.swf, sample bank 2.
6. MuteNoiseToy3.swf, sample bank 3.

3. The sound toy's elements
■ Loading screen
This screen appears as the toy loads and shows a visual progression.

■ Main screen
When the toy is loaded the screen displays 32 cubes that each play sounds when the red diamonds pass through them. There are four lanes with eight samples in each. You can add new playheads, which means that a sample can be played more than once in a lane. Clicking a cube results in that sample not being played (it mutes the sample), click it again and it will reactivate the sample. You can turn all samples on or off in a lane.

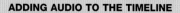

ADDING AUDIO TO THE TIMELINE

1. Open Flash and also the folder(s) where you keep your audio files—for example, WAVs or AIFFs prepared in a music or sound application.

2. Either drag audio files onto the Flash work area, or go to File > Import and click through to your destination folder.

3. Go to Insert > Layer to create a layer for the new audio element in your animation. Name this something appropriate, e.g. "Sound."

3. Choose the point in the movie where you want to trigger each sound file. Click on that keyframe in the timeline once to bring the cursor to that position. Click on the same point in the Sound layer. Now go to Insert > Keyframe.

4. Doubleclick at the same point in the Sound layer and choose the Sound tab under Frame Properties. Click and hold the arrow next to "Sound – None" to see the sound file. Drag the blue bar to your sound file. And make it a Sync Event. You can also add effects at this stage, and also change the volume settings by dragging the squares in the Sound window up or down.

5. When you Export your finished movie, you will be prompted to choose the Audio stream type and sample rate of the audio, and also any (data) compression algorithms you wish to apply. If it's vital to go for the top audio quality, preview the Movie in your browser to ensure that the files do not take too long to download.

■ **Flash and generative music and sound**
The plugin version of the Koan generative music system, via its API (application programming interface), can send out events that can be used to drive generative Flash animations from generative music files.

Some Flash animation examples are here:
http://www.sseyo.com/showcase/flash-demos/index.html

4. The music and sound elements
Farrington outlines his creative process. "I first used Ableton Live to preview the sounds by dragging them one by one into the vertical preview tracks in the software. I then cut up all of the samples, morphing and beatmatching them in Live [using the Warp dialog] so they all shared the same tempo and sample length. The result is that when the various samples are triggered, the beat- and tempo matching is tight. All the samples were saved as AIFF files and then imported into Flash, where each automatically gets placed in the library.

"When creating a Flash movie, Flash exports audio in an MP3 format—which helps with file size and with your movie playing smoothly. You change the quality (bitrate) of the MP3 format when you publish your movie—so it's best to play around with the audio you're using and how it feels at different settings.

"When using audio in Flash there are two ways that sound can be played: one is to add audio to a Frame on the main timeline [see box, left], but my preferred option is to keep sounds in the Library and link to them with action script. As this toy used 32 samples in each bank, I decided to link to my sounds in the library."

To link to sounds from the library first choose a sound file that you want to use, click it and hold the mouse down and then select Linkage. In the Linkage Properties window you need to give it a unique identifier—e.g. mute1, mute2, mute3 etc.

5. Programming the sound to play
Farrington explains how he put the finishing touches to this simple toy. "By using the above method I was able to have the sounds play when the red diamond passed through a graphic cube. For this I used the code [image 4, previous page]. This code allows for a sound to be activated and played once only."

http://www.mute.com/distract/noisetoy

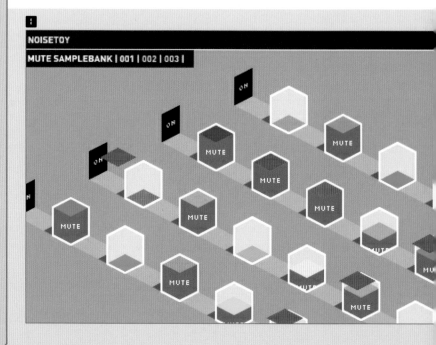

NOISETOY

MUTE SAMPLEBANK | 001 | 002 | 003 |

PAUL FARRINGTON'S THREE STEPS TO DIGITAL CREATIVITY

"My work is more than just creating images that simply illustrate music. I create visuals that are directly generated by sound, or which generate sound themselves. These pieces—sound toys, installations, and live music visuals—link noise and image in a manner that renders them completely inextricable. In each of my projects, I adopt a system through which to match the audible to the visual."

1. Inspiration
"Early on in my career I was always interested in how music was packaged and how it sounded, as for me the physical links between a printed record cover and a piece of music was never enough. What interests me is how you can interact with music and graphic animations to create new spaces for music to be played with and experienced. For Studio Tonne music has always been the passion that drives our work to date, which has taken us to find new and interesting ways in which music can be experienced on the Web and in other digital spaces."

2. Using the real world in the virtual
"[During my studies] I experimented with theremins, which are physical musical instruments that generate tones in response to movement. In my final year show at the RCA [the Royal Academy of Arts, London], I created a space that contained three theremins, each connected to a computer screen. As they approached the piece, visitors became aware that their movement in the vicinity of these instruments controlled both the sound in the space and the images onscreen. In other words, the project allowed the user to create music, which then resulted in animations that responded to the music. It was a physical sound toy. That process then became a virtual one."

3. Technology
"Before anything is programmed my designs always start off in a sketchbook while I listen to the music. The second stage is to design simple 2D interfaces and try to get an idea of how they will work, function, behave, and be played with. Then I start to play with the audio, cutting-up samples, stretching sample lengths, pitchshifting sequences, and so on, and then create a bank of samples that I can work with."

■ Software
Design: Macromedia Flash; Director; Macromedia Freehand.

Music and Sound: Reaktor 5 [a Native Instruments soft synth and synth modeler]; Absynth [a Native Instruments synth]; Ableton Live; Logic Audio.

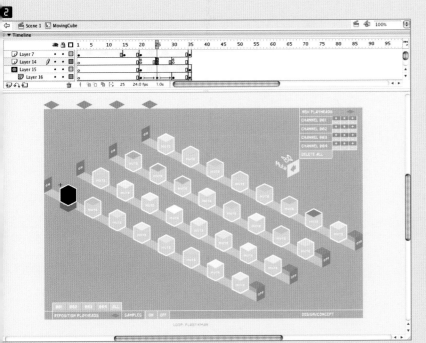

1. THE FINAL TOY
The final build of the Mute Noise Toy, showing the optional sample banks.

2. ACTION SCRIPTS
Here the action script is triggered to play when the cube is activated.

DEPECHE MODE SOUND TOY

Paul Farrington explains the genesis of his collaboration with the band Depeche Mode and its label Mute Records to create another Flash-based, online sound toy. "This was for a Depeche Mode Remix album in 2004. Mute Records provided me with a CD of samples that had been taken from the album in an MP3 format, and then it was up to me to decide on how the toy would work and behave.

"I created two interfaces (Amateur and Professional), which allow for the user to create simple mixes at first, by selecting colored sample icons and placing them into a standard music sequencer grid. The user then can build up a song and save it online. But visitors to the site also have access to a second set of samples that are cut to varying lengths, so the user then has to take the time and trouble to make a more complex mix work. For me, when I have tried to DJ with vinyl it's never that easy, so I wanted to try to make something digital that was a similar experience in this regard—you have to work at the mix; it's not all done for you."

Elements of the sound toy

Farrington explains how the individual elements of this Depeche Mode project were put together. For instructions on how to build a sound toy yourself and also work with music and sound within Flash, please see the preceding spreads in this section.

User interface: elements

Screen 1: Audio format/Loading screen
The initial screen asks the user to select a toy based on their Internet connection speed. Farrington had a bank of 64 samples. "We saved three separate versions of the samples by simply using i-Tunes, as this gives you the ability to import audio files at different bit rates."

- **High Quality: 192kBps**
- **Medium Quality: 128kBps**
- **Low Quality: 64kBps**

When the mouse rolls over a format quality, information is shown that tells the user how long a download would take on both Broadband and Modem connections.

Screen 2: Loading Screen

The loading screen was designed so that it reflected how samples needed to be placed into the toy, and secondly spelled out the word LOADING.

Screen 3: Main interface

Once the toy has loaded, the screen is split into various sections:

- **Sequencer**

The sequencer is split into eight lanes and a maximum of 16 samples can be placed in any one lane. To add sounds to the sequencer the user has first to select a sample from the Samples window, and then click an empty space in the sequencer. This method allows the user to visualize where samples are placed and onto which lanes, so when a mix is being created the user can build a graphic representation of their creation.

- **Global mixer**

This panel allows the user to control various aspects of the mix:

Stop/Play
Speed (Tempo)
Level (Volume)
Pan

- **Track mixer**

As well as being able to control all eight lanes of the sequencer, the user can also individually control each lane independently of the main mixer. This allows for each lane to have its own setting. For example, if the main mixer's speed is set to 30, the user can change the speed of Lane 1—making it faster or slower—which allows samples to move out of phase and alignment with each other, creating interesting audio effects.

- **Samples**

Each sample is labeled with its own track title, and is also color-coded.

Sequencer patterns

This area allows the user to draw pictures and then save them to the sequencer. This panel allows for mixes to be made that are free from any fixed viewpoint of making music—and allows for the user to draw patterns, write their name, and so on, and then apply this pattern to the sequencer. This then becomes part of the main mix.

MOBY HOTEL SOUND TOY

"On the mobyhotel site (www.mobyhotel.com) there were a lot of deadlines as the label [Mute Records] has prerelease dates, so every week was intense. I have a very good client and we work very well together—and luckily we both share the same passion for how things will be created.

"Because of copyright issues, music is quite a difficult thing to have control over [online]. At the start of the Moby project, because of the fact he was releasing a new album, I wasn't allowed to use any audio from the main album, so I had to use samples from an Ambient album he was releasing at the same time, and then as singles and tracks were released I was given more leeway about how I could use the audio."

- On the Moby site, music is presented in various formats: Windows Media, Real Audio, and embedded into Flash movies.

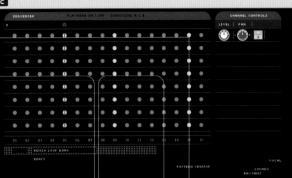

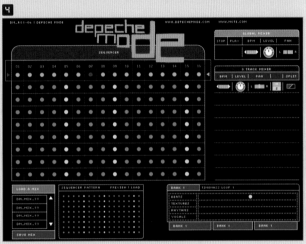

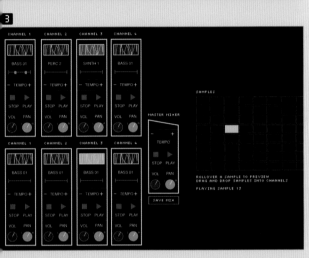

1–4 EVOLUTION
Various sequencer-like
builds of the sound toy.

5. THE FINAL TOY
The toy showing the
sequencer controls and
pattern interface.

AUDIO FOR VIDEO AND MOVIES

MUSIC AND SOUND IN MOVIES AND VIDEO

SOUND IN VIDEO SOFTWARE

VIDEO LOCATION SOUND

MUSIC FOR LOW-BUDGET MOVIES AND VIDEOS

SOUND DESIGN

VIDEO SYNCHING

SURROUND SOUND

The relationship between music, sound, movies, and video began at commercial cinema's birth, with live musicians–pianists, organists, and sometimes whole orchestras–accompanying movies as they were projected, dramatizing the onscreen action in a way that told audiences (used to watching live theater and vaudeville) what to feel. Sometimes sound effects and narration were provided live in the theater by actors employed by the cinemas.

In 1926, the motion picture *Don Juan* was the first movie with a prerecorded (but unsynchronized) musical soundtrack. In 1928, *The Jazz Singer* became the first "talkie" with synchronized dialog and songs, and in the same year Walt Disney's *Steamboat Willie* introduced Mickey Mouse to the world in the first movie to have a complete soundtrack (dialog, music, and sound effects) recorded in post-production. The original *King Kong* (1933) terrorized audiences with the first notable use of sound design, using multilayered sound effects and varying tape speeds to create Kong's supersized roar–techniques that predate Peter Jackson's remake by over 70 years. In 1940, Disney's orchestral tour de force, *Fantasia*, introduced many techniques that we think of as recent innovations: multitrack recording, stereo panning, and the use of optical sound recorders. To synchronize them, Disney pioneered the use in movies of the "click track," or timecode, which remains standard in your desktop music software. Throw in Dolby, THX, IMAX, and the emerging worlds of digital 3D projection and you are in the present, but with only subtle evolutions to the pioneering work of the early 20th century.

Of course, during cinema's formative years many techniques were developed to escape the limitations of available technology. For example, it was often easier to create naturalistic sounds artificially in the studio rather than attempt to record them on location and synchronize them with actors' voices. That remains true today, but you can use your digital music and sound software to create sounds that are "bigger than life," and which add new dimensions to video.

When making short movies and videos on zero to low budgets, the challenges in creating a professional soundtrack can be enormous. Poorly recorded location sound, voice distortion, cheap audio effects and hardware, noisy outdoor scenes, and no money for a professional audio dub are just some of the issues that can arise at any stage in the process.

"Creating great sound for your own movies and videos is often an area that is overlooked compared to the visuals, because a lot of first-time directors think that visuals rule over everything else," says freelance movie and video editor Gary Miller, whose own short movies have won him festival awards in the US and UK. "If you don't try to get the best possible sound both creatively and technically you are selling your work short. From my own experience the best way to learn about sound is to try and gain an overall understanding of the process from pre- to post-production. From my [video, movie, documentary, and TV] editing background I had an understanding of music and sound editing–or at least I thought I did.

But I discovered that the processes involved in creating a soundtrack were much more involved."

The main areas of soundtracks for short movies and videos are:

- overall sound design
- location sound recording, including dialog
- sound effects
- the musical score.

In this section, we're going to examine each in turn, plus the technologies, techniques, and inspiration behind them.

LR:000002

FN.73 9696 5579+12   02:03:38:02.

IMPORT VIDEO FOOTAGE
Bring video into your audio and music suite...

WORK ON THE TIMELINE
Synchronize it with music and sound...

APPLY FULL AUDIO PROCESSING
EQ your soundttrack and apply effects.

AVID XPRESS
The "cutdown" version of AVID's professional suite, affordable to some home budgets.

Creating and editing music and sound within video software is an increasingly exciting area for several reasons. First, some of the desktop video NLE (non-linear editing) suites are made by the same manufacturers as some of the best music and sound applications–Apple, Adobe, AVID/Digidesign, and Sony. That means well-integrated technology.

Second, many desktop video-editing applications open an upgrade path to truly professional equipment, such as the full AVID video-editing suite. This means you can acquire the skills to set you on the road to a professional career.

Third, entry-level video-editing software is now standard on most PCs and Macs, so home family videos and movies can share some of the production values of professional work–something that would

have been impossible just a few years ago. Fourth, you can work with video within many music and sound software, such as Logic, Cubase, and CoolEdit, while many video apps such as Adobe Premiere, Apple Final Cut Pro, and Steinberg's Nuendo video/broadcast application incorporate some of the same tools and effects as their audio siblings (Cubase is built on the Nuendo engine.) There is enormous creative potential up for grabs, and no barriers to taking part.

TIMELINES
All video-editing software works on the same principle as most music and sound-creation tools, namely a scrolling timeline onto which you place video files, control events, effects, and audio files, and then manage the relationship between each of these events, which are represented in graphical form.

TECHNOLOGY OPTIONS
Sony's Vegas video software is good enough to be used solely for audio production, offering unlimited audio tracks (depending on your processor, RAM, and free disk space), 24-bit audio recording to sampling rates as high as 192kHz (depending on your soundcard), punch-in recording, 5.1 surround mixing, and effects automation. It also offers customizable, real-time audio effects including EQ, reverb, delay, and so on–facilities that rival Logic Express and other affordable tools in terms of their audio capabilities. Vegas also supports VST audio plugins.

Apple's Soundtrack Pro is the soundtrack-editing companion to its Final Cut Pro video software, and includes effects directly ported in from Logic Pro, plus more than 5,000 specially selected loops

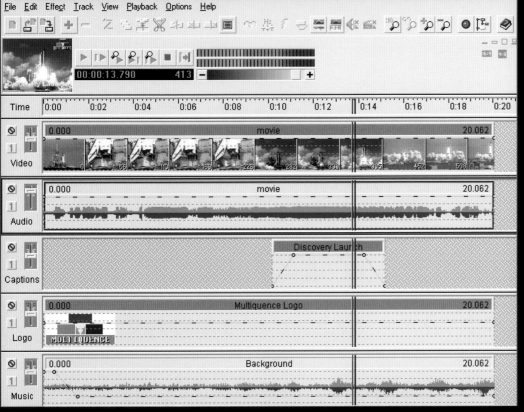

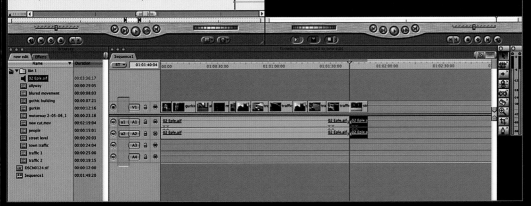

1-2 WORKING REGIME
When editing music and sound within video suites, you'll find the same basic functionality and concepts as you do in your music or audio sequencer.

3-5 SOUNDTRACK PRO
Editing loops and sounds on the timeline; editing the spectral frequency of sound; and browsing for loops of sound effects—just like in Garageband and Logic.

of movie sound effects. Among the effects is Logic's Space Designer plugin, which allows you to create precise virtual spaces and ambiences, from cathedrals to basement rooms—useful for applying to any looped dialog, for example (see page 146 for more on dialog recording).

You also get all the features you would expect from an audio application, including multitrack mixing and external control surface support. You can send video from Final Cut Pro directly into Soundtrack Pro. Final Cut Pro itself provides 24 channels of 24-bit audio at a sampling rate of 96kHz.

In recent years, Adobe has moved toward bundling separate applications into creative suites, recognizing that the boundaries between media are falling, and that people increasingly want to share work between different applications. Adobe's full Production

Studio suite is beyond many budgets, but individual applications include its Adobe Premiere video suite (available in Pro and consumer variations) and Audition (soundtrack creation tool). The latter allows you to mix an unlimited number of tracks in a low-latency environment with ASIO support. Another ingredient in the suite is the Encore DVD authoring package—although you can create DVDs directly from the Premiere timeline.

AVID, which has become a byword for professional video editing, is also available to consumers in a cutdown, desktop version (which, like Pro Tools, comes with integrated desktop hardware). AVID Xpress interfaces with Pro Tools LE and M-Powered, so for a relatively small outlay you can purchase a quality video editor, a video-editing hardware controller, professional sound tools, and an integrated audio interface for the cost of a new computer.

SOUND IN THE SIMPLEST TOOLS
In Apple's iMovie application (part of OS X and iLife), the working methodology is simple: dump all of your files into the "Bin," including captured video clips, audio files (such as location sound, music files, dialog, and library sound effects), and transitions between video clips. Then simply drag files from the Bin onto the timeline.

To add music and narration to your video first turn off the pre-existing audio you may have captured in-camera with your original footage. Clicking the Audio icon will display the contents of your iTunes library, into which you can load all of your audio clips—which might be in WAV, AIFF, MP3, or other formats.

Drag the playhead along the timeline to the spot where you want the music to start, then hit the Place at Playhead button. You can add narration directly by

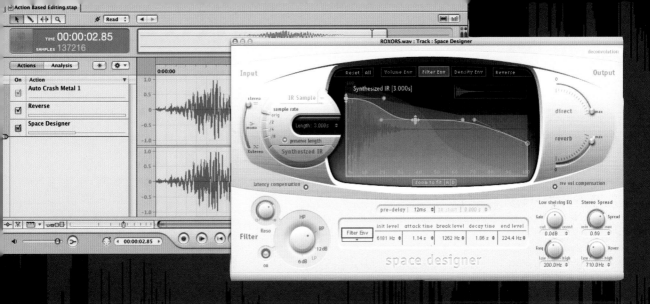

ROXORS.wav : Track : Space Designer

6. SOUNDTRACK PRO
Apple's video soundtrack suite includes the Space
Designer plugin, from Logic Pro.

7. AVID MOJO
This portable FireWire interface allows you to record
audio and video on location, and in the studio.

simply activating a new audio track and
hitting record, using a mic connected to
your soundcard or breakout box. This
might be a good strategy, as you could
then export the audio into your audio-
editing package and fine-tune it, EQ it,
remove noise, and perhaps add
additional audio processing. As long as
you don't alter the overall length of the
file, then importing it back into your
video timeline after editing will leave the
audio file in synch.

In iMovie you can adjust the audio levels
in the same manner as you can apply
control curves in Logic using the Pen
tool. Go to View > Select Audio
Waveforms > Show Clip Volume Levels.
The waveform displays the peaks and
troughs of the audio, while the black line
through the middle represents the
volume. Drag the line up or down for an
overall increase or decrease. Alternatively,
click at different spots on the line to

make pegs appear. Drag these pegs up
and down and the volume line between
them will adjust accordingly.

Movie Maker is the Microsoft Windows
equivalent of iMovie. The principles of
working with audio are nearly the same
as in iMovie—indeed, the basic principles
apply to working with audio in all video
suites. To add audio go to Import Audio
or Music from the menu to the left of the
screen. The files should now appear in
the Collections window, and can be
dragged onto the audio track.

AN OLD-TIME CLAPPERBOARD
A simple aid to synching sound and movie or video footage.

Welcome to the real world. If you are working on an ambitious production rather than simply editing together your own video footage, then recording location sound well, including dialog and natural atmospheres, is a must.

In movies it is sometimes impractical to use location recordings of what the actors say on set because of noisy or difficult locations. In these cases, actors can repeat the lines in a recording studio after the movie has been edited–a process called "looping," or automated dialog replacement (ADR). For more on these, turn to page 146 and the interview with Academy Award nominated movie and sound editor, Kant Pan.

There are a whole range of less technical drawbacks when recording sound digitally on location, such as on a laptop or a digital recorder. Workflow and file management are vital factors. "On one location shoot the sound recordist recorded the sound directly into his laptop–which seemed incredibly convenient," says video editor and moviemaker Gary Miller. "However, with so many soundfiles with similar names representing different takes it was only a matter of time until one got deleted. Whether it was a finger slipping onto the Delete key, or giving a file the same name as another, it lost me the scene."

"THE 'WILHELM SCREAM' SOUND EFFECT THAT WAS ORIGINALLY RECORDED FOR THE 1951 MOVIE, *DISTANT DRUMS*, HAS BEEN USED IN HUNDREDS OF DIFFERENT MOVIES SINCE, INCLUDING EVERY *STAR WARS* EPISODE"

LOCATION SOUND
Consider using a small mixer to manage lots of different audio feeds on location.

YOUR LOCATION SOUND MENTOR

■ If recording sound separately onto a laptop, plan your file management at the outset and ensure you name all of your digital files accessibly and intuitively.

■ Have your sound recordist capture the ambient location sound of any location so that it can be blended under the scene in the audio edit. If you're doing this yourself, try to record enough ambient sound to play under an entire scene and add it in software at the editing stage on your desktop or laptop. In an emergency loop a shorter segment.

■ The audience expects certain sounds from an environment. There is nothing to beat hearing the sound of the real location, as opposed to one from a sound library.

■ Many "library" sounds (thunder, screams) are recognizable from movies and TV shows and can detract from the reality of a scene. The "Wilhelm Scream" library sound was originally recorded for the 1951 movie *Distant Drums*, and later accompanied the shooting of Private Wilhelm in the 1953 movie *The Charge at Feather River*. It features in every *Star Wars* episode, and hundreds of other movies.

■ If you have a digital video camera (DV cam), then you can record sound via the onboard microphone. The mic might be integral to the camera, or mounted over the lens.

■ Most DV cams record sound in stereo using the same technology that CD recorders and soundcards use, PCM. However, Dolby Digital 5.1 Creator is available on some models, allowing in-camera surround sound recording.

■ Dolby Digital Creator requires less data than stereo PCM, resulting in savings in disk space, allowing you to store higher-quality video by assigning a higher data rate to the video.

■ If you are working with a filmmaker, it's vital you discuss the use of surround sound before the final mix.

CAPTURING SOUND ON, AND FROM, VIDEO CAMERAS
■ Depending on the quality of your onboard mic, you might benefit from purchasing an external mic if you need professional-quality sound from location recording. However, not all digital camcorders have an external mic socket.

■ It makes sense to buy a camera that includes a headphone socket, as headphones are vital tools for monitoring what the mic is picking up on location.

■ To avoid recording the sound of the wind hitting the mic, make sure you use a foam-rubber shield over the front of the mic.

■ Some cameras have a Wind-cut function to reduce wind noise, but this often involves switching to mono sound recording. You could try limiting the signal to avoid sudden peaks.

■ Expensive, highly sensitive vocal mics that are built for the recording studio are easily damaged. Consider a rugged, basic unidirectional mic with a decent frequency range.

■ Check whether your camera can phantom power any mic that needs a low voltage to make it work.

■ Remember to consider the polar patterns of any mic you use for location recording work—e.g. a supercardioid mic for picking up sound from in front, but also ambient sound from behind.

■ "Shotgun" mics pick up sound only from directly in front, and are mounted above the lens on some DV cams.

■ Lavalier mics are the ones you see clipped on to television newsreaders' lapels. They are extremely useful for accurately recording speech in interviews or documentary-style work.

■ If you have access to a specialist home studio equipment supplier, ask them about radio mics. These contain a small built-in transmitter—or connect to a transmitter pack that you wear in your pocket—and you'll also get a separate receiver station that you can connect to your camera or soundcard. Radio mics give you much greater freedom of movement without worrying about leads and connections on location.

■ Remember, any strongly (sound-) reflective location ambience may be impossible to remove from your recording later, unless you've recorded the sound source and any ambient reflections (echoes and reverb) separately.

■ The most important rule for good location sound is to get as close as possible to the source, otherwise you may have trouble isolating it from the ambient sound.

■ One option for getting close to a sound is to use a boom. Fix your directional mic securely on the end of one and hold it out of shot directly above the sound source.

■ Listen carefully through headphones for unwanted background noises (airplanes, the hum of electrical devices and lights) that may be picked up by your microphone.

■ You can add to your location sound "in camera" by using the Audio Dub function. Ordinarily, DV cam records 16-bit audio onto two channels. By switching this to 12-bit, however, you leave one 8-bit channel free onto which you can dub music or narration without using a PC.

■ Depending on your computer connections, you can use FireWire or USB ports to transfer video and sound onto your computer for editing.

■ On your DV cam, the FireWire connection may be known as DV-Out. Some DV cams have a DV-in/out, meaning you can also send images and sound back to your camcorder.

■ If you do have DV-in/out then it might be possible to use the FireWire port to connect an external digital audio interface. This could allow you to plug in a pair of mics and balance the sound before it reaches your camera.

■ If recording the sound onto your camera is not giving you satisfactory results, you can always record the sound onto a separate device—such as a laptop; a good-quality MP3 recorder/media-player/portable hard disk, or either a DAT (digital audio tape) recorder or a minidisk recorder (if either of these formats are still available from your local supplier).

■ It might be worth investing in a sold-state recorder. This is essentially a radio-sized portable drive with tape-recorder-like controls designed especially for professional location-sound recording. Such devices are sometimes flash-memory based—the same technology used in the iPod Nano, SmartMedia cards, and memory sticks.

■ Solid-state recorders are useful because they have no moving parts, motors, lasers, or sensitive tape heads, which means they can be safely carried without compromising your recording or damaging the device. Many sound designers for movies and computer games use them when they are gathering the raw sound samples for editing and manipulation later on in the studio.

■ If you're planning to add location sound to your video at the editing stage, rather than straight from the camera (where it will already be in synch with the visuals), it will be useful to synchronize it with a visual cue. This is the function of the clapperboard in the movies: it allows directors and editors to synchronize the short, percussive "clap" sound with footage at the moment the clapperboard is snapped shut. In software, you can line up clips using this audio cue by looking for the sharp, hairline signal peak on the timeline.

1. DV CAMS
On-camera mics can be used on set.

2. SHOTGUN MICS
Directional; can be boom-mounted.

3-4. HIGHER-SPEC DV CAMS
Can offer more sophisticated audio input and control options.

- Consider making a clapperboard of your own with one large piece of wood (about the size of your favorite movie magazine) and a smaller one on a hinge. If you are shooting dozens of different scenes in a homemade or independent drama, paint the front of the clapperboard with blackboard paint and write the name of each scene in chalk on the front as an additional aide memoire for collating your material later.

- In professional movies, electronic clapperboards are often used that are linked to both camera and sound equipment. These generate a digital timecode, which allows the subsequent synchronization of video and audio in the edit.

- When on location, musician and composer Nitin Sawhney says he records a short, percussive sound on his laptop immediately before recording local musicians' performances on his global travels. Later on in the studio he synchs his location recordings with his studio work visually by locating the percussive "hit" on the audio timeline.

- This is a good lesson to remember with digital audio: because sound is represented visually by waveforms that correspond to a signal's amplitude and time-based elements, you can locate certain types of sound by looking for them on the timeline.

"DON'T FORGET THAT EDITING MUSIC AND SOUND ON GRAPHICAL TIMELINES MEANS THAT YOU CAN LOOK FOR AUDIO CUES TO SYNCHRONIZE ONSCREEN AND AUDIO EVENTS"

AVID MOJO
This "video breakout box" can be an invaluable resource on location, as it can be a single, integrated connection point for audio and video inputs and outputs to a laptop running AVID Xpress (and Pro Tools for audio editing).

Q&A: SIMON FISHER TURNER, MOVIE MUSIC COMPOSER

Simon Fisher Turner was born in London in November, 1954. He is a movie music composer, musician, and sound designer. As a composer he is perhaps best known for his collaborations with the late director, Derek Jarman, scoring many of his movies, including, among others, *Caravaggio* (1986); *The Last of England* (1988); *The Garden* (1990); and Jarman's last film, *Blue* (1993). More recently he has composed and performed the music for *Croupier* (1998); the TV series *Nature Boy* (2000); *I'll Sleep When I'm Dead* (2003); and various documentaries.

In 2004, Simon was invited, along with musicians such as Cornelius, David Byrne, Roots Manuva, and Elizabeth Fraser to create environments in music and sound for rooms and public spaces at London's Victoria and Albert Museum (the V&A). The exhibition, called "Shhh...Sounds in Spaces," ran until August 2004. Examples of the work can be found at http://shhh.vam.ac.uk.

Please tell us some things about yourself...
"My name is Simon, and I make noise, and enjoy putting people together to make more noises. In short, I'm lucky."

What inspires you?
"Having read Birgit Nilsson's obituary [the great Swedish soprano passed away on Christmas Day, 2005] I have to say she was a massive influence on my life, and inspired me enormously. People inspire me. Movies, music, and silence inspire me. Architecture, art, love, and children inspire me. Nature. Sound."

Can you share a good strategy for composition?
"Listen to your collaborators and your betters. Don't be mean. Share."

How do you approach a new commission and work with other creative people, such as moviemakers?
"Every time I work I try to make my best work. With moviemakers I listen and ask questions. I like to see images, and if I can bring a new opinion to the end result this is an achievement I can be pleased with, perhaps.

"Listen. Think. Always think, and ask. Be honest with yourself. Images excite me if I'm not directed too much. Imagination is important. Also talking about anything else but what you're supposed to be talking about makes interesting progress in a new working relationship."

How important are process and technology tools to you?
"Process is natural. My process is now dictated by time, then money. I do use laptops in a rather simple fashion. I bought my first computer in 2000. I use electricity, but needn't. A piano will do. I use recording studios, home recording equipment, cassette machines, DAT machines, Minidisk machines, Revox [tape recorders]."

Could you do what you do without digital technology?
"Yes. Easily."

Is it a limiting factor to have so much choice of software, plugins, hardware, and so on, given that a lot of incredibly creative things can be done by pushing the limitations of primitive technology?
"Less is more, but more is fun. Again, time is changing, and I believe demands are changing. Too fast is sometimes too much. Take the long way round."

How do you approach editing and arranging your work once you have the basics of a composition?
"I edit roughly to rough pictures, and then tighten it all up later when the pictures are locked and secure—which, of course, these days they never are."

How do you monitor your work?
"I used to monitor on damaged speakers with no bass, and broken woofers. Now I monitor on straight speakers, laptop, beatbox, stereo, and mono. It's not so easy to find a mono button these days, either."

What are your tips for mastering a good mix?
"Go to a good masterer. Do not hurry. Let them listen for you. This is the most detailed time you will ever listen to the sounds you have made. Frequencies are vital at this stage, and I need all the help I can get to make it sound even better. A good mastering engineer will change your music radically and pull out many unheard changes. Be positive."

MUSIC FOR LOW-BUDGET VIDEOS AND MOVIES

Imagine these movies without music: *Jaws*; *Blade Runner*; *American Beauty*; *King Kong* (2005); *Psycho*; *Titanic*; *Amélie*; *Easy Rider*; *Ghost in the Shell*; *The Great Escape*; *2001: A Space Odyssey*; the James Bond series... When we think of a movie, we often think of the music. Music and sound are perhaps 50% of the experience of going to the movies. Hearing a familiar theme evokes and invokes the same feelings we had on seeing the movie for the first time. Even at the most basic level the application of music to an edited piece of visual material can transform onscreen images. The downside is that the powerful emotional effect of music can overwhelm the visuals if it is not used in the right way. Music can act as a counterpoint to visuals; it can mislead an audience and be an unreliable witness; it can alert us to something hidden, or known only to one character; it can create comedy or terror when neither is present onscreen; it can evoke one emotion when the dialog suggests another; and it can reveal a character's innermost feelings as they develop across the arc of the story. Bring two characters and their respective musical themes together and you might have harmony, or dischord. That is not to say that music should be used to dramatize every frame of celluloid, as it was in the silent-movie days for an audience that was learning how to respond to two-dimensional actors and an absent stage. Music can be sparse and minimal and be just as effective—think of the unsolved mysteries suggested by the brief incidental music interludes for the US TV series, *Lost*.

The story is the primary reason you have edited the visuals in the way that you have. Everything else merely enhances the telling of that story, including sound design and music. So use them to enhance the story!

MUSIC FOR LOW-BUDGET VIDEOS AND MOVIES: MOVIEMAKERS

- Source or compose your own music if you plan to show your work publicly, because most festivals will not accept the use of commercially released music unless you have the license to use it.

- Establish a friendly working relationship with a composer who will be right for the kind of films you want to make. First, this will set your work apart from the crowd; and second, it may add a new dimension to your own ideas.

- Advertise on one of the moviemakers' crew-sourcing discussion boards (e.g. http://shootingpeople.org/index.php); many composers use them. Ideally, find a composer or musician who is at the beginning of their career—the relationship will be mutually beneficial. Don't worry about not being able to describe your ideas—use examples of music and movies you like.

- Some composers may take on your project for free if they simply want their music to be heard. If you have a budget, negotiate a fee with your composer and give him an initial timescale for production and post-production and an idea of how much music you want. Let him take the script away and start to form his own ideas.

- It's common in moviemaking to put together a "temp track" of well-known music that conveys the mood you want to communicate in a musical soundtrack. For composers, this can be a mixed blessing—temp tracks are often a source of dread more than inspiration! It may be more rewarding to let your composer put together his own temp track, showing what he thinks about your story and characters.

- Discussing the story with a composer may bring to the surface a whole range of creative strategies, moods, and intepretations of the story that take your work into new areas. It's no coincidence that most of the great moviemakers are people who use music and sound in challenging and sophisticated ways. Have the confidence to forge relationships with other creative people.

- Find out if your composer can produce and mix the music in surround sound, if you plan to show your work in a fully equipped cinema, or on DVD in a home cinema environment. Many audio and music production suites can produce mixes in up to 7.1 surround sound. See Surround Sound, page 158.

MUSIC FOR LOW-BUDGET VIDEOS AND MOVIES: COMPOSERS

■ Use music to establish character. Creating a theme for a character means the theme could appear in different musical guises to dramatize changes the character is experiencing: a switch from major to minor key, perhaps; a blending of one character's theme with another when they meet, exploring the emotional interplay between the two musical ideas.

■ Don't always go for obvious approaches to scoring your work—i.e. a sad theme for a sad moment, then a fast-paced rhythmic piece for an action scene (although these are valid approaches). This can have the effect of breaking up the story into self-contained blocks on the movie's timeline rather than establishing a real arc for a character.

■ Just because you are using software that divides music and sound into blocks and events doesn't mean that you have to think in a building-block fashion. In movies, the character or story is your timeline, not your software.

■ In a drama, consider introducing "interior" themes in the music that reveal the character's hidden feelings, perhaps introducing the motivation for whatever happens next in the story. An example of this is John Powell's music for *The Bourne Supremacy*. Powell introduces rhythmic elements underneath sad themes to bridge the transition into action scenes, but retains the sad themes during the action to reveal the character's emotional landscape.

■ Consider creating a pallette of characteristic sounds and musical ideas for each main character. These will help establish personality and envelop the audience in the storyline.

■ Consider using music in unexpected ways to reveal unusual aspects of a character: for example, big expansive themes when the character is in an enclosed space, or claustrophobic themes when the character is in a wide-open space. This is one way in which music can communicate information about a character that is not onscreen. This is a technique often used by David Lynch's composer, Angelo Badalamenti, and in Peter Gabriel's scores for films such as *Birdy*, and *Rabbit Proof Fence*.

■ Would silence be more effective?

Movie sound is an elaborate deception, an agglomeration of location recordings and sounds added later from different sources. In some movies, perhaps only a small proportion of sound has been recorded on location. From a gunshot to a speeding car, you are often seeing one thing but hearing something very different. In fact, you are listening to the work of a sound designer or sound editor and his team.

Part of the reason for this is the practical problems of noisy locations; but another impetus behind sound design is that real location sounds, such as gunshots or revving engines, are often disappointing, thin, or even unconvincing when laid to picture—or else difficult to record in situ while filming. It's usually simpler and more cost-effective to add sound later. Once you do that, you can get really creative.

Some sounds created in studio backlots become iconic—just think of the lightsabers in *Star Wars*, created by sound designer Ben Burtt by blending the sounds of faulty wiring, a humming cathode ray tube, and an old projector. With digital software you can experiment yourself by mixing together different sounds to create new ones, and then edit and master the finished soundwave and synch it with video.

1. DESIGN YOUR OWN SOUNDS
Import onto your timeline, slice, process—and then export into your video suite!

2. REAL SOUNDS
Sounds from real items are often thin and unconvincing in a movie.

KANT PAN, ACADEMY AWARD NOMINEE

Kant Pan is a Hong Kong-born movie editor turned movie producer, whose first film in the West as editor, *The Crying Game* (1992), gained him an Oscar nomination. He has also worked as sound editor, supervising sound editor, and dubbing editor on numerous feature films, including *Dangerous Liaisons*, *Orlando*, and *Never Say Never Again*. This gives him a unique perspective on movie editing, sound design, and music.

"First and foremost we are dealing with a visual medium," he says. "Sound and music should enhance the visual experience, which if executed well should help immerse the audience into the visuals. Respect the internal rhythm and pacing of the performances and how actors have been directed."

On set, sound is recorded by a person called the sound-recording mixer, either from boom mics, mics placed about the set, or concealed radio mics worn by the actors. His job is also to record ambient location sound—which can run beneath a scene, regardless of the number of cuts between shots—but sets are mainly miked for dialog. Indeed, dialog is recorded separately so that it can easily be replaced in foreign-language editions of the movie, on DVDs and so on.

The location sound—whether it has been recorded to DAT (digital audio tape), hard disk, or solid-state recorder—is then passed to the sound department. A vital consideration here is that the audit trail of location recordings is clear: files are clearly labelled to match each take of each scene, and so on.

"When you reach the stage of editing called the 'locked picture'—the final edit—you start the process of sound editing," says Pan. "The sound editor or dialog editor will start to work on the dialog, preparing it for the next stage, mixing. If the original sound recorded on set is not up to standard, the actors will be recalled to do an ADR session [automated dialog replacement] in a sound booth, where the dialog of that scene is re-recorded in pristine conditions to picture. This is also called 'looping,' or 'post-synching.'"

GARY MILLER'S DIGITAL SOUND DESIGN HINTS AND TIPS

- Sit down with your locked [final] script and study every potential aspect of sound within your project. If you are working on a drama, imagine how sound and music might be used, either realistically or in ways that might inform the mood, enhance the themes, or highlight the character arcs.

- Imagine your script is a radio play, not a screen-based experience. How would you sell your story to the audience if you couldn't use any visuals? It is important to free your mind with regard to the sound design of your movie.

- Mark the script where you plan to record sounds on location. How will you replace these if the location sound proves to be poor or unusable?

- Also mark the script where you want to add sound effects in post-production. Then go deeper and start to enhance the emotion of each scene by the application of other sounds and effects. (Don't overdo this: resist the temptation to be didactic).

- If you have a scene where there is conflict simmering below the surface you can use audio in a subtle way to influence your audience's response. I had such a scene and the audio mixer suggested we put roadworks and beeping horns in the background of the mix. It worked to great effect because up until that point the "atmos tracks" had been tranquil.

- Another effective technique is to use sound to build anticipation of something happening offscreen. In another movie I worked on, there was a scene with two characters in bed who are disturbed by the sounds of a room being smashed up. We didn't have the budget or screentime to show the room being trashed, so I decided to do it with sound. I got the actors to react to imagined sounds and added sound effects in the final audio dub. This was all done by just studying the script before we'd shot a single frame—such is the power of sound."

The sound editor or sound effects editor also enhances the edited picture by adding other sounds in addition to those recorded on set. This creative process of making sounds symbolic or naturalistic to create a mood, set a tone, provide a unique or unusual soundscape, and so on, is what is now known as sound design."

So how does someone make a name as a sound designer? Pan explains that it is not about technology, but about imagination and creative flair. "If I was asked to create the sound of a witch's cloak moving across the camera, I'd think: I'll slow down a flame-thrower's 'whoosh' rather than record a flapping sheet of canvas; perhaps combine it with a wind noise, or the backwards sound of a soccer crowd shouting. If you can think of something interesting, then it might work emotionally—a symbolic sound. Take a door opening and closing: there's also the outside noise coming in, then closing off." For many "everyday" sounds and sound effects, a Foley editor creates "footsteps" sessions, says Pan. The term "Foley Editor" or "Foley Artist" is something you'll see scrolling by on every movie's

closing credits. The term comes from the late Jack Foley (d. 1967), the Universal Studios sound editor who found it was much quicker and more effective to create sounds such as footsteps himself in a studio than by attempting to synchronize the (often poor) location sound with the visuals.

The process is similar in some respects to the work of "Spot Effects" artists in radio dramas, who slam doors, walk on gravel, and so on, in the studio while the actors are reading, but Foleying is also necessary so that dialog and sound effects can remain on separate audio tracks for foreign language distribution.

"Next, the music is composed and then arranged and recorded in a studio session with an orchestra or musicians, ideally to picture," continues Pan. "Afterward, the music editor 'lays up' the music."

How does Pan see the collaboration between director, sound editor, sound designer, and composer? "The director is the captain of the ship and the producer is the owner of it—as an editor you are a

sidekick. Depending on the director, the movie editor as the head of editing department cuts the film and then oversees the sound-editing process and· collaborates with the director when briefing sound editors and composer. The director and his producer will generally have the final say!"

"I tend to work with the composer after the movie has been edited," Pan explains. "The composer's music should help enrich our experience of watching the film, guiding us emotionally through the story. Music—like editing, which is storytelling with moving pictures—contains motion, forward movement with rhythm, tempo, and pacing to accommodate the visual experience.

"To understand the process of storytelling in a piece—the emotional through-line; the spine of action, the continuing questions and delayed answers, the suspense, what's happening next; the uncertainties of the resolution, and the driving towards the climax... the finale—movie music and sound must accommodate all of these.

1. MOVIE SOUND-EDITING CONSOLE
Matched with professional music, sound, and video-editing software to create the sound envionment we experience in the cinema and at home.

2. CROSS OVER TO SUCCESS
The crossing outside Abbey Road studios in London, made famous on the cover of The Beatles' *Abbey Road* album, is so closely connected with the studio it has become a part of their identity. Abbey Road studios is the venue for a lot of major motion music recording—and they also regularly take students who have studied sound-engineering degrees from UK universities and colleges.

3. AVID XPRESS SUITE
Like Pro Tools in audio production, the AVID Express desktop suite gives you an upgrade path to more professional software and hardware interfaces.

AbbeyRoad

"The work of the sound editors and music editor on completion comprises laid-up dialog, sound effects, and music tracks, and these are all taken into a mixing session where the sound mixer combines these into the final soundtrack for the motion picture. The sound mixer can clean the tracks provided [remove unwanted noise and artifacts], balance the levels between the various elements, add equalization, and so on. When the mixing session is completed you walk away with a mixed track, which is the sound printing master. This will eventually be 'laid back,' onto your graded motion picture."

Has digital technology simplified all of the above—or made it more complex and difficult to manage? "Professionally, I work with AVID non-linear editing software, while on my own projects I have Final Cut Pro," says Pan. "Professional equipment and tools are much more sophisticated these days, but [their wide availability creates] a gap that is more to do with the person operating the gear than with the equipment itself. That can only be bridged by experience and talent, not by technology.

"Technology has made it simpler and cheaper, but it has also taken away some important thinking and 'digesting of material' time. Knowledge is not always passed down. For example, in the US they farm some TV drama sound work out to people who work on their own on computers at home, like secretaries!" Professional versions of software may have many more tools and options than the consumer versions, says Pan, but a good video editor, sound editor, or musician could work with the least expensive tools as long as they have that magic ingredient: flair.

"Personally, I don't read magazines, I sit with professionals," he says, "it's the best way to learn. Software programs are great in themselves, but they don't show you how to cut."

THE BOURNE IDENTITY CAR CHASE

Ninety-nine percent of all of the sound for this iconic car chase through Paris in an old Mini was created in a recording studio by supervising sound editor Per Hallberg, re-recording mixer Bob Beamer, and sound effects editor Chris Assells from dozens of different stereo tracks, including the combined sound of different car and motorbike engines (solely for the Mini); screeching brakes; in-car sounds, such as seatbelts being buckled; looped dialog; whooshes, crashes, and ambient sounds; other traffic sounds; people shouting, and policemen talking on walkie-talkies. "The misconception that the audience has [that the sound is "real"] is what we work very hard for them to get," said Hallberg at the time.

1. IN THE CONTROL ROOM
A producer in the control room at Abbey Road prepares the desk for an orchestral session that will synch up with an edited movie.

2. THE COMPOSER'S TASK
Everything shown by, and implicit in, the story needs to be reflected in the sound and music environment.

SYNCHING SOUND TO VIDEO

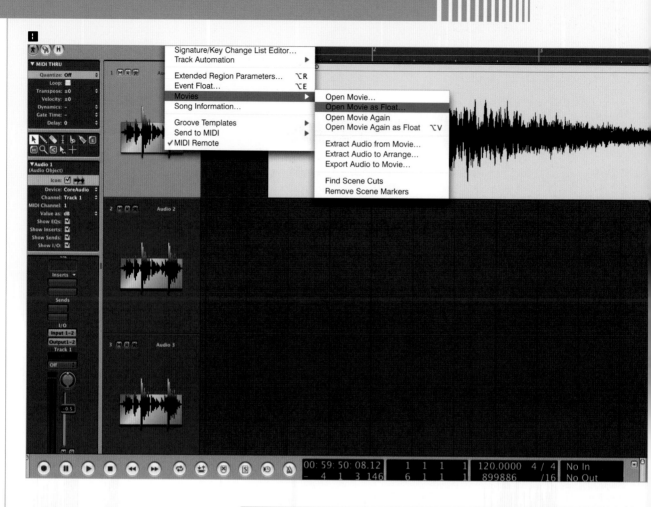

OPENING A MOVIE AS A "FLOAT" IN LOGIC (MAC)

Many music- and audio-production packages, such as the different versions of Logic and Cubase, make it easy to synchronize audio with video footage.

Here is one way you can do it:

1. Create a new Logic project (Arrangement).

2. Now import the movie as a "float." Go to Options > Movies > Open Movie as Float.

THE BRIEF

In this instance, a low-resolution version of the director's final cut has been supplied in QuickTime, complete with a visible timecode. The director has decided to go into an editing suite to do the post-production on the main soundtrack—the voices and sound effects—but has asked me to provide the music for specific scenes in the movie to a tight deadline. The un-mixed voices, minus sound effects (but plus background noise) are on the QuickTime file.

THE SOLUTION

I had already produced some short pieces of music in Reason based on an earlier rough cut, and I imported these, jigsaw-puzzle-style, into Logic to begin compiling the final music track—making some minor edits and fades on the way. But how to synchronize everything with the footage?

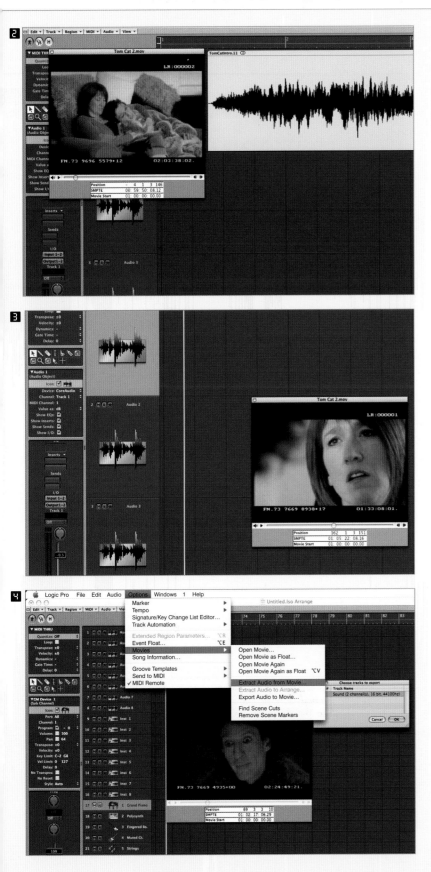

3. A window containing the movie will now appear, floating above the main Logic timeline. Simple.

4. Now go to Options > Movies > Extract Audio. This will extract the unmixed voice soundtrack from the QuickTime file and import it into Logic. If you don't do this, you won't be able to hear the existing video soundtrack once you've started work on the music.

5. Logic analyzes the QuickTime file and links itself with the length of black that has been striped onto the video. If you're not familiar with video terminology, this essentially means that it synchronizes itself with the entire length of the video file, including the empty black frames at the top and tail where the credits will later be added. In a video-editing suite, video files are "(crystal) blacked" before the visuals are added because otherwise the screen will be filled with the kind of distracting noise you get on a blank VHS. The process sets a fixed timecode for the required length of the video.

6. Now if you hit the Play button in Logic, you will not only activate the Logic timeline but also the QuickTime file. Likewise, if you hit the Play, Rewind, or Fast-forward buttons in the self-contained Movie window these will control the audio in Logic. This means that if you drag the cursor along Logic's timeline the video will fast-forward in the Movie window until you let go of the mouse. Use the Logic cursor in the audio timeline to nudge the video along frame by frame so that you can then position each piece of your music "puzzle," as it were, exactly where you want it.

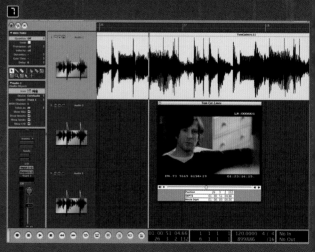

- Although this is a low-res copy of the video, the timings will be exactly the same because it is a final cut that has been striped with a synchronizing timecode.

7. Once all the elements of your music soundtrack are in place you can mix it, apply effects, and master it—but first check with the director or editor whether they prefer to do this themselves as part of the final pass through the dubbing suite.

- After editing the music clips I had already prepared, I also recorded a piano piece live into Logic while watching one scene play in the Movie window—an echo of the silent movie days when musicians would play along with a movie in the cinema.

- The director wanted the finished soundtrack in 5.1 surround sound—for which Logic Pro was also a good choice as it allows mixing in anything from mono all the way up to 7.1 (see Surround Sound, overleaf).

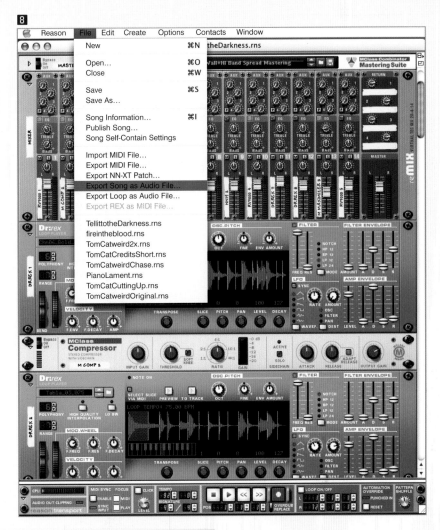

CREATIVE TIP: CUT TO THE BEAT

Some movie- and video-editors will admit to cutting a movie while listening to music that doesn't appear in the movie itself. Editors who do this often search for a song that suits the mood and pace they want to convey with the final cut, and have the song playing (or going through their heads) while they're working. One editor sent me a scene from a movie that he said he'd cut while playing the David Bowie song *The Man Who Sold the World*—in fact, the version by Nirvana. When I watched the scene I could see what he meant: although the music was not in the scene, the edits had the same insistent, rhythmic momentum as the camera stalked the central character. He asked me to come up with an instrumental piece that evoked a similar atmosphere—the dreaded "temp track." Like many composers in this situation, I looked for a visual cue in the scene for the music to play against and found it in the pounding rhythm of the character's footsteps.

8. PREPARING CLIPS IN REASON
Before working on the audio and music in Logic, I prepared some short music clips in Reason for specific scenes and then exported them as individual audio files using the dropdown option from the File menu. If you do this, you will then be asked which file format and resolution you wish to use for the exported file. As we explored in the introduction, ensure that you work at the same resolution in any program you import the files into to avoid them playing at the incorrect speed.

If you are working on just one piece of music rather than several clips, then you don't necessarily have to import your track into your audio application if you've prepared it in a music-only package, such as Reason. You can trigger the track from within Logic or Cubase, for example, via the ReWire protocol.

SURROUND SOUND

The relationship between non-linear film and video editing, computer games, and digital sound can only get more exciting as entertainment moves further into the digital age. The latest advances in 3D digital projection and digital surround sound will become standard in multiplexes, while home cinema systems, the Xbox 360, PlayStation 3, high-definition (HD) TV and advanced optical storage media mean that astonishing detail in sound and vision is available to most homes. Soon, 16-bit listening will be the sole domain of the Web, replaced on disk, cable, and satellite in the home by 24-bit, 96kHz audio in a surround environment. If you have a soundcard and a music/sound production package capable of dealing with 24-bit sound, then you have a golden opportunity to capitalize on this!

5.1, 6.1, AND 7.1 SURROUND SOUND

Surround sound systems consist of no fewer than five speakers, delivering five separate, full-bandwidth (3Hz–20kHz) channels of sound—front left, center, and front right, positioned as a traditional stereo pattern; rear left, and rear right speakers, which can be positioned to diffuse the sound across walls; plus a low-frequency effects (LFE) channel. This is devoted to audio frequencies from 3Hz to 120 Hz—the bass end of all those rumbles and explosions that shake your living-room floor. The positioning of this subwoofer speaker is not critical.

The LFE channel uses one-tenth of the bandwidth of the other channels, hence the ".1". 6.1 surround sound adds a full-bandwidth rear center channel, while 7.1 adds side left and right full-bandwidth channels to the 5.1 matrix.

Today's surround sound systems tend to be synonymous with Dolby Laboratories, the company set up by American engineer and physicist Ray Dolby in London in 1965. As a result, the technology's complex origins are often neglected (see box, page 159).

DOLBY SURROUND TECHNOLOGIES

Dolby Digital is the standard 5.1 surround sound technology. Nearly every DVD-video player offers a two-channel mixdown of any Dolby Digital 5.1 movie soundtrack, as well as a digital output for connection to any 5.1-channel-compatible unit. Dolby Digital is also the most widely accepted multichannel audio standard for satellite and cable. In the movie industry, Dolby Digital soundtracks are optically encoded between the filmstrip's sprocket holes, alongside the analog track.

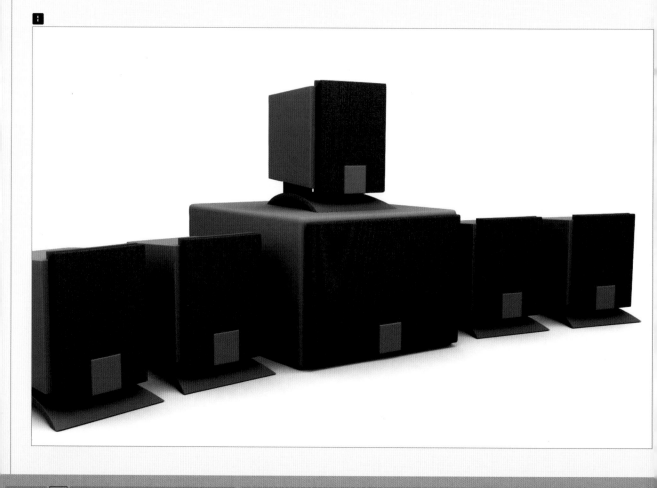

All Dolby Digital decoders can "downmix" 5.1 sound to stereo. Producers of 5.1-channel programs need only provide an original 5.1-channel mix. The **NTSC** broadcast TV standard specifies at least one soundtrack in either Dolby Digital or WAV (PCM Linear), while **PAL** mandates at least one soundtrack in either Dolby Digital, WAV (PCM Linear), or MPEG. Most Region 1 and 2 DVDs include a Dolby Digital track.

Dolby Digital Creator is a DV cam recording system that allows you to record home videos in 5.1 surround. **Dolby Headphone** creates a surround sound like presence on standard stereo headphones. **Dolby Pro Logic II** processes any stereo soundtrack into up to 7.1 playback channels of full-bandwidth surround sound by analyzing audio cues in a stereo mix.

1. SIX SPEAKER SEPARATION

A typical 5.1 system. For an illustrated guide on how to set up a surround sound system creatively in your own work, turn to the diagram on page 160.

2. SURROUND ON HEADPHONES

Technologies have been around since the 1980s to allow us to hear a simulation of surround sound on a normal pair of stereo headphones.

VITAL CONNECTIONS
You need a soundcard that can handle up to eight outputs and software, such as Logic, Cubase, or CoolEdit that allows you to mix in anything up to 7.1 surround sound.

MIXING FOR SURROUND SOUND

- First you need to be able to monitor in surround, so ensure you have your soundcard and multiple speaker system set up to do so (see separate box).

- When you bring up the Surround Panner control in Logic, Cubase, CoolEdit, and other programs, it's fun throwing tracks around the sound circle you're sitting in. However, in videos, movies, and games, we're still dealing with a screen placed in front of the viewer. The camera tends to locate whoever is speaking near the center of the screen, so the center audio channel is often most associated with speech, while the front left and right channels provide the dominant sound environment and context (sound effects, music, and so on). As the character moves across the screen, pan the sound to follow them left or right by dragging the cursor within the Surround Panner circle. Remember, you can also use this to fly sound in over the audience's head by panning from back to front (think of the opening of *Star Wars Episode IV: A New Hope*).

- The rear left and right speakers help create depth and a sense of place in the sound circle, and are often used as "ambience" channels. In a DVD of a stage performance, for example, much of the music will come from the front speakers, while the rear channels provide audience sounds, plus acoustic reflections from the back of the hall. In this way the viewer feels as though they're seated in the auditorium. You can fake this sense of place by adding reverb to the stereo signal and flying it around the back at low volume.

- In music, there are fewer rules, but realism remains vital if you're recording a band performance, for example. You'll create far greater impact using the rear speakers to create space and atmosphere rather than by spinning the sound around too much. Remember also that if you create a dazzling surround-sound mix, this might be downmixed to a confusing stereo performance.

- The key, then, is restraint if you want to create a realistic soundscape.

Turn to the diagram overleaf for an explanation of how to set up and use surround sound creatively.

SETTING UP FOR SURROUND SOUND

LOGIC (MAC)

■ First set up up your surround-ready soundcard—for example, the M-Audio 410, or upward. Opening the soundcard's onscreen interface gives you the option to activate eight audio outputs.

■ In Logic, go to Audio > Surround… This brings up a window where you can assign up to eight channels (7.1) of sound to the eight outputs of your soundcard. The default settings are: Left (channel 1); Right (2); Rear Left (3); Rear Center (3); Rear Right (4); Front Center (5); LFE (6); Side Left (7); and Side Right (8).

■ Bring up a Mixer by double-clicking on the name of an Audio Track. Now in the I/O (Input/Output) section of each track, click on the Out and scroll to Surround in the popup menu. This creates a Surround Panner icon in place of the L/R stereo panpot. Moving the cursor around in the circle will move the sound between whatever surround channels you have set up.

CUBASE, ON THE PC

■ Go to Devices > Setup. Select the VST Multitrack driver and ensure it is also set to ASIO. In the VST Outputs window select your Outs by clicking on "Visible: Yes."

■ Now route the surround sound by going to Devices > VST Connections. Alternatively hit F4. Click the Add Bus button and choose your Configuration (let's assume it's 5.1). Click OK to bring up your six outputs (including LFE) in the left-hand list. Now match these to your speaker placements and soundcard setup.

THE ROOTS OF SURROUND SOUND

Surround's origins are the same as stereo's, namely in engineer Alan Blumlein's 1931–1935 development of "binaural" sound. His experiments alongside colleagues at EMI gave birth to what we now know as sound separation and stereo. Walt Disney explored these in the multitrack panning techniques used to create and "stage" the 1941 movie, *Fantasia*.

In 1952, the "Cinerama" process laid the foundations for today's big-screen experiences, recording up to seven separate channels of sound from microphones placed around a movie set.

In the 1970s, quadrophonic (four-channel) sound became popular among hi-fi buffs, and English rock band The Who went as far as using the idea in a concept album, *Quadrophenia* (1972). At the same time, Pink Floyd pioneered quadrophonic sound in live rock performances, taking inspiration from composer Karlheinz Stockhausen (www.stockhausen.org). The band designed a joystick device called the Azimuth Coordinator to spin sound around the audience. As anyone toward the back of a large auditorium would hear the rear-speakers sound before the stage PA (because of the time it took for the stage sound to reach them), small delays were placed in the signal path to ensure the front and rear sound arrived simultaneously. This same principle applies to today's home cinema systems.

The 1979 movie *Apocalypse Now* was the first to use 70mm Dolby Stereo Surround technology (combined with stunning sound design).

www.doramusic.com/Stereo.htm
www.cineramaadventure.com/theworks-sound.htm

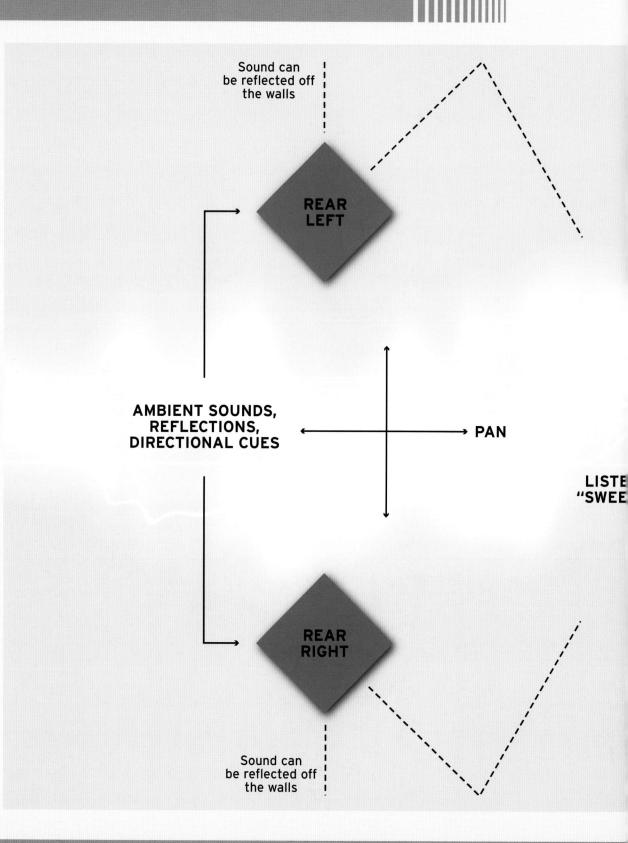

Sound can
be reflected off
the walls

REAR
LEFT

**AMBIENT SOUNDS,
REFLECTIONS,
DIRECTIONAL CUES**

PAN

LISTE
"SWEE

REAR
RIGHT

Sound can
be reflected off
the walls

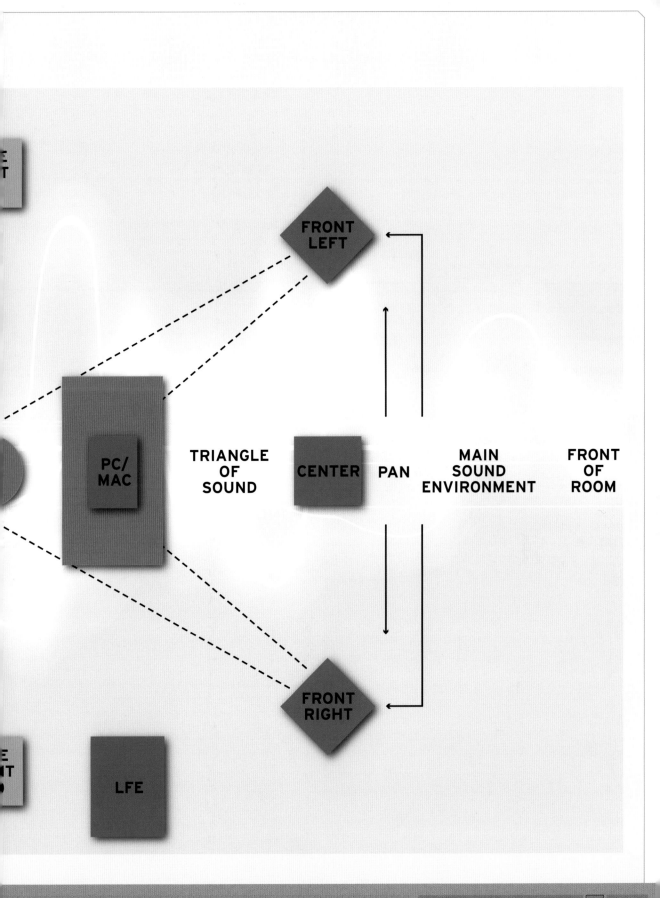

WHEN WORLDS COLLIDE...

Technology and media convergence has been with us for centuries, but it has found its purest expression in the merging of digital music, sound, video, graphic design, movies, games, and the mobile environment of multimedia ringtones and superdistributed content (content sent peer to peer without proprietary restrictions). D-Fuse is a creative collective of motion graphics designers, artists, graphic designers, sound designers, and musicians. As worlds collide, roles become less important and people simply make things. Mike Faulkner (video) and Matthias Kispert (audio) tell us about their world.

Q&A: D-FUSE

 Please introduce yourselves.

(Mike Faulkner; Video) "I consider myself a video artist, motion-, and graphic designer. Some people within D-Fuse are quite clear about their aims and outcomes, but I consider what I do is freeform and experimental. In simple terms I "paint sound.""

"We have produced DVDs–*Nonplace* and the groundbreaking *D-Tonate*, both initially released in Japan–and this has led to more profitable projects, such as the Beck DVD/UMD *Guero* (2005), plus tour. We also perform live A/V [audiovisual] performances. We've released video ringtones in Japan–some D-Fuse, and some Beck. We're planning to release these in the US."

(Matthias Kispert, Audio) "My work ranges from electronica-style music, via ringtones to abstract sound pieces, but I'm mostly interested in connecting sounds with concepts, so that in audiovisual terms, video and sound together create an integrated communication. We also collaborate with a wide range of musicians on live performances and DVD releases."

What (and who) inspires you about what you do?

(MF) "In the 1980s, movie and cut performances of people like 23 Skiddoo, Cabaret Voltaire, and Throbbing Gristle. Music has always had an important influence."

How important is process to you? And what is your process?

(MF) "Processes are different depending on the project. We devise strategies during the conceptual stage, and then test and modify them while we are working on a project. Something like the Beck DVD, *Guero*, was completely freeform. We were asked to produce 26 movies without storyboarding, approval from record labels, or any interference. We were commissioned as artists to interrupt Beck's tracks in whatever way we felt fit."

Could you do what you do without digital technology? If so, how would you go about it?

(MF) "Yes, but the beauty of technology is that it speeds the workflow and helps you produce things that would not be possible before. Another factor is cost–computers have become affordable to the masses. I always remember, pre-personal computers, seeing the work Vaughan Oliver's V23 did for the 4AD music label and thinking how good it was that they had access to that 'expensive' technology. But now everybody has access to it, which is good, but it also raises other issues."

THE LIVE VJ
Triggering synchronized music and sound live in a club environment.

D-FUSE LIVE A/V SHOW

You can do a lot of interesting work with analog technology. We see computers as good tools, but not as the only answer to producing the work."

What technologies do you use?

(MF) "We work in Final Cut Pro, Adobe After Effects, Photoshop, Freehand, Illustrator, and [photography suite] Aperture. We also have Shake and we're looking into this program. Our hardware is Mac based, and we've been working with HDV camcorders."

Is it a limiting factor to have so much choice of technology? Does it stop us realizing the creative potential of the simplest tools?

(MF) "Technology—especially the Internet—means that everybody in the world can produce almost anything, anywhere. It's great that technology is more affordable and opening things up to the masses, but it does undermine people's perceptions of your work. It can also be overwhelming—so many programs to learn and to keep track of is exhausting, but exciting at the same time.

"Of course, it's important to consider how much of this is driven by software manufacturers. Shake and Aperture are great programs, but at the same time I'm a little lost about how much more productive the latest version of Photoshop is over the last one! Sometimes, I still use an old version of After Effects simply to use some of the old filters..."

How do you work with sound and music and interpret it visually?

(MF) "In terms of synching video to sound, that was the case with Beck and *D-Tonate*, but recently we've been creating video first and working with audio later. Some of our work is moving away from the classic A/V method where video is created in response to music. In *Brilliant City*, the audio alternates between musical material and field recordings. This gives us the freedom to play with the meaning and impact of images through the manipulation of sound."

D-FUSE LIVE A/V SHOW

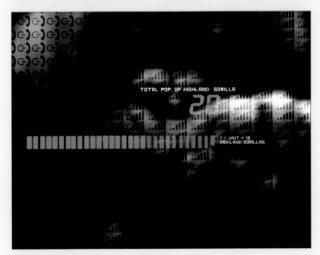

IMAGE FROM D-FUSE LIVE A/V SHOW

SUPPLEMENTARY GLOSSARY OF OTHER USEFUL TERMS

MANY OF THE MOST COMMON DIGITAL RECORDING, MUSIC, AND TECHNOLOGY TERMS HAVE ALREADY BEEN DEFINED ELSEWHERE IN THIS BOOK—FOR EXAMPLE, IN THE INTRODUCTION, AND IN THE SECTIONS ON FILE FORMATS; STORAGE FORMATS; SEQUENCING; RECORDING AND CONNECTIVITY TERMS; MICROPHONES; MIXING; AND DYNAMIC AND TIME-BASED PROCESSORS. PLEASE REFER TO THESE SECTIONS, WITH REFERENCE TO THE INDEX, FOR AN EXPLANATION OF THE MOST COMMON TERMS, PROCESSES, AND ACRONYMS YOU'RE LIKELY TO ENCOUNTER IN YOUR JOURNEY THROUGH THE WORLD OF MUSIC AND SOUND. WHAT FOLLOWS IS A SUPPLEMENTARY GLOSSARY OF SOME OTHER USEFUL TERMS, AND CONCEPTS, WITH FURTHER CLARIFICATION OF CONCEPTS MENTIONED IN THE BOOK WHERE NECESSARY.

ADAT

Alesis Digital Audio Tape. The ADAT was originally a very popular, easy-to-use hardware device for multitracking digital audio onto video cassettes. Through the 1990s, the modular ADAT machines were standard in many types of studio, with some studios stacking multiple ADAT recorders on top of each other to allow them to record 8, 16, 24, 32, or more individual tracks of digital sound. In more recent years ADAT has become more of a brand name for its manufacturer, Alesis. The ADAT HD-24, for example, resembles its tape-based forebears, but is in fact a modular hard disk recorder.

COSM

Proprietary technology developed by Roland Inc., enabling software modeling of the characteristic sounds, frequency curves, and responses of some classic microphones. Other companies, such as Antares, also produce mic-modeling software that can be run as a plugin to your main recording application. Using a mic modeler allows you to record audio with any mic and then, to some extent, model the sound of a different, perhaps superior, mic to enhance vocals, and so on.

destructive editing

Edits on a digital file that are applied to the original data itself, overwriting the original, rather than being stored on a separate file that modifies the original (as is the case with non-destructive editing). In analog, tape-based recording, all edits are usually destructive as they involve physically splicing the tape—as is also the case with any film-editing process that involves leaving celluloid on the proverbial cutting room floor. Also see NLE.

dongle

Colloquial term for a small piece of hardware, usually key-fob sized, that plugs into your computer, often via the USB port. Dongles can contain extra memory, for example, but are increasingly used as hardware security keys to authorize expensive pieces of software. For example, many fully featured, pro versions of studio suites such as Logic and Cubase come with a dongle, so if the software is illegally copied or shared, the copy will only work if the user also has the dongle that came with the authorized copy. This strategy makes perfect sense if you're a software maker, but for users it ties up a USB port permanently. If regularly removed and shared between a desktop and a laptop, for example, then dongles are easily lost, which means your expensive, legal copy of your studio suite will no longer work. So take great care of any dongle that comes with your software, and ensure you register any packaged software you've purchased just in case. Some other software suites need to be authorized online and will lock up unless they are registered within a specific time period, or will limit the number of functions that can be used.

dry (signal)

A dry signal is one that has no effect or processor added to it. Many effects or processors, such as Reverbs or Delays (in software or hardware), include a sliding control to make the signal more "wet," i.e. to apply increasing amounts of the effect to it. A 100% wet signal is one where the original signal has been replaced by an entirely processed version. In most cases—such as adding reverb to a vocal or a snare drum, for example—you only need apply a percentage of the effect so you can hear a mix of the original sound with the added effect, hopefully so that the effect does not draw any unwanted attention to itself.

hubs

One of the inherent problems with digital music-making is that you can swiftly accumulate a lot of separate hardware devices, from soundcards and controllers to effects units, mixers, multitrackers, and so on. This can become a problem if you only have a couple of spare USB or FireWire ports (sockets for connections) on your computer into which to plug them. One solution to this is to purchase a USB or FireWire hub, which is essentially a junction box into which you can plug a number of separate USB or FireWire cables and then output that information in a single feed to the USB or FireWire port on your computer. Ensure, though, that if you are running FireWire 800 you purchase a FireWire 800 hub—the connections are different sizes, so the mistake will rapidly become apparent. You can also purchase MIDI hubs. These are useful if you want to connect to your computer one or more hardware MIDI devices that do not have FireWire or USB outputs—for example, older-generation synths and samplers. MIDI hubs normally give you a USB output, allowing you to send MIDI data to the USB input of your PC or Mac.

iPod

Apple's generation-defining portable media player, onto which hundreds or thousands of songs can be downloaded and stored as compatible digital files, depending on the capacity of the machine, via Apple's iTunes music (and video) service. Some iPods, such as the iPod Nano, are flash-memory based, and have no moving parts; others are essentially music-specific portable hard disks—indeed, many people use their iPods to transfer digital files from one place to another. Some versions of the iPod can store and display images and video files. The main difference between iPods and other media/MP3 players is that users are limited to buying music and other content via the iTunes service and WMA (Windows Media Audio) files are not compatible. To use them on an iPod, users have to "rip" the files into a compatible format by processing it through their iTunes software. At present, however, Apple's iPod dominates the market by dint of good design in every respect.

modulate

Usually, to modify a (carrier) signal's amplitude, phase, and frequency elements in order to use it to convey additional information.

monophony, monophonic

A single voice, or tone. See polyphony for more information.

motorized flying faders / total recall

On some hardware mixing desks and top-of-the-range digital multitrack recorders, the faders—the volume sliders that govern each individual channel on the desk—are motorized and programmable so that changes in the level of each fader can be memorized by the machine within each mix. With total recall, the desk can be reset automatically so that all of the faders snap to the correct position for each song, avoiding the need for the user to have to memorize the controls for each song, or to keep detailed written notes. Obviously, within software-based recording setups, mixer settings are memorized as a matter of course within each file, and mixes can be automated using the Read and Write controls, among other options. See the chapter on mixing for more information about this.

multitrack

To record music or sound onto separate, individual tracks of a recording device, or software package, either simultaneously, or to build up a complex recording track by track over time. Each track, or group of tracks, can then be individually edited, equalized, and mixed. From the multitrack original recording(s), stereo or surround-sound master recordings can then be made. In the case of a stereo recording, all of the individual tracks are mixed down to a two-channel signal.

NLE

Non-linear editing. Related to non-destructive editing, NLE is a common term in digital video and movie-editing, whereby any frame of a moving image can be accessed instantly, or near instantly, without having to scroll through the entire length of a piece (in a linear fashion) to locate the desired frame. Edits are usually non-destructive and stored as modifiers to the original data on a separate file. Video-editing packages such as Adobe Premiere, AVID Xpress, Apple Final Cut Pro, and Sony Vegas are common NLE packages for video.

polyphony, polyphonic

Deriving, like many audio terms, from the Greek word "phone," meaning "voice" or "sound," polyphony means "multiple voices." In digital and analog synthesis, a "voice" does not refer to the human voice, but instead to whatever components are needed to

enable it to produce a single tone.
A polyphonic synthesizer is one that
has multiple voices—enabling the
playing of 64, 128, or 256 simultaneous
tones, for example. This capacity allows
a musician to play chords, but also to
play complex layers of different
sounds simultaneously. Monophonic
synthesizers, on the other hand, are
only capable of generating a single
tone at a time, so hitting a chord on a
monophonic synth will only trigger one
of the notes within that chord. As a
result, monophonic synths tend to be
used for lead lines, bass sounds,
sequences of single notes, or effects.

wet (signal)
A wet signal is one that has had
noticeable amounts of an effect or
processor applied to it, modifying the
original signal—the opposite to a "dry"
signal. See dry (signal) for more.

WEB SITES AND RESOURCES

IN ADDITION TO THE VARIOUS WEB SITES MENTIONED IN THE BOOK, HERE IS A SMALL SELECTION OF OTHER USEFUL RESOURCES, IN ALPHABETICAL ORDER. SOME OF THESE ARE MANUFACTURERS' HOMEPAGES, WHILE OTHERS ARE PRIVATE MUSIC AND SOFTWARE SITES. THE PUBLISHERS ACCEPT NO RESPONSIBILITY FOR THE CONTENT OR SECURITY OF ANY OF THESE WEB PAGES.

LOOPS, SAMPLES, AND RELATED

http://mapage.noos.fr/bigweb
http://reason.fan.free.fr
www.acid-project.com
www.artificialear.com
www.audiowarrior.com
www.beatfreax.nl
www.bigfishaudio.com
www.combinatorhq.com
www.container.to
www.doctorfilter.com
www.dorumalaia2.com/index.htm
www.getimo.de/linkpage
www.hitsquad.com
www.insaneguitartools.com
www.kreativsounds.com
www.lapjockey.com
www.ninevoltaudio.com
www.peff.com
www.powerfx.com
www.reasonbanks.com
www.reasonfreaks.com
www.samples4.com
www.soniccouture.com
www.sonicflavours.com
www.sonicreality.com
www.sonicshack.com
www.soundlabel.com
www.toontrack.com
www.trackteamaudio.com
www.zero-g.co.uk

MUSIC HARDWARE, SOFTWARE, AND RELATED

www.ableton.com
www.adobe.com
www.akg.com
www.alesis.com
www.apple.com
www.avid.com
www.behringer.com
www.cakewalk.com
www.dbpoweramp.com
www.digidesign.com
www.dolby.com
www.easywma.com
www.fender.com
www.goldwave.com
www.korg.com
www.line6.com
www.macromedia.com
www.marshallsamps.com
www.m-audio.com
www.minimixa.com
www.motu.com
www.nativeinstruments.de
www.propellerheads.se
www.roland.com
www.seelectronics.com
www.sennheiser.com
www.shure.com
www.sibelius.com
www.sonymediasoftware.com
www.sseyo.com
www.steinberg.de
www.syntrillium.com
www.tannoy.com
www.tao-group.com
www.winamp.com
www.yamaha.com
www.zoomeffects.net

LINUX RESOURCES

http://amsynthe.sourceforge.net/amsynth
http://audacity.sourceforge.net
http://gmorgan.sourceforge.net
http://linuxsound.atnet.at
http://linuxsound.jp
http://linux-sound.org
http://mixmagic.bengburken.net
http://protux.sourceforge.net
http://smack.berlios.de
http://sourceforge.net/index.php
http://tkeca.sourceforge.net
www.agnula.org
www.ardour.org
www.eca.cx/ecasound
www.euph0r1a.net/projects
www.lcsaudio.com/Products/CueStation.html
www.les-stooges.org/pascal/midiswing/index.php
www.notam02.no/notam02
www.procomposer-software.com
www.rosegardenmusic.com
www.slabexchange.org
www.xowave.com/whatyouget.shtml

CREATIVE MOVIE AND VIDEO CREW SOURCES (ENGLISH LANGUAGE)

www.creativecircle.co.uk
http://shootingpeople.org

PODCASTING AND INTERNET RADIO

http://podcasts.yahoo.com
www.backbone.com
www.ipodder.org
www.libsyn.com
www.itunes.com
www.podcast.net
www.podcastalley.com
www.podcastingnews.com
www.podcasting-tools.com
www.shoutcast.com
wwwportablemediaexpo.com

OTHER USEFUL SITES

www.sibeliusmusic.com (downloadable music scores)
www.songwriter.co.uk (songwriters' resources)
www.bbc.co.uk/radio1/onemusic/fatguides (music business guides and other advice)
www.vocalist.org.uk (singers' noticeboards)

S

S/N (signal to noise) ratio 33
samplers 26-28, 31, 38, 48, 50, 60
samples 18, 34, 36, 38, 48, 50, 52, 64, 84, 88, 101, 128, 130, 140
sampling frequency 18
sampling rates 17-18, 28, 42, 98-99, 134
Sawhney, Nitin 20, 142
scrubbing 54
seed files 116-17
sequencers 38-41, 50, 60, 62, 94, 123, 130
sequencing 33, 36-38, 42, 44
shaped frequency response 66
shock-mounts 68
shotgun mics 139
SHOUTcast 105-8
signal processors 28-29, 35, 48, 50, 79
signature tracks 107
simulators 60
SMIL (synchronized multimedia information language) 108
social media 120
software settings 16
solid-state recorders 140, 146
sound design 148-49
sound separation 73
sound toys 126-31
soundcards 22-24, 27-29, 35, 38, 42, 44-45, 60, 64, 74, 102, 116, 134, 137, 139, 156, 158-59
Soundtrack Pro 134
soundwaves 12-17, 19, 32-34, 38, 54, 56, 64-65, 101
S/PDIF outputs 29
speakers 17, 29, 72, 74, 76-77, 80, 113, 156-58
spectrum analyzer 77
spikes 54, 113
SPL (sound pressure level) 12
spot effects 148
stacks 74
Steinberg 52, 134
step sequencing 33
stereo 35, 38, 40, 56, 69, 76, 78-84, 86, 88, 94, 98, 103, 139, 156-59

Stockhausen, Karlheinz 159
storage 19, 23, 25, 98-99, 103, 112, 123-24, 156
streaming 101, 104, 108-10, 112, 118, 123
strings 65, 72
subscriptions 118
supercardioid mics 66, 68, 139
surround sound 22, 29, 78, 84, 139, 156-61
sustain 27
sweet spot 76
Symbian 118-19
synching 152-55
synthesizers 16, 26-28, 30-31, 34, 36, 44, 48, 50, 60

T

tape phasing 56
TDM (Time Division Multiplexing) 18
temp tracks 144, 155
tempo 32-33, 36, 42, 48, 52, 56, 88, 107, 128, 130
terminology 32
texturizing 70
THD (total harmonic distortion) 34
theremins 26, 60, 129
threshold 58-59, 82
time signatures 52
timecodes 132, 152
timelines 33, 36-38, 52, 54, 128, 134, 136-37, 142, 145, 153
timing problems 19
transducers 16-17
transient response 65
triggers 40, 44
Triton 31
Turner, Simon F. 143

U

UMD (universal media disk) recording 99
unidirectional mics 66, 68, 139
Unix 23
USB (universal serial bus) 22, 27-30, 32, 35, 45, 139

V

vector audio 116, 124
velocity 27
video 8, 10, 22, 31, 35-36, 38, 42, 52, 104, 108, 124, 126, 132-61
virtual guitar rack 74
virtual instruments 60-61
viruses 24
VJing 162-63
vocals 29, 32-33, 48, 54, 56, 62, 64-66, 68-71, 80, 82-88, 90, 92
Vodafone Radio DJ 118
voiceovers 62
volume 54, 58-59, 64-65, 73, 76-77, 83, 130, 158
VST (virtual studio technology) plugins 60, 134

W

Walter, Andrew 76, 94, 157
warping 32, 49, 52
WAV files 94, 97, 113, 128, 136, 157
waveforms 12, 15-16, 18, 36, 54, 56, 101, 137
wavelength 14, 16, 98
Web sites 8, 10, 101-4, 110, 112, 114-15, 125
whispering 70
WiFi 118
WiMAX (wireless data transfer systems) 118
Windows PCs 8, 20-25, 28, 118, 134, 159
word length 19
workspace 62-63
workstations 30-31

X

XLR inputs 29-30, 35

THANKS

Many thanks to (in no particular order):
Suzanne Elston and Andrew Walter at Abbey Road; Tim Didymus for inspiration, tea, and generative contributions; Tim Cole for his contributions, help, and inspiration over the years; Hakan Lidbo for all his help and work; Paul Farrington for his major contribution to this book; Geoff Pryce, Marco Migliari, and Owen Leech at Real World Studios in Box for earlier conversations; Simon Fisher Turner for the Q&A; Gary Miller for his help and major contribution to the movie and video section; Kant Pan for conversation, ideas, and dim sum; Liz Cox at AVID; Colin at M-Audio; Mike Faulkner and D-Fuse for their contributions; Andy Hobsbawm for all things e-related; Neil Gibb for being a non-stop source of ideas, contributions, and encouragement (thanks for being our rock star for the day); to my dear friends Gary Eastwood for editing and Vicky Eastwood for modeling; Jamie Freeman; Jane at Brian Eno's office; Steve Rockett of Chrome Audio/Climax Games; the Sanctuary, Hove, for the mocha and giant cookies without which this book would have been impossible; Mr. Jack Daniels; Andy Cruse for a quarter-century of friendship and the emergency Marshall amp; Chris Allen and the Light Surgeons—with apologies for material not used in this book; Drew Hemment; Luke Herriott for the design; April, Tony, Jane W, Jane R, Lindy, and all at RotoVision; and finally—and most importantly—to Nathan for putting up with me so willingly.

Illustrations:
Commissioned photography at ghostWorld music, Brighton, UK: Calvey Taylor-Haw;
Diagrams and mic polar pattern images: Jane Waterhouse;
Additional photography and cover shot: Chris Middleton;
Abbey Road and Andrew Walter images, courtesy of Abbey Road studios, London;
Hakan Lidbo, Kant Pan, D-Fuse, Tim Cole, and Simon Fisher Turner images courtesy of the contributors;
Studio Tonne sound toy images courtesy of Paul Farrington;
Tom Cat movie stills copyright Gary Miller/Akira films, 2005;
Additional images courtesy of iStockphoto.